Coach	Year	W	L	T	Conference
Bob Williams (5 games)					SoCon
Josh Cody	1927	5	3	1	SoCon
	1928	8	3	0	SoCon
	1929	8	3	0	SoCon
	1930	8	2	0	SoCon
Jess Neely	1931	1	6	2	SoCon
	1932	3	5	1	SoCon
	1933	3	6	2	SoCon
	1934	5	4	0	SoCon
	1935	6	3	0	SoCon
	1936	5	5	0	SoCon
	1937	4	4	1	SoCon
	1938	7	1	1	SoCon
	1939	9	1	0	SoCon
Frank Howard	1940	6	2	1	SoCon
	1941	7	2	0	SoCon
	1942	3	6	1	SoCon
	1943	2	6	0	SoCon
	1944	4	5	0	SoCon
	1945	6	3	1	SoCon
	1946	4	5	0	SoCon
	1947	4	5	0	SoCon
	1948	11	0	0	SoCon
	1949	4	4	2	SoCon
	1950	9	0	1	SoCon
	1951	7	3	0	SoCon
	1952	2	6	1	SoCon
	1953	3	5	1	ACC
	1954	5	5	0	ACC
	1955	7	3	0	ACC
	1956	7	2	2	ACC
	1957	7	3	0	ACC
	1958	8	3	0	ACC
	1959	9	2	0	ACC

Coach	Year	W	L	T	Conference
	1960	6	4	0	ACC
	1961	5	5	0	ACC
	1962	6	4	0	ACC
	1963	5	4	1	ACC
	1964	3	7	0	ACC
	1965	5	5	0	ACC
	1966	6	4	0	ACC
	1967	6	4	0	ACC
	1968	4	5	1	ACC
	1969	4	6	0	ACC
	1970	3	8	0	ACC
Hootie Ingram	1971	5	6	0	ACC
	1972	4	7	0	ACC
	1973	5	6	0	ACC
Red Parker	1974	7	4	0	ACC
	1975	2	9	0	ACC
	1976	3	6	2	ACC
Charley Pell	1977	8	3	1	ACC
Charley Pell (11 games)	1978 *				ACC
		11	1	0	
Danny Ford (1 game)					ACC
	1979	8	4	0	ACC
	1980	6	5	0	ACC
	1981	12	0	0	ACC
	1982	9	1	1	ACC
	1983	9	1	1	ACC
Danny Ford	1984	7	4	0	ACC
	1985	6	6	0	ACC
	1986	8	2	2	ACC
	1987	10	2	0	ACC
	1988	10	2	0	ACC
	1989	10	2	0	ACC
Ken Hatfield	1990	10	2	0	ACC
	1991	9	2	1	ACC

Coach	Year	W	L	T	Conf
	1992	5	6	0	ACC
Ken Hatfield (11 games)	1993				ACC
		9	3	0	
Tommy West (1 game)					ACC
Tommy West	1994	5	6	0	ACC
	1995	8	4	0	ACC
	1996	7	5	—	ACC
	1997	7	5	—	ACC
	1998	3	8	—	ACC
Tommy Bowden	1999	6	6	—	ACC
	2000	9	3	—	ACC
	2001	7	5	—	ACC
	2002	7	6	—	ACC
	2003	9	4	—	ACC
	2004	6	5	—	ACC
	2005	8	4	—	ACC
	2006	8	5	—	ACC
	2007	9	4	—	ACC
Tommy Bowden (6 games)	2008				ACC
		7	6	—	
Dabo Swinney (7 games)					ACC
Dabo Swinney	2009	9	5	—	ACC
	2010	6	7	—	ACC
	2011	10	4	—	ACC
	2012	11	2	—	ACC
	2013	11	2	—	ACC
	2014	10	3	—	ACC
	2015	14	1	—	ACC
	2016	14	1	—	ACC

Dabo Swinney	2017	12	2	0	ACC
	2018	15	0	0	ACC

Total Games 1,251
Seasons   123
Total Wins   748
Total Losses 452
Total Ties   45   * Prior to Overtime Rules
Stats from   1896 Through August 2019

Clemson Tigers
Championship
Seasons

From the beginning of football all the way to the 2018/2019 Clemson National Championship

This book is written for those of us who love Clemson University and especially the CU Fighting Tigers Football Team. You'll like all the stories from the University's founding in 1889, just about 130 years ago, to the beginning of the football program, through the great coaches to CU as an annual National Championship contender.

You will learn that Clemson Tigers are fierce and passionate competitors. From the stadium to the classroom to the research lab, the Clemson Tigers always play to win.

You will learn that CUs first official football game was in 1896 even before American football rules had been completely defined. You'll also learn why the immortal Walter Riggs is known as the father of Clemson Football and it is not just because he hired the famed John Heisman as the fourth Tiger coach shortly after the official beginning of football on campus.

From here, the book moves you one coach at time through the early championships of the John Heisman years on to Frank Howard, the longest tenured Clemson Coach. Then, on the way to today, we stop for coaches Jess Neely and Danny Ford who brought in CUs first modern era National Championship in 1981 and of course we take you to Coach Tommy Bowden and on to the great Dabo Swinney and the reigning 2018/2019 National Champion Clemson Tigers. Go Tigers!

The history of Clemson Tiger Championship Football as told here is just fascinating. This book captures the many great moments and the contributions of each of the 25 coaches and standout players such as Tajh Boyd, Refrigerator Perry, C.J Spiller, and of course DeShaun Watson. We look at every season and we take the reader through great chapters about all of the Clemson championship teams with great stories and accounts of 123 seasons worth of great games (1251 games) with many great championships.

This book is your finest source for a great read on your favorite college football team. It is the closest thing to an all-encompassing blow by blow history of clemson championships—with tales of the many great championships. We capture all the action and all the top winning moments of Tigers football. This book is for your reading pleasure but also a great reference for checking out a particular Clemson championship game or a great bowl game in any year .

If you are a Clemson Tigers fan. you will not want to put this book down.

Brian Kelly

Copyright © August 2019, Brian W. Kelly   Editor: Brian P. Kelly
Title: Clemson Tigers Championship Seasons   Author Brian W. Kelly

Referenced Material: *Standard Disclaimer: The information in this book has been obtained through personal and third-party observations, interviews, and copious research. Where unique information has been provided, or extracted from other sources, those sources are acknowledged within the text of the book itself or in the References area in the front matter. Thus, there are no formal footnotes nor is there a bibliography section. Any picture that does not have a source was taken from various sites on the Internet with no credit attached. If resource owners would like credit in the next printing, please email publisher.*

Published by: ....LETS GO PUBLISH!
Editor in Chief ....Brian P. Kelly
Email: ....info@letsgopublish.com
Web site .... www.letsgopublish.com

Library of Congress Copyright Information Pending
Book Cover Design by **Brian W. Kelly**
Editor-in-Chief—**Brian P. Kelly**

ISBN Information: The International Standard Book Number (ISBN) is a unique machine-readable identification number, which marks any book unmistakably. The ISBN is the clear standard in the book industry. 159 countries and territories are officially ISBN members. The Official ISBN for this book is

978-1-947402-94-2

The price for this work is:..........   **$ 19.95 USD**

10	9	8	7	6	5	4	3	2	1

Release Date   August 2019

1. WALTER RIGGS

2. WM. WILLIAMS

3. JOHN PENTON

4. JOHN HEISMAN

5. SHACK SHEALY

6. EDDIE COCHEMS

7. BOB WILLIAMS

8. FRANK SHAUGHNESSY

9. STEIN STONE

10. FRANK DOBSON

11. WAYNE HART

12. JIGGS DONAHUE

13. E. J. STEWART

14. BUD SAUNDERS

15. JOSH CODY

16. JESS NEELY

17. FRANK HOWARD

18. HOOTIE INGRAM

19. RED PARKER

20. CHARLEY PELL

Clemson University Seasons by Year/Coach

Head coach	Year	Wins/ Losses/Ties			Conf.
Walter Riggs	1896	2	1	0	Indep
Wm. M. Williams	1897	2	2	0	Indep
John Penton	1898	3	1	0	Indep
Walter Riggs	1899	4	2	0	SIAA
John Heisman	1900	6	0	0	SIAA
	1901	3	1	1	SIAA
	1902	6	1	0	SIAA
	1903	4	1	1	SIAA
Shack Shealy	1904	3	3	1	SIAA
Eddie Cochems	1905	3	2	1	SIAA
Bob Williams	1906	4	0	3	SIAA
Frank Shaughnessy	1907	4	4	0	SIAA
John N. Stone	1908	1	6	0	SIAA
Bob Williams	1909	6	3	0	SIAA
Frank Dobson	1910	4	3	1	SIAA
	1911	3	5	0	SIAA
	1912	4	4	0	SIAA
Bob Williams	1913	4	4	0	SIAA
	1914	5	3	1	SIAA
	1915	2	4	2	SIAA
Wayne Hart	1916	3	6	0	SIAA
Edward Donahue	1917	6	2	0	SIAA
	1918	5	2	0	SIAA
	1919	6	2	2	SIAA
	1920	4	6	1	SIAA
E. J. Stewart	1921	1	6	2	SIAA
	1922	5	4	0	SoCon
Bud Saunders	1923	5	2	1	SoCon
	1924	2	6	0	SoCon
	1925	1	7	0	SoCon
Bud Saunders (4 games)	1926	2	7	0	SoCon

Acknowledgments:

I appreciate all the help that I received in putting this book together, along with the 208 other books from the past.

My printed acknowledgments were once so large that book readers needed to navigate too many pages to get to page one of the text. To permit me more flexibility, I put my acknowledgment list online at www.letsgopublish.com. The list of acknowledgments continues to grow. Believe it or not, it once cost about a dollar more to print each book.

Thank you all on the big list in the sky and God bless you all for your help.

Please check out www.letsgopublish.com to read the latest version of my heartfelt acknowledgments updated for this book. Thank you all!

In this book, I received some extra special help from many avid football friends including Dennis Grimes, Gerry Rodski, Wily Ky Eyely, Angel Irene McKeown Kelly, Angel Edward Joseph Kelly Sr., Angel Edward Joseph Kelly Jr., Ann Flannery, Angel James Flannery Sr., Mary Daniels, Bill Daniels, Angel Robert Garry Daniels, Angel Sarah Janice Daniels, Angel Punkie Daniels, Joe Kelly and Diane Kelly, Angel Ben Kelly, and Budmond Arthur Kelly.

References

I learned how to write creatively in Grade School at St. Boniface. I even enjoyed reading some of my own stuff as a toddler.

At Meyers High School and King's College and Wilkes-University, I learned how to research, write bibliographies and footnote every non-original thought I might have had. I learned to hate ibid, and op. cit., and I hated assuring that I had all citations written down in the proper sequence. Having to pay attention to details took my desire to write creatively and diminished it with busy work.

I know it is necessary for the world to stop plagiarism so authors and publishers can get paid properly, but for an honest writer, it sure is annoying. I wrote many proposals while with IBM and whenever I needed to cite something, I cited it in place, because my readers, IT Managers, could care less about tracing the vagaries of citations and their varied formats.

I always hated to use stilted footnotes, or produce a lengthy, perfectly formatted bibliography. I bet most bibliographies are flawed because even the experts on such drivel do not like the tedium.

I wrote 208 books before this book and several hundred articles published by many magazines and newspapers and I only cite when an idea is not mine or when I am quoting, and again, I choose to cite in place, and the reader does not have to trace strange numbers through strange footnotes and back to bibliography elements that may not be readily accessible or available. Academicians knowing all the rules of citation are not my audience. In this book, if you are a lover of Clemson Tigers football, you are my intended group of readers

Yet, I would be kidding you, if in a book about the great moments in Clemson University Football, I tried to bluff my way into trying to make you think that I knew everything before I began to write anything in this book. I spent as much time researching as writing. I might even call myself an expert of sorts now about the Tigers, a team that I have recently begun to watch and enjoy, especially when a great coach such as Dabo Swinney is on the sidelines.

Without any pain on your part you can read this book from cover to cover to enjoy the stories about the many great moments in the Clemson University of Football Program.

It took me about two months to write this book. If I were to have made sure that a thought of mine was not a thought somebody else ever had, this book never would have been completed or the citations pages would more than likely exceed the prose. Everybody takes credit for everything in sports writing—at least that's what I have found.

I used CU Season summaries and recaps from whatever source I could to get the scores of all the games. I verified facts when possible. There are many web sites that have great information and facts. Ironically most internet stories are the same exact stories. Who's got the original? While I was writing the book, I wrote down a bunch of Internet references and at one time, I listed them right here en masse in this article. They were the least read pages. No more. Unless I am citing a reference in a section of the book, you will not see the URL.

I am not a South Carolinian, but I love vacationing at Myrtle Beach, I want to visit SC and below often as winters in PA are very harsh and grey. Still hoping for a 50-yard line ticket for telling the truth..

I have no favorite source for information to put in my books. However, I continually hunt for articles written by students to amplify the text I present.

While I was writing this book, because I was not sure that my citations within the text would be enough, and I was not producing a bibliography, I copied URLs into some of the book text in those cases in which I had read articles or had downloaded material and had brought articles or pieces of articles into this book. Hopefully, this will satisfy any request for additional citations. If there is anything which needs a specific citation, I would be pleased to change the text. Just contact me. Your stuff is your stuff.

Most of the facts in this book are also put forth in the Clemson Media Guide. Our thanks for the use of this material for the accurate production of this book. Additionally, when I was looking for some special games to highlight, I used a piece by Bob Bradley, Sports Information Director as a source for my facts.

http://www.clemsontigers.com/ViewArticle.dbml?ATCLID=205510943.

Preface:

This book is all about the great moments in Clemson Tigers football over the years. Along the way to today, we study the founding of Clemson football, including some preliminaries before CU football officially began, and then we delve right into the storied Clemson University Football Program--its struggles; its greatness; its many championships from ages ago to 2018's championship season.

As a Pennsylvanian, I admit I wrote a similar book about Penn State Football but only after I had fulfilled the family Irish wish to write about Notre Dame Football. Then, before Clemson whooped Alabama twice in three years, I had figured Nick Saban could not be beaten—though I was not necessarily rooting for him—and so I selected Alabama as the third football team about which I would write about substantially.

You've got to admit, they are a competent team. Now, I find myself writing about the National Champions, the Clemson Tigers, and I am honored to take up this challenge. As I am reviewing the preface right before publication, I have concluded that I think you are going to like this book.

Since none of the three, ND, PSU, or UA, invited me on campus to sign books, and none of them have appealing locations anyway, especially those in the North, I figured why not pick a state where I vacation such as Florida. But, I am not a fan of the Seminoles. I have friends in the Gainesville area so I picked the Gators and my first book on the Gators came out over a year ago. I brought some copies to a Gators game when I was staying in the Villages in Florida. But I did not hear anoything about those 50-yard seats from the Gators. a few months ago. I am waiting for the Clemson invite.

I remembered how rivetted I was to my seat watching DeShaun Watson and the Dabo Swinney squad on January 9, 2017 put a stinging defeat on Alabama. I like Clemson

I also got to thinking that I like South Carolina as a state. It is so nice that I choosc to go thcrc on vacations. Though Myrtle Beach is on the other side of the state from Clemson, the weather is fine in both sections of the state and the Tiger country is beautiful.

This is not the first book I wrote about South Carolina. I am the proud author of a book with a catchy title called Take the Train to Myrtle Beach, which I wrote several years ago and updated last summer. I look forward to my first trip to Clemson to sign some books in the Fall 2019. Don't forget to invite me.

When you are ready to invite me to "Death Valley," aka Frank Howard Field at Clemson Memorial Stadium, I will be pleased to arrive in Clemson, SC with bells on. Perhaps somebody could get me fifty-yard line seats in a game in which CU is playing against one of my old-time favorites, ND or PSU, or quite frankly, any team. I'd be happy to do some signing before and after the game, and at the bookstore the day before and after. I'll wait 'til the signing is finished to move on to the whistle wetting period. I'll sign until you tell me "No more!"

I respect Clemson an awful lot, especially now that I have completed all the research necessary to print this book. I am sure long-term Clemson fans will admit that as a Pennsylvanian, for me it was easy to grow up a Penn State Fan. ND of course has always been as close to me as a family religion.

I began to pay attention to Clemson a few years ago when DeShaun beat Deshone in one of the toughest games of my life. Clemson beat both Notre Dame and the torrential rain. It was tough for me because ND lost and because I was in the first couple days of a herniated disc recovery that sidelined me for two months. Thank God for laptops. I noted that those Clemson players sure know how to play great football.

I watched the end of season games and would not miss the January Championship game in which Clemson was barely beaten by less than a touchdown. I was in awe of the Clemson Team and I was again amazed by the outstanding play of QB Deshaun Watson. What a football player. What a team And how about those two National Championships since then.

Of course, in 2017, I was attached to the TV for the Alabama rematch nail-biter game and saw the best player in the country, Deshaun Watson win the game for Dabo Swinney and for Clemson. Well deserved. It's time for another. I have enjoyed writing this book immensely. Go Tigers!

Supporters who love Clemson University will read this book and get an immediate burst of emotions such as warmth and love for their favorite team. You will love this book because it has it all – every great championship game. Go Clemson Tigers!

This book walks you through the whole CU championship journey. Then, we look at some sepcific players on the early teams who succeeded despite Clemson not yet having a big-time program. This period began in 1896. Like all new teams, you can imagine the struggle of playing on a college football team when getting the right equipment was one of the biggest issues.

The 25 great CU coaches's pics are inside the front covar a couple pages in. Then, they are listed within the football seasons in which they coached--from season 1 in 1896 to season 124 in 2018. In other words, the seasons are examined chronologically and the coaches and certain games and certain players are highlighted within the seasons in which the championship games and almost championships were played. I sure hope you enjoy this unique approach.

Before Frank Howard put in a thirty-year stint starting in 1940, few of CU's 16 coaches to that point took the team for more than a couple years. Yet, they still produced some powerful teams with powerful players. Of the 25 coaches in the Fighting Tigers history, just six had losing seasons. That's a lot of winning for any football program.

Clemson Tigers are a long-time football power

One hundred twenty-three years is a long time to be playing football. The Clemson Tigers are recognized today as one of the finest teams in the nation, ready to win a national championship at the drop of the next hat. In fact, it was less than a year ago that the hat dropped for the second time in three years.

In 1953, Clemson joined the ACC and have been playing many of the best football teams in the nation ever since by competing in the NCAA Division I Football Bowl Subdivision. Some say the SEC was better in 2016 than the ACC but then again, Clemson, a mainstay of the ACC is the reigning national champion. I rest my case.

You can read about Clemson success before and after it joined the ACC right here in this book and decide for yourself how great the Fighting Tigers play the game of Football.

Your author would like you to know that when the college football season closes in the second week of January each year, there is now a great football item—this book—that is available all 52 weeks of the year and in fact all 365 days each year. It does not rely on the stadium gates being open for you to get a great dose of Clemson Tigers Football. Just begin reading right here.

It is now available for you to add to your Clemson Football experience. and your book collection. Once you get this book, it is yours forever unless, of course you give it away to one of the many who will be in awe, and who will accept it gladly. For those who love to use gadgets to read, this book is also available on Kindle.

We open the book with the first story set shortly after the beginning of college football as a sport in America. It then moves on to the first official game with the first official coach and all the way to Coach Swinney's National Championship games. It tells a story about all the football seasons and the great coaches and great players and great moments and great championshps from the first coached game in 1896 to today.

You are going to love this book because it is the perfect read for anybody who loves the Clemson Tigers and wants to know more about the most revered athletes to have competed in one of the finest football programs of all time.

Few sports books are a must-read but Brian Kelly's *Clemson Tigers Championship Seasons* will quickly appear at the top of Americas most enjoyable must-read books about sports. Enjoy!

Who is Brian W. Kelly?

Brian W. Kelly is one of the leading authors in America with this, his 209th published book. Brian is an outspoken and eloquent expert on a variety of topics and he has also written several hundred articles on topics of interest to Americans.

Most of his early works involved high technology. Later, Brian wrote a number of patriotic books and most recently he has been writing human interest books such as <u>The Wine Diet,</u> <u>Thank you, IBM,</u> and this summer's favorite, <u>The Big Toxic School</u>. His books are always well received.

Brian's books are highlighted at <u>www.letsgopublish.com</u>. Quantities from 20 to 1000 can be made available by emailing the author. You can order most of Brian's works by taking the following link <u>www.amazon.com/author/brianwkelly</u>.

The Best!

Sincerely,

Brian W. Kelly, Author
Brian P. Kelly, Editor in Chief
I am Brian Kelly's eldest son.

Yes, I do love the great work of the Clemson Tigers, God bless!

Table of Contents

About the Author

Brian Kelly retired as an Assistant Professor in the Business Information Technology (BIT) Program at Marywood University, where he also served as the IBM i and Midrange Systems Technical Advisor to the IT Faculty. Kelly designed, developed, and taught many college and professional courses. He continues as a contributing technical editor to a number of technical industry magazines, including "The Four Hundred" and "Four Hundred Guru," published by IT Jungle.

Kelly is a former IBM Senior Systems Engineer. His specialty was problem solving for customers as well as implementing advanced operating systems and software on his client's machines. Brian is the author of 209 books and hundreds of magazine articles. He has been a frequent speaker at technical conferences throughout the United States.

Brian was a candidate for the US Congress from Pennsylvania in 2010 and he ran for Mayor in his home town in 2015. He loves Clemson Tigers Football and can't wait to get back down to South Carolina in the fall. When he comes he'll be glad to sign your books. God bless the Tigers!

Chapter 1 Introduction to Clemson University (CU) Football

Clemson's 120th Year in 2015!

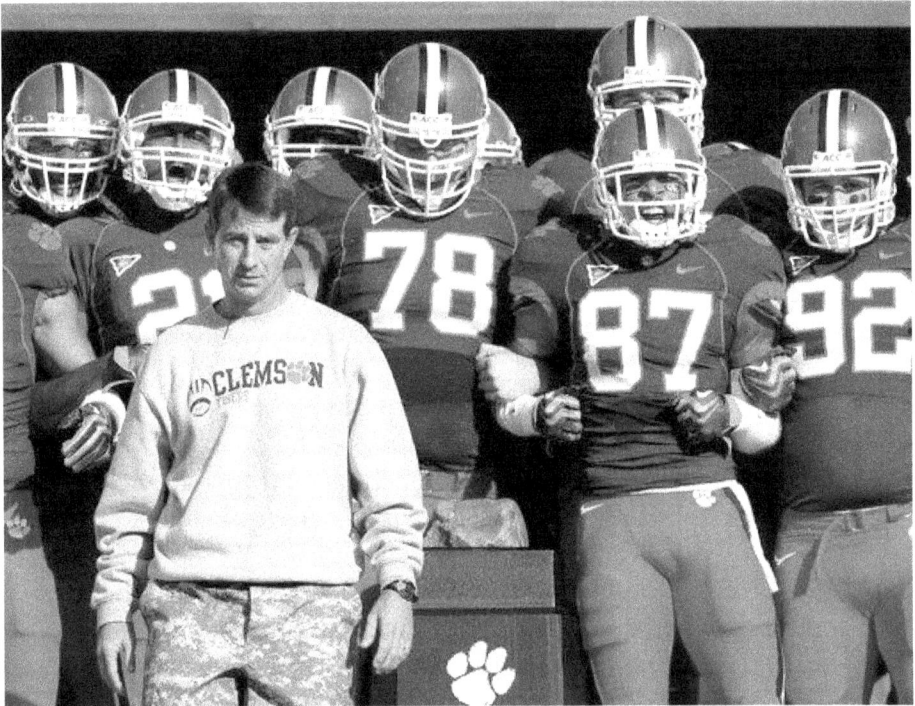

Coach Swinney leading the Tigers onto the field

The Clemson Tigers have fielded a team every season since the inaugural 1896 season. That's a lot of football games. To be exact, it's 1,251 games in its 123 seasons, and the Tigers have a fine all-time record of 748 wins, 452 losses, and 45 ties. That's a lot of great Clemson football, folks.

Officially the Clemson prganization recognizes a long football history that dates back to 1896. If you are from South Carolina, or some other rival school, you might not be so kind. Such rivals might ask if Clemson even had a football team before 1981 with Danny Ford and the Clemson University First National Championship. Of course, they don't know how to read as the immortal Frank Howard had an extremely successful thirty-year tenure from 1940 through 1969.

After Howard, Hootie Ingram and Red Parker had a tough time getting wins for the team. They combined for a seven-year losing record of 29-46-2 before even the great Charlie Pell, who stopped by Clemson for two years (1977 & 1978) could not put them back on the plus side of the win column even though he picked up 18 wins with just four losses and a tie. Combining the trio's record post Frank Howard and pre-Danny Ford, we come up with 47-50-3. Knowing what we know now, however, once Pell arrived the wins began to accumulate. The Clemson team was built to win.

So, IMHO, it is an unfair shot to suggest the Tigers were no place as the program has produced well over 700 wins with a late start in 1896 when many of the legendary teams had already been legends for ten or twenty years or more. Like most startups, CU did have its share of medsa mediocre seasons but they more or less ended in the1940's with Frank Howard and those great coaches who followed.

From the time of Danny Ford in 1980, to 2017, the Clemson Tigers have been on a rip with 338 wins, 153 losses, and 5 ties. With the great three years and national championships after this, the record is as good as it gets. Sometimes I wish the NCAA would just go away.

This is the fifth book that I have researched and written about big-time college football, and I am beginning to see a pattern. When a team that is trying to break into the big-time has a good or great year, the NCAA is likely to impose sanctions. Perhaps they have allegiances to certain teams that just don't happen to be our teams. Perhaps!

I could have predicted it from heuristic analysis. During the Danny Ford years, Clemson was not supposed to be such a winning team and so, the NCAA stepped in with its sanctions. It is OK to say Boo!

1. Clemson University shall be publicly reprimanded and censured, and placed on probation for a period of two years, effective November 21, 1982, it being understood that should any portion of the penalty in this case be set aside for any reason other than by appropriate action of the Association, the penalty shall be

reconsidered by the NCAA; further, prior to the expiration of this period of probation, the NCAA shall review the athletic policies and practices of the university.

2. The university's intercollegiate football team shall end its 1982 and 1983 football seasons with the playing of its last regularly scheduled, in-season contest and the university shall not be eligible to participate in any postseason football competition.

3. During the 1983 and 1984 football seasons, the university's intercollegiate football team shall not be eligible to appear on any television series or program subject to the administration or control of this Association or any other television programs involving live coverage.

There are more.

My point is that it was only when Clemson began to make trouble for the expected winners with people on the NCAA Board did the NCAA clamp down. Maybe I am wrong but I have seen this pattern before. Yes, I am looking for 50-yard line free seats but I am kidding about everything else. I do not expect to get anything from writing the truth.

Danny Ford was a great coach and brought home all the bacon one time during his tenure. The NCAA spots great programs and great coaches and the sanctions bomb comes down. Only mediocre coaches want to win because another

Dabo Swinney is a great coach and he takes a back seat to no other coach in college football. He brought in a National Championship and a ton of great seasons even before that. Check out his Clemson record below. His football legacy is from hard work. He came to Clemson in 2008 and there was not even a hint of losing season upon his arrival. By 2012, Clemson was a major contender for national laurels. In the 2015 Championship game. Just five points separated Clemson from dethroning Alabama but five points made the difference.

With an even more determined team, in 2016, Swinney's offense and defense would not be picked apart even in the big games. They won the ACC and then went on the beat the vaunted SEC Champion Alabama in a great game to cap their season. Dabo Swinney is being compared to Danny Ford, and that sure is a compliment but the comparisons have to do with the NCAA sniffing around and finding violations. I hope none of this is true. Like I said. We might be better off as a country without the current NCAA.

Year	School	G	W	L	T	Pct
2008	Clemson	7	4	3	0	.571
2009	Clemson	14	9	5	0	.643
2010	Clemson	13	6	7	0	.462
2011	Clemson	14	10	4	0	.714
2012	Clemson	13	11	2	0	.846
2013	Clemson	13	11	2	0	.846
2014	Clemson	13	10	3	0	.769
2015	Clemson	15	14	1	0	.933
2016	Clemson	15	14	1	0	.933

OK, you insist on me showing you the last two years. OK:

Dabo Swinney	2017	12	2	0	ACC
Clemson	2018	15	0	0	ACC

Ask any other college team to try that recent record on for size. The shoe will not fit.

This book that you are reading celebrates Clemson University of South Carolina; its founding; its struggles; its greatness; and its long-lasting impact on American life. People like me, who love the Tigers, will love this book. Clemson Haters will want their own copy just for additional ammo. Yet, it won't help them! Hah!

We begin the rest of the Clemson Fighting Tigers football story in Chapter 2 with the founding of Clemson University institution almost 139 years ago and we continue in subsequent chapters, right into the founding of the full Clemson football program in 1896 after the students had been begging the argument by playing American football on the campus in intramural fashion. The Clemson athletes even played other colleges to help sharpen their game and add some zip to their unofficial seasons.

In defining the format of the book, we chose to use a timetable that is based on a historical chronology. Within this framework, we discuss the great moments in Clemson University football history, and there are many great moments. No book can claim to be able to capture them all, as it would be a never-ending story, but we sure do try.

No Heisman's for Clemson???

Though there still are no Heisman Trophy's yet for Clemson but a few close calls, nobody can deny that the founder of the Heisman award, John Heisman, shown below, was the third head coach at Clemson. Heisman was as good as it gets as a coach and his record was 19-3 in four seasons. of coaching the Tigers.

John Heisman with famous Heisman Pose at Oberlin Before Clemson

The Coolest Pre-Game Tradition in College Football

The Clemson Tigers have the coolest pre-game tradition in College Football. When you go to a Clemson Home game, make sure you do not miss it. It culminates in the most exciting 25 seconds in college football.

Clemson Players "Running Down the Hill"

The following is courtesy of Clemson University

When Don Munson ran down the hill for the first time, he didn't know what he was in for. This was in 2010, the year he began working full-time for the Clemson athletic department. Before the Tigers' home opener that September, Munson turned to coach Dabo Swinney, shook his hand, and told him how much he appreciated being part of the team's pregame ritual. Swinney responded by slapping Munson on the back and saying, "You have no idea." "It was absolutely true," said Munson, who's in his first year as the Tigers' radio play-by-play announcer. He was about to participate in what Brett Musburger (and many others) have called "the most exciting 25 seconds in football."

Every Clemson entrance is an event. Ten minutes before the start of each home game, the Tigers leave their locker room (located underneath the west end zone stands) and board buses [yes busses for a home game—with the bus route lined with fans. that take them on a short ride to the north side of Memorial Stadium. At that point, the players file out and assemble on top of a hill above the east end zone. Then, after rubbing Howard's Rock (more on that later), a cannon fires, sending the team down the hill and onto the field.

"You're up on that hill looking over the sea of people and I'm telling you it gets your blood flowing, man," Munson said. "It's crazy. I've had players describe it as [feeling like] gladiators. They look upon themselves as kind of walking into that Roman Coliseum.

"The guy that's in the booth with me, Rodney Williams, he was a great player at Clemson in the '80s. I can tell the effect that it has on him. It still is an emotional thing. I've seen ex-players cry at this thing. Literally, just weep. They know what it's all about."

According to the university, the tradition was borne out of necessity: The first 20,000 seats in Clemson Memorial Stadium were built and ready for use before the 1942 season. The shortest entry into the stadium was a walk down Williamson Road from Fike Field House's dressing rooms to a gate at the top of the hill behind the east end zone.

There were no dressing facilities in the west end zone-only a big clock where the hands turned, and a scoreboard, which was operated by hand. The team would dress at Fike, walk down Williamson Road, come in the gate underneath where the big scoreboard now stands and jog down the hill for its warm-up exercises.

Things changed in the 1960s, when S.C. Jones, a Clemson alum, gifted then-coach Frank Howard a hunk of white flint from Death Valley, California. (By then, Memorial Stadium had been nicknamed Death Valley.) Howard hated the present at first, but eventually came around. In 1966, the rock was positioned on top of a pedestal located on top of the hill. The players didn't begin rubbing what became known as Howard's Rock until September 23, 1967. Before the Tigers beat Wake Forest that day, Howard allegedly told his team: "If you're going to give me 110 percent, you can rub that rock. If you're not, keep your filthy hands off it."

Members of the Clemson University ROTC guard Howard's Rock. Photo by Joshua S. Kelly-USA TODAY Sports

Since then—except for a stretch from 1970 to early 1972 when coach Hootie Ingram was at the helm—the Tigers have rubbed Howard's Rock and run down the hill before every game at Memorial Stadium.

"What other entrance in America is like that?" Munson said. "There isn't one."

This is Munson's first season in the booth. For four years, he ran down the hill with Swinney and the Tigers.
"I'll be really honest with you," he said. "I actually miss it."

Clemson Football: The All-Time Dream Team

http://bleacherreport.com/articles/1296550-clemson-football-the-all-time-dream-team

ON AUGUST 15, 2012, BLEACHER REPORT'S COLBY LANHAM wrote a great piece about the all-time Clemson Dream Team. It covers bases we have not seen over the past few years of great Dabo Swinney led Clemson football so we include it here as another perspective of the great football players to have one-time played for Clemson University. When you have an opportunity, take the link below and read this recent perspective. It is worth your time.

Here is Colby Lanham's beginning in italics below:

Clemson football is a celebrated, major NCAA Division I college football program. That's a dictionary definition of it.

But to its devoted fanbase, it is tradition and a way of life in college football.

Clemson has seen plenty of greatness within Death Valley stadium, from back in its high days in the '80s, claiming its only national championship, all the way to today, where fans are more excited than ever after winning its first ACC Championship since 1991.

But what would the Clemson Football All-Time Dream Team look like? If you could put together the greatest Tigers on one team and watch them all touch Howard's

Rock as they run down The Hill, who would be a part of that unit on offense and defense?

Here's a possible roster of what that All-Time Dream Team would look like.

Here is the link for those who want to read the whole piece:

http://bleacherreport.com/articles/1296550-clemson-football-the-all-time-dream-team

How would anybody construct a dream team covering 121 years of Clemson football if given the mission. Many have tried and I read their works to help me find the consensus great players in Clemson history. My thanks to them all.

There have been many surveys that included fans, former Clemson players, coaches, and administrators to select their top Clemson football players of the Century. In most cases, the participants in the surveys and interviews have followed Clemson football for at least 20 years and some for over 50 years. Some of the players that we highlight in the proper chronological order in this book are from some of those surveys. In all cases, the player is clearly a great Clemson gridiron stalwart. Whenever you see the term Player Highlights, you can expect a well-researched snap biography of a great Clemson Player. When possible, I include a picture. Enjoy!

Chapter 2 CU "Un-Official" Football Teams

Early Clemson Football Team

1890's: Nearly 50 years from the founding

You could not find a football game on South Carolina campuses at any college through most of the 1890's but by the end football was on its way. There was lots of baseball, which was the main sport on South Carolina college campuses during this early period.

Recreational levels (intramural) of football began at some institutions by the 1880s. Founded in 1889, it was not too long afterwards that spot games of football were being played wherever students could find a field to play the game. South Carolina College (later became the University of South Carolina) played football before all other schools. It became a very popular sport between groups of students who just seemed interested in its recreational value.

In October 1888 a student wrote, in a half joking manner, that football was good for health, because after playing a game players bloodied themselves to the point that they "never need to be bled by a physician." Though we do not see it much today, for thousands of years, physicians relied heavily on a single treatment for hysteria, heart disease and just about every other malady. They called it *bloodletting*. The theory behind the practice changed often over time, but the practice itself remained much the same -- with doctors often bleeding patients until they were weak, pale and, sometimes, unconscious. The student was joking but he may have been right.

Two other South Carolina Schools, Wofford and Furman seemed to have gained knowledge of football prior to their first game in December 1889 through recreational contests held on their campuses. Unlike pure intramural sports, however, they played each other. And even after the first game between the two schools, intramural contests between classes at various campuses became an annual contest in the late fall.

In 1911, long after varsity football came to South Carolina campuses, and after the intercollegiate season, the University of South Carolina conducted a competition between the four classes for the Football Trophy. Similarly, class competitions were held on campuses from Greenville to Newberry even when intercollegiate competition was suspended by most upstate schools during the first decade of the 20th century. South Carolina loved its football as did one of its sons, Clemson University.

John Heisman is one of the great immortal notables who coached at Clemson. He was respected nationwide as a football guru. Heisman first coached in 1892 at Oberlin College in Ohio. That College was founded way back in 1833. The Oberlin Review wrote about Heisman in 1892: "Mr. Heisman has entirely remade our football. He has taught us scientific football." They did not name the trophy after him because he was a slouch.

The Akron (Ohio) Beacon noted: "Trainer Heisman has shown what can be done with a new man, even in one short month of training. The advancement of the men has been remarkable."

Soon to be a head football coach at Clemson, even before Clemson began its program, Walter Riggs, the father of Clemson football, tracked down John Heisman. He was growing tomatoes and strawberries in Texas for supplemental income in 1894. Riggs offered Heisman $500 to coach football at Auburn. Heisman agreed. In 1890, John Heisman would be coaching at Clemson College (not yet a University).

There is very little written to almost nothing written about Clemson intramural football other than that we know it did exist. Unlike other schools, there appeared to be no documented unofficial intercollegiate games between pickup teams from Clemson and other colleges or universities or even athletic clubs before Clemson began its varsity football program. But, this history more than likely is inexact.

In my research, I was fortunate to find a wonderful article that appears to have been produced by the SC state government that puts the beginning of football at Clemson in perspective. Since it is public domain, and it provides great insights about South Carolina Football, with copious insights into Clemson Football, I have included it here. There is a huge bibliography following the article and for your edification, I have included it also. The States of both North and South Carolina primed their colleges and universities to be the best in college football. Clemson was one of the SC colleges that definitely got that message.

Origins and Development of College football in South Carolina, 1889-1930

Another source of early football is a book that I wrote in early 2017 titled, *American College Football: The Beginning* – available on Amazon and Kindle. ALs, Chapter 6 of this book has some great insights. Clemson began its football program in 1896. It is written by Fritz P. Hamer. Enjoy it at the following link if you want to explore SC football—the environment in which Clemson football grew up.

https://core.ac.uk/display/49236202

Here is the beginning of the article from the State of South Carolina:

"The colors of the two institutions were conspicuous. Furman's banner of purple and white floated in the air and the students wore badges of the same color . . . the players were dressed in canvass cloth uniforms and wore caps of purple and white. The old gold and black of Wofford was everywhere to be seen . . ."[1]

Such was the splendor surrounding the second year of intercollegiate competition between the two upstate college rivals in January 1891 as the teams formed on the field of Wofford's home ground in Spartanburg. Although the new game of "football" had only begun to take root in the Palmetto State less than a decade before, it was gaining a significant following on these two upstate campuses. At this early stage, though, the rules were different from what they have become. In fact, it probably resembled a rugby match more than what we see in college stadiums today. Scrimmage lines were unbalanced, the forward pass was illegal, and scoring a touchdown only earned four points, while the extra point, or goal, as it was called then, earned two.

. . .

Chapter 3 CU Launches First "Official" Football Team

Riggs,   Coach #1
Williams   Coach #2
Penton   Coach #3
Riggs   Coach #1 repeat

Year	Coach	Record	Conf	Record
1896	Walter M. Riggs	2-1-0	SIAA	0-0-0
1897	Wm. M. Williams	2-2-0	SIAA	0-1-0
1898	John Penton	3-1-0	SIAA	1-1-0
1899	Walter M. Riggs	4-2-0	SIAA	1-2-0

Finally, after the college had been operating as an academic institution for seven years, just in time for the fall season in 1906, Clemson threw its hat in the football ring. Actually, CU had its hat gently placed there by a great man and a great coach, Walter Riggs.

1896 Team Picture below: Clemson's First Varsity Football Team

Clemson's football program is a long and storied one. Some say that the Clemson program does not necessarily command the prestige of

programs like Oklahoma, Notre Dame, or Michigan. However, the coaches over the past thirty years have really made the nation notice Clemson, especially with its second National Championship in the 2016 season.

Walter Riggs--Clemson's 1st Head Football Coach

Quite Frankly, Clemson has always been a great team from its first season in 1896 to its last season 120 years later in 2016. After all, John Heisman was brought to Clemson by Walter Riggs as he was preparing to be the Clemson president. Only a few teams in the nation have a John Heisman on their immortal coaches list.

So, with two National Championships, a winning tradition, having beaten state rival South Carolina often, and having celebrated many influential head coaches and players, Clemson surely needs to make no apologies for its record.

The man who made it all happen was named Walter M. Riggs. He was responsible for the creation of an official Clemson University football program as well as its continuation and livelihood throughout the beginning of the twentieth century.

Riggs was quite a guy. He graduated from what is now Auburn University in 1892 where he played on their newly formed football team, back when American football rules were just being created by another Walter. Walter Camp worked hard to perfect the game of American football so as to differentiate it from Rugby and Soccer.

Riggs was a versatile young man and his interests were many. He was a natural leader. For example, he was the head of the Auburn Glee club and was a member of Phi Delta Theta. He was pretty good with the books also as he earned a Bachelor of Science degree in both mechanical and electrical engineering.

Riggs loved football at a time when many schools were just toying around with the notion of Walter Camp style American football. He soon became the head coach of the Auburn Tigers (1893), but he chose to move to Clemson after the 1895 season. At Auburn, Riggs had recruited John Heisman for the coaching staff and when Riggs came to Clemson, he was so respected that he was able to hand over control of Auburn's program to this same John Heisman. Yes, this is the Heisman that the trophy is named after.

And, so, as the Administration was ready to give in to pressure to form a team, they were able to snag Walter Riggs to be their first Clemson football head coach in 1996. Like everybody in football back then, when temporary bleachers were often unaffordable by colleges, Riggs had to improvise.

He ignored the property of Auburn on the older, very worn Auburn jerseys and because he and his new team were low on money, Riggs stole a few of the Auburn practice jerseys for the newly minted

Clemson players. The navy color was mostly faded out. Only a discerning eye could detect a blue. Auburn was orange and blue and so Clemson's official colors became orange, and later on, a faded navy-purple color called Regalia.

Riggs did not bother innovating on silly things like names because after all everybody has one. So, while he was stealing the jerseys, he stole the mascot name – Tigers. The Auburn Tigers never missed it as they still have it. So, Clemson also owes its mascot, the Fighting Tiger to Riggs's Auburn affections for the Tiger. Like I said, Riggs was quite a guy. In a time when nobody had anything, Riggs made due and he got the Clemson football program off the ground.

Not only did he bring the notion of football to Clemson, but he received the honor of being the head coach to start the program and then again in 1899 when there were no finds for the athletic department. Ironically, this year, 1899, was the first year that Clemson ever played Auburn.

Riggs was not the finesse and mathematical strategy coach that John Heisman was and so Auburn, under Heisman took advantage of Riggs years away from the game in 1900. Under the guidance of John Heisman, Auburn won that first meeting of "cousin by coaches' teams" 34-0. In 1900, Riggs had had his fill as he was destined for other tasks at Clemson. He officially stepped down as head coach.

John Heisman really liked Walter Riggs and that says something nice about both of the men. So, Riggs hired Heisman to coach from 1900 to 1903. Clemson's first home game under Heisman was against Davidson College on Bowman Field in 1900.

Riggs continued to work for the university as a professor in engineering, but his real passion was for athletics. He created the position of athletic director, which is currently held today by Dan Radakovich. Riggs became the president of the Southern Intercollegiate Athletics Association (SIAA) in 1912. The SIAA had 72 members when it was dissolved and comprised almost all of the members of the current Southeastern Conference (SEC), six from the Atlantic Coast Conference (ACC) and the University of Texas at Austin in the Big 12, as well as other schools that are not in Division I football.

In order to alleviate the usage of Bowman Field, a rag tag field that had served its time, a new field was to be built on the north side of campus. In 1915, it was finished and it was aptly named Riggs Field. Riggs Field was the first of many solely athletic facilities to be built on Clemson's campus. It was where the Clemson football team played until they moved to Memorial Stadium in 1942. Now it is currently being used by the men's and women's soccer teams and has been since 1980.

Walter Riggs died in 1924, two days before his 51st birthday. Some say that he worked himself too hard. In the end, his dedication and sacrifice has led Clemson to be a home for one of the top athletic programs in the nation.

In a fitting turn of events, the Clemson football team played Auburn to kick off its 2016 football season on September 3. Knowing that Clemson became National Champions, we all know it would have been quite difficult if the C Tigers lost to the A Tigers. It did not happen that way. On its way to the Championship, the Clemson Tigers survived a tough battle against an always tough Auburn Tigers squad, and won the game W (19-13). The stadium crew spent the next day cleaning up all the bitten nails. Go Fighting Tigers!

OK, so now that we have introduced the first official encounter with an oval shaped ball (football), made possible by the perspicacity of Walter M. Riggs, the first coach of the Clemson Fighting Tigers, let's look at the game as played on 1896 in the Clemson football inaugural season, known forever to the common folk such as you and me as Clemson's first football game.

1896: Clemson Tigers Coach Walter M. Riggs

The 1896 Clemson Tigers football team represented the Clemson Agricultural College during the 1896 college football season. Professor / Coach Walter Riggs brought the game to Clemson from his alma mater, Auburn, where he was a member of Auburn's first football team. The Tigers completed their first season with a record of 2–1. They became members of the Southern Intercollegiate

Athletic Association (SIAA) from day one and continued from 1896–1921, at which time, they joined the Southern Conference (SoCon).

They got their wins over upstate neighboring SC colleges Furman and Wofford, and they got their only loss of the season in the first installment of what immediately became a rivalry with South Carolina.

All Clemson games were played in the opposing school's home city as the Clemson Tigers were not yet prepared to play at home. The rivalry matchup with South Carolina was held on a Thursday morning at the South Carolina state fair, a tradition that would endure until 1960. In this encounter, Riggs served as the team's coach while R. G. Hamilton was the first team captain. Rules at the time prohibited the coach from offering direction from the sidelines.

The games of the season

The season opened up on October 31 at Furman, a team that had been playing for several years. The game was played in Greenville, SC. The Clemson Tigers emerged victorious with a nice but close win W (14–6).

Not many Clemson fans know R.G. Hamilton, but you should. Hamilton was the captain of Clemson's first football team in 1896. Below is some information on Clemson's first football team from an article on Clemson's web site:

After grueling practices, the first-ever Clemson football game day finally arrived. On October 31, 1896, Clemson traveled to Furman (probably by train). George Swygert, center on the first Clemson football team, recalls the Furman game and the first season as follows:

"With Professor Riggs as our coach we got in shape fairly well. Our first game was with Furman, the biggest men I have ever seen, and believe it or not we won that game. We had a few trick plays. One was when the play ended near the side lines, our lightest end would hide the ball under his sweater and as the two teams moved toward the center of the field for the next play, he appeared to be injured, and then when things were clear, he made a bee-line for the goal.

This worked maybe once a game, it worked against Furman our first game."

Very few details of the Clemson-Furman game are known, but it is known that Charlie Gentry scored Clemson's first touchdown in history. The Tigers defeated Furman 14-6 at Greenville, SC. Below is a rare photo of Clemson's first football team.

Clemson's First Football Team 1896 Another Picture

On November 12, the Tigers traveled to South Carolina to play in Columbia against the Gamecocks. It was called Big Thursday. SC had much more experience with American Football and were able to defeat Riggs' Tigers by a close score of L (6-12. On November 21, the Saturday before Thanksgiving, another more experienced team, Wofford played the Clemson Tigers at their home field in Spartanburg, SC. The Clemson Tigers were a tough team and took no prisoners as they beat Wofford, W (16–0)

And so, the inaugural season with professor / coach Riggs was very successful at 2 wins and just one loss. The Tiger had become unleashed and many great games and a great winning tradition would come from this, Clemson's first football season.

There was a contagion of great coaches spawned by the greatness of one coach to a protégé at the time. For example, Jack "Pee Wee" Forsythe, was the first Head Coach for the Florida Gators. He was a former Clemson Tigers lineman who played for coach THE John Heisman from 1901 to 1903. Isn't football great?

<< The 1st Gator Coach. Jack Forsythe was a real coach but he also played on the team as an end, just like Knute Rockne was an end. Forsythe used a technique known as the Minnesota shift to get the advantage over opponents.

Since 1906, when Clemson's own Jack Forsythe enabled the Gators' debut, Florida has had a football season every year until 1943 when the war demands were such that even if a university could field a team, they would have a tough time finding another team to play.

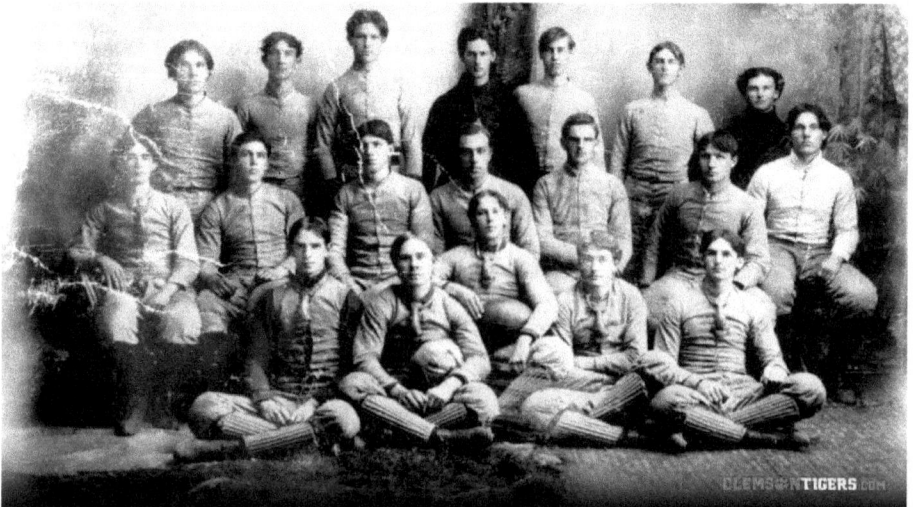

Another pic of the 1896 Team is shown above:

1897: Clemson Tigers Coach William M. Williams

The rules of football were in flux at this time. One rule was changed in 1897. A team scoring a touchdown received five points, and the goal after touchdown added another point. This scoring value would remain until 1912.

<<< Coach William Williams

The 1897 Clemson Tigers football team represented the Clemson Agricultural College during the 1897 college football season as a member of the SIAA. William M. Williams served as the team's coach for his first season while W. T. Brock was the captain. The Tigers completed their second season with a record of 2–2-0 and an 0-1 record in the SIAA. They had nice wins over South Carolina and a Charlotte YMCA team, and they lost to Georgia and North Carolina. Since there was no home field yet, all games were played in the opposing school's home city. Despite this disadvantage, and the small number of games played, the team was state champion.

Games of 1897 the season.

The Fighting Tigers kicked off the season at Georgia at Herty Field in Athens, GA. This matchup would blossom into a rivalry over the years. The Tigers lost the game. Next, on Oct 23, Clemson traveled to Charlotte to play their YMCA team. The Tigers won the game W (10-0). The next trip was to play North Carolina at Chapel Hill and the Tigers suffered their second loss L (0-28). In a game that gave the Tigers their first state championship, they beat South Carolina at Columbia on what has been dubbed Big Thursday W (18-6).

1898: Clemson Tigers Coach John Penton

The 1898 Clemson Tigers football team represented the Clemson Agricultural College during the 1898 college football season as a member of the SIAA.

<<< Coach John Penton— Penton served as the team's coach for his first season while Shack Shealy was the captain. The Tigers completed their second season with a record of 3–1-0 and a 1-1 record in the SIAA. They had nice wins over Bingham Military School, South Carolina and Georgia Tech and they lost to Georgia again. For the first time, Clemson played a home game in Calhoun SC on October 20 against Bingham Military School, and a neutral site game at Augusta, Georgia against Georgia Tech.

The season opener was Oct 8 at Georgia in an SIAA game. The Tigers got their one loss out of the way in the first game played in Herty Field in Athens GA. L (8-20). The next game was Oct 20 at an undisclosed location on campus against the Bingham Military School W (55-0) The Tigers were on the rod on Nov 17 after a month off up to Columbia SC on Big Thursday and they claimed a fine win v SC's Gamecocks W (24-0). Finishing up the season, on Nov 24, Clemson shut out Georgia Tech W (23-0) for their first SIAA victory. Nice season

1899: Clemson Tigers Coach William M. Riggs

The 1899 Clemson Tigers football team represented the Clemson Agricultural College during the 1899 college football season as a member of the SIAA. William Riggs, who was a professor at Clemson, and who had coached its first team, came back for an encore. So, he served as the team's coach for his second season while J. N. Walker was the captain. The Tigers completed their fourth season with a record of 4-2-0 and a 1-2 record in the SIAA. As you can see, the team was able to secure more games each season.

They had nice wins over Davidson, South Carolina and SIAA Georgia Tech and they lost to SIAA Georgia again. They also lost to SIAA Auburn. Clemson again did not host any games, but played a mix of away and neutral site games. Walter Riggs picked up a labor of love again as coach, having also led the team in its inaugural 1896 season.

The season opened on Oct 7 at Georgia. Again, the SIAA Conference Georgia Bulldogs beat the Clemson Tigers but each time the score is closer. This game was played in Herty Field in Athens, GA L (0-11). On Oct 14, the Tigers beat Davidson at Rock Hill, SC W (10-0). Another tough SIAA team, Auburn beat Clemson two weeks later on Oct 28 at their stadium in Auburn, AL L (0-34). On Nov 9, the Tigers beat the Gamecocks of SC on Big Thursday W (24-0).

On Nov 18, the Fighting Tigers traveled to play North Carolina. A&M at Rock Hill, SC in the first Textile Bowl W (24-0) Later historians think the series began in 1981 but it has been played 85 times including 1899. The Textile Bowl is an American college football rivalry game played annually by the Clemson Tigers football team of Clemson University and the NC State Wolfpack football team of North Carolina State University. The rivalry game has been formally known as the Textile Bowl for some time. The south is big on textiles. On Nov. 30, Clemson played at Greenville SC against Georgia Tech and the Tigers beat the Yellow Jackets in a blowout W 41–5. The next season, John Heisman came to town.

Before John Heisman came to Clemson for the 1890 season, Clemson's record was 9-6-0 overall and 2-4-0 in the SIAA. 9-6-0 is not a bad start for a brand- new football program. Winning in a tough conference always take some time. John Heisman's time had come.

Chapter 4 Historic Clemson Fields & Stadiums

First there was Bowman Field

This is Bowman Field *then*

From its initial land donation, the Clemson Campus began huge. Its setting is suburban, and the campus size is 17,000 acres. With such a huge land mass, there would be no excuse for the University to not have terrific athletic fields with plenty of space for both varsity play and pure fun for students.

This is Bowman Field *now*. . . .

Though Clemson opted to play all away games for many of its early football years while the campus was being prepared for sports, eventually, one of their academic instructors worked hard enough to make sure Clemson was able to play home games. Cut from some of the 17,000 acres, Bowman Field is an extremely large, open grassy area located in front of Sikes Hall, Tillman Hall, Godfrey Hall, Holtzendorff Hall, and Mell Hall. It is the front lawn of the campus.

The field is named for Randolph T. V. Bowman, an instructor in forge and foundry, at Clemson Agricultural College of South Carolina from February 1895 to April 1899, just after the college opened in 1889. who also served as an assistant football coach.

Bowman met with an early death at 23 years of age on April 14, 1899. The field became the parade ground for Clemson cadets and the home of Clemson University's first football, baseball, basketball teams, track and even soccer teams.

Randolph Bowman had apparently suffered from ill-health from his early years, yet he persevered as if he had no handicaps. He received a great tribute from Clemson President Henry Simms Hartzog who noted that "Though physically unable to take any considerable part in athletics, he helped [...] by his counsel and presence."

Just before his death, Bowman finished carving the commemorative plaques for Professor Henry Aubrey Strode, Clemson College's first president, and Professor W. L. McGee, now displayed in Tillman Auditorium. Bowman Field, Clemson's "front lawn", of course is named in his honor: Bowman is said to have personally cleared the former sedge field of rocks and other detritus so that it could be used as an athletics ground.

Yes, while serving as an assistant coach, Bowman took responsibility for much of the hard work required in clearing of the field area for use as an athletics field.

The two 19th-century cannons located on the field were nicknamed Tom and Jerry by the class of 1952. Bowman Field sure has a lot of history.

It is a great testimony to the spirit of Randolph Bowman that he received the honor of the first Clemson field being named after him. He was quite a young man. Like many other greats in life, Bowman was not blessed with all the physical gifts that assure a successful life, yet, he not only persevered, he conquered all the Bogeymen he faced in life but one.

Despite his powerful spirit, even he could not chase away the Grim Reaper and so he died a young man, with many accomplishments and many accomplishments that would have come. The Randolf Bowman story is inspiring. In many ways, it resembles two of my favorite perseverance fables-- The Little Engine That Could and The King and The Spider.

Randolph Bowman was in many ways like Vikram, the brave king who learned to believe in himself as noted in his own words: "If a small spider can face failure so bravely, why should I give up? He was also like the little Blue Train, The Little Engine That Could, who would not give up when bigger trains said no, and he carried the toys to the other side of the mountain so as not to disappoint the children.

But, even more special than the heroes in these fables, Randolph Bowman was just like the real Randolph Bowman. He was true to himself and all those he met. He never said no to a worthwhile challenge and he would succeed when others would give up without even picking up the cup. Clemson University is honored to have Randolph Bowman in its proud institutional and football legacy. I was very moved by his personal story.

Clemson continued over the years to improve Bowman Field even after Riggs Field and Memorial Stadium were built. I am sure Randolph Bowman would humbly approve. Today Bowman Field is regarded as "sacred soil," having played such a large part in Clemson's history and being the central location for leisure activity for students. On most any day with nice weather you are likely to see students laying out, tanning, studying, throwing frisbee, playing football, volleyball, soccer, or even playing with their dogs.

Bowman Field is used by many organizations throughout the year for a whole variety of different activities. Clemson AFROTC can be seen using the field for practice marches on most Thursday afternoons. Clemson fraternities and sororities also use Bowman Field for their many activities like Powderpuff Football. First Friday activities are usually held here and once a year, Homecoming floats are built on Bowman Field, in full view of all passing pedestrians and motorists. Habitat for Humanity builds a house for charity right on Bowman Field every year at Homecoming. Its use for parking vehicles for football games was discontinued in the 1990s over concerns of the damage done to the lawn.

Riggs Field

Bowman Field served all of Clemson's needs from 1889 to 1915. Riggs Field became Clemson's second football field, with a tour of duty from the football program lasting from 1915to 1941. Just like Bowman Field is still in high use today, so also is Riggs Field. It has now been remodeled into the university's soccer stadium.

The Original Riggs Field Circa 1915

As you recall, the founder of Clemson Football was Walter Merit Riggs who was Clemson's President and the first (and fourth) head football coach. Riggs is given credit for being the "Father of Clemson Football" insofar as his bringing the game from Auburn to the new Clemson campus is concerned.

When Clemson played its first football game against Furman on October 31, 1896, only two people on the Clemson campus had ever seen a football game - Riggs, and Tiger backfielder Frank Thompkins, a Tiger team plank-holder.

Riggs Field was designed in 1915 to replace Bowman Field. It was located right behind the Rudolph E. Lee-designed YMCA building, and it was finished the following year. Players would dress inside the Y and then come down the staircase from the rear portico of the structure to field level. Having the Y so close meant no locker room facilities were required at Riggs.

Riggs Field was dedicated October 2, 1915, prior to the football game with Davidson College. A parade to the field formed in front of the main building at 3 p.m. led, in this order, by the Cadet Band, speakers, Athletic Council, Alumni, faculty, and the Corps of Cadets.

"Upon entering Riggs Field, the body took a 'C' formation and poured forth a thrilling volume of patriotic Tiger yells and songs." (The Tiger, 5 October 1915, Volume XI, Number 3, page 1.)

Presentation of the field to the Corps of Cadets by Dr. Walter Merritt Riggs followed. Prof. J. W. Gantt, President of the Athletic Association, introduced Dr. Riggs as "the man who has done more for the athletics at Clemson and probably more for Southern athletics than any other man." "In presenting the field to the corps of cadets, Dr. Riggs said in part; 'This magnificent field is a token of recognition by the Trustees of Clemson College of the importance of military and athletic training for the cadets. It is to be a place for the teaching of the principles of team work and fair play.

On the crest of the hill stands the main Building which represents the intellectual side of life. In the immediate fore-ground you can see the Textile Building. Here the brain and hand are trained to work together. Just to our left is the magnificent new Y. M. C. A. Building, standing for the development of spirit, mind, and body. In the immediate vicinity in the back are the churches, which are agents in the influencing of our spiritual natures.

This large and beautiful athletic field was built to stand for the development of the physical man, and, whether in real work or in play the hope was for the field to be used as an agency in the developing of high and honorable men. (Mostly from The Tiger, 5 October 1915, page 1.)

Prof. Gantt then introduced Mr. H. C. Tillman, Class of 1903 and President of the Clemson Alumni Association, who christened the new playing field. Tillman offered these words: "Students who have been and are to be, no matter how much we love other things, we love our athletic field best. Therefore, this field should be named for him who has done most for our athletics. Dr. Riggs is not only the father of athletics at Clemson but has coached our teams. It is not alone for gratitude, but for a sense of love and esteem that we name this field. May it bring victory to the Tigers' lair, and may it be represented by the honor and spirit Dr. Riggs has always shown. In the name of all students and lovers of Clemson, I christen this Field Riggs Field."

A few minutes later, Dr. Riggs made the initial kick-off in the first football game to be played on the new field. Clemson and Davidson play to a 6-6 tie.

Riggs Field was the place for football for many years. Construction got underway for the new Memorial Stadium in October, 1941. The last game played on Riggs Field was against Wake Forest, on November 15, 1941. It was a fitting sendoff to the old Riggs football venue as the Tigers shut out the Demon Deacons, 29-0. Three weeks later, the Japanese Navy attacked Pearl Harbor, Hawaii, setting America's involvement in World War II into motion.

As football games were played in Memorial Stadium, Riggs Field, just like Bowman Field began to be used for other worthwhile athletic and recreational purposes. For example, in 1973, Riggs Field was the location for a closing scene of the Burt Lancaster film The Midnight Man.

Riggs Field, with its large half-mile oval cinder track, remained an intramural space through the 1970s, providing a site for Greek Week, Dixie Day, and the Special Olympics. In late March 1980, without informing anyone, the athletic department began grading of the historic Riggs Field site for transformation into the new soccer stadium. Dixie Day was moved to the soccer field located north of Death Valley on short notice.

The remodeled facility, seating 6,500, opened its new era on September 1, 1987 with a Men's soccer team win over UNC-Asheville, 8-0.

In early September 2011, the stadium which surrounds Riggs Field was named Ibrahim Stadium after the late Dr. I.M Ibrahim, who is credited with starting Clemson's men's soccer program in 1967 and who led the team to national titles in 1984 and 1987.

Riggs Kept Improving

In 2013, Riggs Field completed another round of renovations. As part of the renovation, stands were constructed to replace bleachers on the north side of the stadium. Additionally, a new entrance was constructed on the side of the stadium and pedestrian improvements were installed along the north side between the stadium and highway SC 93. A memorial to Walter Riggs was constructed at the new entrance on the north side. Renovations were completed in time for the 2013 soccer season.

Celebrating 100 Years of Riggs

On October 2, 2015, Clemson University celebrated Riggs Field's 100th anniversary. The Clemson University men's and women's soccer teams both played vs Virginia Tech and Wake Forest, respectively. Special promotions included a museum in the nearby indoor track to display artifacts and photos from Riggs Field's history, 2000 commemorative scarves to celebrate the occasion, and one uniform was given away during the women's game.

Riggs Field 2015 Construction

Historic Riggs Field Now Built for Soccer

Memorial Stadium – AKA Death Valley

Courtesy of Clemson tigers.com

Clemson Memorial Stadium is the third venue in which the Clemson Tigers played the game of football. With this latest iteration, many more fans could enjoy the game. Everybody has an opinion of "Death Valley." Opposing players from the 1970s and 1980s, professional players from the 1990s, and just about everybody else enjoy the ambiance of this special setting and most understand that this is what college football is all about.

The storied edifice added to its legend when the first meeting of father and son head coaches (Bowden Bowl I) took place before a sellout crowd of more than 86,000 fans in 1999. Clemson has ranked in the top 20 in the nation in average attendance 22 consecutive seasons. That includes 2001 when Clemson set an ACC record for total attendance. Last season, the streak continued when Clemson averaged nearly 79,000 fans per game.

The facility's mystique is derived from its many traditions, which date to its opening in 1942, the legendary games and players, and Clemson's corresponding rate of success. Clemson has won 227 games in 63 years there and has won over 71 percent of the contests (227-88-7). Thirty-nine times since 1983, a crowd has exceeded 80,000.

The stadium has definitely been good to the Tigers, but the stadium was constructed against the advice of at least one Clemson coach. Just before Head Coach Jess Neely left for Rice after the 1939 season, he gave Clemson a message. "Don't ever let them talk you into building a big stadium," he said. "Put about 10,000 seats behind the YMCA. That's all you'll ever need."

Instead of following Coach Neely's advice, however, Clemson officials decided to build the new stadium in a valley on the western part of campus. The place would take some clearing-there were many trees, but luckily there were no hedges. The crews went to work, clearing, cutting, pouring, and forming. Finally, on September 19, 1942, Memorial Stadium opened with Clemson thrashing Presbyterian by a score of 32-13. Those 20,000 seats installed for Opening Day would soon grow; and grow and grow.

When the original part of the stadium was built in the early 40's, much of the work was done by scholarship athletes, including many football players. The first staking out of the stadium was done by two members of the football team, A.N. Cameron and Hugh Webb. Webb returned to Clemson years later to be an architecture professor, and Cameron went on to become a civil engineer in Louisiana.

The building of the stadium did not proceed without problems. One day during the clearing of the land, one young player proudly announced that he was not allergic to poison oak. He then commenced to attack the poison oak with a swing blade, throwing the plants to and fro. The next day, the boy was swollen twice his size and was hospitalized.

There are many other stories about the stadium, including one that Frank Howard put a chew of tobacco in each corner as the concrete poured. Howard said that the seeding of the grass caused a few problems. "About 40 people and I laid sod on the field," he said. "After three weeks, on July 15, we had only gotten halfway through." "I told them that it had taken us three weeks to get that far, and I would give them three more week's pay for however long it took. I also told them we would have 50 gallons of ice cream when we got through. After that it took them three days to do the rest of the field.

Then we sat down in the middle of the field and ate up that whole 50 gallons."

Howard said that on the day of the first game in the stadium, "the gates were hung at 1:00 and we played at 2:00." But that would be all of the construction for a while. Then in 1958, 18,000 sideline seats were added and in 1960, 5,658 west endzone seats were added in response to increasing attendance.

With the large endzone, "Green Grass" section, this expansion increased capacity to 53,000. Later, upper decks were added to each side of as crowds swelled - the first in 1978 and the second in '83. This increased capacity to over 80,000, which makes it one of the largest on-campus stadiums.

The effect of spiraling inflation has had in this century can be dramatically seen in the differences in stadium construction. The original part of the stadium was built at a cost of $125,000 or at $6.25 a seat. The newest upper deck was finished in 1983 at a cost of $13.5 million, or $866 a seat.

The capacity for Clemson Memorial Stadium in 2005 was listed as 77,381 during construction of the WestZone area. The new capacity with the completion of the WestZone in 2006 is 80,301. Previously, capacity was listed as 81,473. When we listed that number in previous years, we counted 6,000 people on the hill. Our new capacities (2005 and 2006) count just 4,000 people on the hill and that accounts for the fact that our new capacity in 2006 is lower than what it had been previously.

Phase II of the WestZone project includes coaches' offices, administrative offices, a new strength and conditioning area, a large team room/auditorium, an expanded equipment room and athletic training facilities. Life improves as time passes and people work hard.

Through the years, Memorial Stadium has become known as "Death Valley." It was tagged this by the late Presbyterian coach, Lonnie McMillan. After bringing his P.C. teams to Clemson for years and getting whipped, McMillan said the place was like Death Valley. A few years later the name stuck.

In 1974, the playing surface was named Frank Howard Field for the legendary coach because of his long service and dedication to the University.

Luckily, the stadium wasn't built behind the YMCA.

Clemson's Top Single Season Attendance Figures

Rank	Year	Home Games	Total	Average	Head Coach
1.	1988	6	490,502	81,750	Danny Ford
2.	2006	7	570,542	81,506	Tommy Bowden
3.	2001	6	480,911	80,152	Tommy Bowden
4.	1990	6	475,174	79,196	Ken Hatfield
5.	1989	6	473,566	78,927	Danny Ford
6.	2004	6	472,939	78,823	Tommy Bowden
7.	1986	5	393,500	78,700	Danny Ford
8.	2000	7	548,647	78,378	Tommy Bowden
9.	1999	5	391,510	78,302	Tommy Bowden
10.	2005	6	469,391	78,232	Tommy Bowden

Pre-Game Festivities

Howard's Rock

Chapter 5 The Evolution of Modern American Football

Yale vs. Columbia

Lots of playing before playing became official

The official agreed upon date for the first American-style college football game is November 6, 1869. If you can find a replay of this game someplace in the heavens, however, you would find it would not look much like football as we know it. But, it was not completely soccer or rugby either.

Before this game, teams were playing a rugby style similar to that played in Britain in the mid-19th century. At the time in the US, a derivative known as association football was also played. In both games, a football is kicked at a goal or run over a line. These styles were based on the varieties of English public school football games. Over time, as noted, the style of "football" play in America continued to evolve.

On November 6, 1869, the first football game in America featured Rutgers and Princeton. Before the teams were even on the field it was being plugged as the first college football game of all time. Penn State did not get a Rugby team until the early 1960's. Nobody at Penn State in 1869, from what I could find, was even thinking about the game of football.

The first game of intercollegiate football was a sporting battle between two neighboring schools on a plot of ground where the present-day Rutgers gymnasium now stands in New Brunswick, N.J. Rutgers won that first game, 6-4.

There were two teams of 25 men each and the rules were rugby-like, but different enough to make it very interesting and enjoyable.

Like today's football, there were many surprises; strategies needed to be employed; determination exhibited, and of course the players required physical prowess.

1st Game Rutgers 6 Princeton 4 College Field, New Brunswick, NJ

At 3 p.m. the 50 combatants as well as 100 spectators gathered on the field. Most sat on a low wooden fence and watched the athletes discard their hats, coats and vests. The players used their suspenders as belts. To give a unique look, Rutgers wore scarlet-colored scarfs, which they converted into turbans. This contrasted them with the bareheaded boys from Princeton.

Two members of each team remained more or less stationary near the opponent's goal in the hopes of being able to slip over and score from unguarded positions. Thus, the present day "sleeper" was conceived. The remaining 23 players were divided into groups of 11 and 12. While the 11 "fielders" lined up in their own territory as defenders, the 12 "bulldogs" carried the battle.

Each score counted as a "game" and 10 games completed the contest. Following each score, the teams changed direction. The ball could be advanced only by kicking or batting it with the feet, hands, heads or sides.

Rutgers put a challenge forward that three games were to be played that year. The first was played at New Brunswick and won by Rutgers. Princeton won the second game, but cries of "over-emphasis" prevented the third game in football's first year when faculties of both institutions protested on the grounds that the games were interfering with student studies.

This is an excerpt of the Rutgers account of the game on its web site. A person named Herbert gave this detailed account of the play in the first game:

"Though smaller on the average, the Rutgers players, as it developed, had ample speed and fine football sense. Receiving the ball, our men formed a perfect interference around it and with short, skillful kicks and dribbles drove it down the field. Taken by surprise, the Princeton men fought valiantly, but in five minutes we had gotten the ball through to our captains on the enemy's goal and S.G. Gano, '71 and G.R. Dixon, '73, neatly kicked it over. None thought of it, so far as I know, but we had without previous plan or thought evolved the play that became famous a few years later as 'the flying wedge'."

"Next period Rutgers bucked, or received the ball, hoping to repeat the flying wedge," Herbert's account continues. "But the first time we formed it Big Mike came charging full upon us. It was our turn for surprise. The Princeton battering ram made no attempt to reach the ball but, forerunner of the interference-breaking ends of today, threw himself into our mass play, bursting us apart, and bowing us over. Time and again Rutgers formed the wedge and charged; as often Big Mike broke it up. And finally, on one of these incredible break-ups a

Princeton bulldog with a long accurate, perhaps lucky kick, sent the ball between the posts for the second score.

It was at this point that a Rutgers professor could stand it no longer. Waving his umbrella at the participants, he shrieked, "You will come to no Christian end!"

Herbert's account of the game continues: "The fifth and sixth goals went to Rutgers. The stars of the latter period of play, in the memory of the players after the lapse of many years, were "Big

Mike" and Large (former State Senator George H. Large of Flemington, another Princeton player) ...

The University of Notre Dame did not get into the football act until the late 1880's. At this time, the rules of rugby kept changing to accommodate the infatuation for the Americanized style of "football" play that would ultimately become the American game of football.

Walter Camp: the father of American football?

EARLY FOOTBALL HEROES

37 USA

2003

WALTER CAMP

Walter Camp was a very well-known rugby player from Yale. In today's world, he would have been characterized as a rugby hero. It was his love of the game, his knowledge of the game as it was played, and his innovative mind that caused him to take the evolution of football even further. He pioneered the changes to the rules of rugby that slowly transformed the sport into the new game of American Football.

The rule changes that were introduced to the rugby and

association style (like soccer) of play were mostly those authored by Camp, who was also a Hopkins School graduate. For his original efforts, Walter Camp today is considered to be the "Father of American Football". Among the important changes brought to the game were the introduction of a line of scrimmage; down-and-distance rules; and the legalization of interference (blocking).

There was no such thing in those days as a forward pass and so the legalization of interference in 1880 football permitted blocking for runners. The forward pass would add another dimension to the game that made it much different than rugby or association football.

Soon after the early football changes, in the late nineteenth and into the early twentieth centuries, more game-play type developments were introduced by college coaches. The list is like a who's who of early American College Football. Coaches, such as Eddie Cochems, Amos Alonzo Stagg, Parke H. Davis, Knute Rockne, John Heisman, and Glenn "Pop" Warner helped introduce and then take advantage of the newly introduced forward pass. College football as well as professional football, were introduced prior to the 20th century. Fans were lured into watching again and again once they saw the game played.

College football especially grew in popularity despite the existence of pro-football. It became the dominant version of the sport of football in the United States. It was this way for the entire first half of the 20th century. Bowl games made the idea of football even more exciting in the college ranks. Rivalries grew and continued and the fans loved it! This great football tradition brought a national audience to college football games that still dominates the sports world today.

This book has little to do with pro-football or any other sport. However, there is no denying that the greatest college football players more often than not eventually found their fortunes in professional football. Pro football can be traced back to the season that Notre Dame brought forth a real football team after a two-year lapse from its last half-Rugby season in 1889. It was 1892 when William "Pudge" Heffelfinger signed a $500 contract to play for the Allegheny Athletic Association against the Pittsburgh Athletic Club.

Twenty-eight years later, the American Professional Football Association was formed. This league changed its name to the National Football League (NFL) just two years later. Eventually, the NFL became the major league of American football. Originally, just a sport played in Midwestern industrial towns in the United States, professional football eventually became a national phenomenon. We all know this because from August to February, in America, many of us are glued to our TV sets or chained to our seats in some of the most intriguing pro-football stadiums in America.

The Heisman

In 1935, New York City's Downtown Athletic Club awarded its first Heisman Trophy to University of Chicago halfback Jay Berwanger. He was also the first ever NFL Draft pick in 1936. The trophy continues to this day to recognize the nation's "most outstanding" college football player. It has become one of the most coveted awards in all of American sports.

Jay Berwanger, 1st Heisman Winner

New formations and play sets continued to be developed by innovative coaches and their staffs. Emory Bellard from the University of Texas, developed a three-back option style offense known as the wishbone. Bear Bryant of Alabama became a preacher of the wishbone.

The strategic opposite of the wishbone is called the spread offense. Some teams have managed to adapt with the times to keep winning consistently. In the rankings of the most victorious programs, Michigan, Texas, and Notre Dame are ranked first, second, and third in total wins.

And so that is as far as we will take it in this chapter about the early evolution of football. With so many conferences and sports associations as well as pro, college, high school, and mini sports, something tells me we have not yet seen our last rule change.

Chapter 6 John Heisman Era 1900-1903

Heisman   Coach #4

Year	Coach	Record	Conf	Record
1900	John Heisman	6-0-0	SIAA	3-0-0
1901	John Heisman	3–1–1	SIAA	1-0-1
1902	John Heisman	5–2–1	SIAA	5-0-0
1903	John Heisman	6–1–1	SIAA	2-0-1

1900 Clemson Football Team Picture Coach John Heisman

John Heisman is one of the most well-known football figures of all time. There would be no reason for me to research his life in full in order to provide you what is already written about this great man and great coach.

The following account of John Heisman and his impact on the
Clemson Football program is presented below in an article written on
October 18, 2000, by Sam Blackman, the Associate Sports
Information Director at Clemson, University. Our thanks to Clemson
University for making this available.

John Heisman
Head Coach Years: 1900-1903
Record at Clemson: 19-3-2
Winning Percentage: .833

A name synonymous with not only the early years of Clemson
football but the collegiate game is John Heisman.

A stern disciplinarian, he expected his players to be of high
character and performance both on the football field and in the
classroom. Heisman coached the Tigers in 1900 to 1903 and was
responsible for putting the Clemson name among the annals of the
great early collegiate teams.

JOHN HEISMAN
COACHED AT
CLEMSON FROM
1900-03 AND
WAS LATER
INDUCTED INTO
THE COLLEGE
FOOTBALL HALL
OF FAME.

Heisman was brought to Clemson by a professor and later University President, Walter Riggs. In the spring of 1894, Riggs was a graduate manager for the Auburn football team, and he was responsible for finding a coach for the 1895 season. Riggs wrote to Carl Williams of Pennsylvania, captain of the 1894 team asking him to suggest a suitable coach. He replied recommending J.W. Heisman, an ex-Penn player, and his coach at Oberlin a few years earlier.

After several weeks, Riggs finally found Heisman in Texas, where he was engaged in raising tomatoes. Having sunk about all of his capital into the tomato venture, he was glad to go back to his old love of football and he readily went to coach at Auburn for $500.OO a year. Riggs later was hired as a professor at Clemson and he hired Heisman at Clemson in 1900. (Riggs started the Clemson football program in 1896 and was head coach in 1896 and 1899).

Heisman began his coaching career at Oberlin in 1892 and lasted 36 years in the profession. His career included positions at Akron, Auburn, Clemson, Georgia Tech, Penn, Washington and Jefferson, and Rice University. He had an overall career record of 185 wins, 70 losses, and 17 ties.

He invented the hidden ball trick, the handoff, the double lateral, and the "Flea flicker." He pioneered the forward pass, and originated the center snap and the word "hike" (previously the center used to roll the ball on the ground to the quarterback).

Heisman took Clemson to a 19-3-2 record in his four seasons. His .833 winning percentage. is still the best in Clemson history. He was also the Clemson baseball coach between 1901-1904.

Clemson was a powerhouse during his tenure and was a most feared opponent. His secret was that he depended on smart, quick players rather than large size and brawn.

William Heisman, a nephew of John Heisman often told a story on how his famous uncle stressed academics.

"I remember a story Coach Heisman used to tell me about this famous football player he confronted in the locker room before a big game. My uncle came busting through the door and went over to this guy and said, 'You can't play today because you haven't got your grades up to par. 'The player looked up at my uncle and said, 'Coach, don't you know that the sportswriters call this toe on my right foot the million-dollar toe?' My uncle snapped back right quick and said, `What good is it if you only have a fifteen-cent head?

Another favorite Heisman story was the speech he used to make before a season began. Heisman would face his recruits holding a football. "What is it?" he would sharply ask. Then he would tell his players, "a football was a prolate spheroid, an elongated sphere-in which the outer leather casing is drawn up tightly over a somewhat smaller rubber tubing." Then after a long pause he would say, "better to have died as a small boy than to fumble this football."

Heisman broke down football into these percentages: talent 25%; mentality 20%; aggressiveness 20%; speed 20%; and weight 15%. He considered coaching as being a master-commanding, even dictatorial. He has no time to say 'please' or `mister', and he must be occasionally severe, arbitrary, and something of a czar."

On November 29,1900, Clemson defeated Alabama 35-0, which allowed Heisman's team to finish the season undefeated with a 6-0 record. This was Clemson's first undefeated team and was the only team to win all of its games in a season until the 1948 squad went 11-0. The Tigers only allowed two touchdowns the entire 1900 season.

Clemson opened the 1901 season with a 122-0 win over Guilford. The Tigers averaged 30 yards per play and a touchdown every minute and 26 seconds. The first half lasted 20 minutes while the second half lasted only 10 minutes. Legend has it that every man on the Clemson team scored a touchdown in this game.

In his third season, on November 27, 1902, Clemson played in the snow for the first time in a game against Tennessee. The Tigers won the game, 11-0, and claimed the Southern Intercollegiate Athletic Association crown. (An early conference that had several southern colleges and universities as members).

In his final season in 1903, Clemson defeated Georgia Tech 73-0 on October 17, 1903. Clemson rushed the ball 55 times for 615 yards, while Tech ran the ball 35 times and collected 28 yards. The second half was shortened to 15 minutes.

On November 24, 1903 Clemson participated in its "First Bowl Game" as Clemson and Cumberland met on this date for the Championship of the South. The contract for the game was drawn up just two weeks before the game was to be played. Cumberland, who had earlier defeated Auburn, Alabama, and Vanderbilt was considered to be champion of the southern states of Louisiana, Mississippi, Alabama, Tennessee, and Kentucky. While Clemson was considered to be the best team in Virginia, North Carolina, South Carolina and Georgia. The game was played on a neutral site, Montgomery, AL. Cumberland and Clemson fought to a 11-11 tie. In this game, John Maxwell scored as a result of a 100-yard kickoff return. After the news came back to Clemson that the game ended in a tie, the students and the local towns people built a bonfire and paraded around the campus.

John Heisman's 19-3-2 record Is still the best in Clemson history on a percentage basis. The man named after the famous trophy that each year honors the best player in college football holds the distinction of building the early foundation of Clemson's football tradition.

1900: Clemson Tigers Coach John Heisman

In 1900, another rule affected how when a touchdown was to count as a touchdown. This year's change was of the definition of touchdown, which was changed to include situations where the ball becomes dead on or above the goal line.

Walter Riggs continued to help the football program. In fact, he led the effort to raise the $415.11 to hire Auburn's football coach John Heisman, the first Clemson coach who had experience coaching at another school. Heisman was already a coaching legend when he came to Clemson.

As Riggs recalled, "By 1899 the Clemson football team had risen steadily until its material was equal to that of any southern college, and the time had come to put on the long-planned finishing touch." Heisman once described his style of play at Clemson as "radically different from anything on earth".

When the team took the field in 1900, they wore jerseys and stockings bearing distinctive orange and purple stripes.

The 1900 Clemson Tigers football team represented the Clemson Agricultural College during the 1900 college football season as a member of the SIAA. John Heisman was the fourth head football coach at Clemson, having been recruited for the Job by William Riggs, well known professor and football coach. This was the first of four years for John Heisman at the helm of the Fighting Tigers. Norman Walker was the team captain. The Tigers completed their fifth season with a record of 6-0-0 and a 3-0 record in the SIAA.

They had a nice win over Davidson on opening day. It was then the largest score ever made in the South and the season's only home game for the Tigers. For the first time this year, the Tigers beat Georgia. They were simply outstanding. In the fifth year of the program, the Tigers outscored their opponents 222–10. As noted, the 64–0 win over Davidson on opening day was then the largest score ever made in the South. That was worth repeating. Also, worth repeating is that the Clemson Tigers were undefeated and untied in 1900 under John Huntsman

Games of the 1900 Season

The season opened on Oct 19 at home in Calhoun SC against Davidson W (64-0). Three days later, on Oct 22, the Tigers were in Spartanburg, SC for a W (21-0) win against Wofford. The real score was not kept as Clemson agreed that every point scored after the first four touchdowns would not count.

Going into the South Carolina game, Clemson had been strong on offense, but weak on defense. Kinsler and Douthit were both injured.

And, so, on Nov 1, on Big Thursday, despite what might have been, Clemson ripped SC W (51-0). The Tigers rolled up a 51–0 score on in-state rival South Carolina. Then, for the first time in five meetings, on Nov 10, Clemson did the impossible. The Tigers beat the well-experienced Georgia Bulldogs at Herty Field in Athens, GA W (39-5). It wasn't even close.

Before the game with Georgia at Georgia, students in the dorms barraged Clemson players with bits of coal. Clemson went on to beat the Bulldogs for the first time, pulling away in the second half to overwhelm the Bulldogs 39–5, and achieve the season's first great victory. The starting lineup on the team was Bellows (left end), Dickerson (left tackle), George (left guard) Kinsley (center), Woodward (right guard), Walker (right tackle), Lynah (right end), Lewis (quarterback), Forsythe (left halfback), Hunt (right halfback), Douthit (fullback).

On Nov 24, Clemson faced its toughest opponent of the year VPI aka Virginia Tech, but the Fighting Tigers prevailed against the Hokies W (12-5). On November 29, Clemson got its rivalry with Alabama started right when it whooped the Crimson White W (35-0). Yes, the history of the two teams battling for dominance goes back to 1900

The season closer was played on Thanksgiving against the Alabama Crimson White, as noted, it was Clemson's first meeting with Alabama, at Birmingham's North Birmingham Park. The Tigers won 35–0. Clemson back Claude Douthit scored four touchdowns. After the Tigers forced an Alabama punt to open the game, Douthit scored three consecutive touchdowns for Clemson en route to an 18–0 lead. Douthit scored first on a 5-yard run, next on a short reception and finally on a second short touchdown run.

M. N. Hunter then scored for Clemson on a long run just before the break and made the halftime score 23–0. In the second half, the Tigers extended their lead to 35–0, behind a long Jim Lynah touchdown run and Douthit's fourth score of the day on a short run. With approximately four minutes left in the game, both team captains agreed to end the game early due to an unruly crowd and impending darkness.

Tigers take all the 1900 SIAA marbles (A championship)

The Tigers ended the season with the outright SIAA title. It was both Clemson and Heisman's first conference championship and undefeated, untied season. The season saw "the rise of Clemson from a little school whose football teams had never been heard of before, to become a football machine of the very first power." Judging from the 2017 results, things have not changed much.

1901: Clemson Tigers Coach John Heisman

The 1901 Clemson Tigers football team represented the Clemson Agricultural College during the 1901 college football season as a member of the SIAA. John Heisman was the head football coach in his second of four seasons at Clemson. The Tigers completed their sixth season overall and sixth in the SIAA with a record of 3-1-1 and a 1-0-1 record in the SIAA.

They had a record-breaking-win over Guilford on opening day W (122-0). On October 5, home at Bowman Field. Rumor was that everybody on the team scored that game. On Oct 19, they tied the Volunteers at Waite Field in Knoxville Tennessee T (6-6). On Oct 26 v Georgia, at Herty Field in Athens, GA, the Tigers beat the Bulldogs for the second year in a row, W (29–5). The next week, Oct 31, it was off to Columbia SC to play a tough VPI team for the second year in a row. The Tigers lost this close one L (17-11). Idle for a month, Clemson picked it up again on Nov 28 and beat North Carolina in Charlotte W (22-10).

1902: Clemson Tigers Coach John Heisman   *Conference Champs*

The 1902 Clemson Tigers football team represented the Clemson Agricultural College during the 1902 college football season as a member of the SIAA. John Heisman was the head football coach in his third of four seasons at Clemson. The Tigers completed their sixth season overall and sixth in the SIAA with a record of 6-1-0 and a 5-0 undefeated record in the SIAA, winning the conference championship. The lone loss was their first to rival South Carolina since 1896. It was a controversial game that ended in riots and banning further play between the teams until 1909.

1902 Clemson Football Team, John Heisman Coach

This year, John Heisman got a raise and was paid $815.11 to coach the football team. The team's captain was Hope Sadler. This was the first season with both Sadler and Carl Sitton at ends. One writer recalls, "Sitton and Hope Sadler were the finest ends that Clemson ever had perhaps."

The season opened on Oct 4 with a home W (11–5) victory over North Carolina A&M in the Textile Bowl. On October 18, at Georgia Tech, Clemson walloped the Yellow Jackets W (44–5). The day before the game, Clemson sent in scrubs to Atlanta, checked into a hotel, and partied until dawn. The varsity sat well rested in Lula, Georgia as Tech betters were fooled. All tricks were permitted without the NCAA's ever watchful eye.

Clemson scored first on an 80-yard end run from Carl Sitton. The starting lineup was Sitton (left end), Barnwell (left tackle), Kaigler (left guard), Green (center), Forsyth (right guard), DeCosta (right tackle), Sadler (right end), Maxwell (quarterback), Gantt (left halfback), Lawrence (right halfback), Hanvey (fullback). Week 3: at Furman On Oct 24, Clemson prevailed at Furman W (28-0). The Tigers made their first touchdown after three minutes of play. On one play, Heisman used a tree to his advantage.

On Oct 20, Clemson lost L (12–6) to rival South Carolina in Columbia, for the first time since 1896, the first year of the rivalry. There were a lot of shenanigans. The Carolina fans that week were carrying around a poster with the image of a tiger with a gamecock standing on top of it, holding the tiger's tail as if he was steering the tiger by the tail," Jay McCormick said. "Naturally, the Clemson guys didn't take too kindly to that, and on Wednesday and again on Thursday, there were sporadic fistfights involving brass knuckles and other objects and so forth, some of which resulted, according to the newspapers, in blood being spilled and persons having to seek medical assistance.

After the game on Thursday, the Clemson guys frankly told the Carolina students that if you bring this poster, which is insulting to us, to the big parade on Friday, you're going to be in trouble. And naturally, of course, the Carolina students brought the poster to the parade. If you give someone an ultimatum and they're your rival, they're going to do exactly what you told them not to do."

As expected, another brawl broke out before both sides agreed to mutually burn the poster in an effort to defuse tensions. The immediate aftermath resulted in the stoppage of the rivalry until 1909.

Clemson gained only 2 and a half yards in the first half. On a triple pass around end, Sitton made a 30-yard touchdown in the second half. More than 5,000 were in attendance.

On Nov 8, Clemson defeated the Georgia Bulldogs at Georgia by a score of W (36–0). One writer called it "the hardest fought football game ever seen here."

On Nov 15, Clemson beat Auburn W (15-0). The Tigers scored three touchdowns on Auburn, using double passes at times.

On Nov 27 Week 7 at Tennessee, Clemson closed the season. Tennessee had already won a then-school record six games, and the beat Clemson W (11–0). Tennessee's Tootsie Douglas still holds the record for the longest punt in school history, when he punted a ball 109 yards (the field length was 110 yards in those days). It was in a blizzard."

1903: Clemson Tigers Coach John Heisman *Conference champs*

The 1903 Clemson Tigers football team represented the Clemson Agricultural College during the 1903 college football season as a member of the SIAA. John Heisman was the head football coach in his last of four seasons at Clemson. The Tigers completed their eighth season overall and also their eighth in the SIAA with a record of 4-1-1 and a 2-0-1-- undefeated record in the SIAA. Clemson won the conference co-championship. Their lone loss was to North Carolina at Chapel Hill in a real nail-biter.

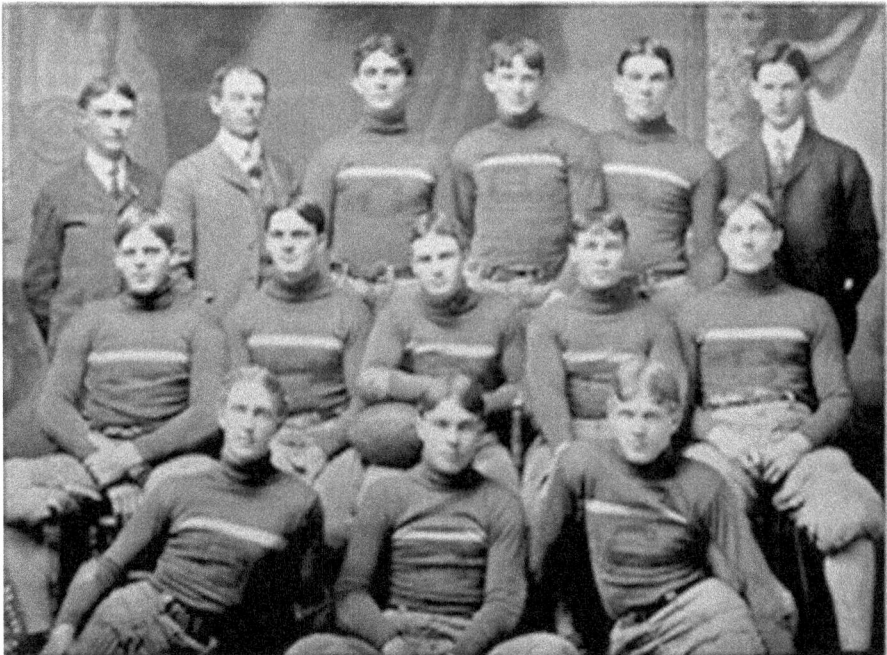

1903 Clemson Football Team John Heisman Coach

During the season, the team competed in an early conference championship game, tying Cumberland 11–11 in the contest. This was John Heisman's last season coaching Clemson. The Tigers had some great moments such as thrashing Georgia Tech's Yellow Jackets 73-0, leading to Heisman's later job-offer at Georgia Tech Even great coaches need to eventually go where other colleges can pay well for their services.

Before the season, teams had to acclimate themselves to the new point system. For the 1903 season, the point values were different from those used in contemporary games. In 1903, for example, a touchdown was worth five points, a field goal was worth five points and a conversion (PAT) was worth one point.

Hope Sadler was again the Tigers'' team captain. This was the last season with both Sadler and Carl Sitton at ends. As noted several times previously, one writer recalls, "Sitton and Hope Sadler were the finest ends that Clemson ever had perhaps."

Games of the 1903 season.

On Oct 10, Clemson shut out Georgia W (29-0) at Herty Field in Athens Georgia. The Bulldogs offered Clemson a bushel of apples for every point over 29 it scored against rival Georgia Tech. Clemson would win W (73-0) v Georgia Tech in Atlanta a week later on Oct 17 on a mud-soaked field, leading to Heisman's later job at Tech. Sitton had to sit out the game.

On Oct 28, it was North Carolina A & M in the Textile Bowl played in Columbia SC W (24-0). While the Aggies gained much using conventional football, Clemson had to use many trick plays Oliver Gardner played for A&M. John Heisman got married soon after the game. North Carolina was next at Chapel Hill. The North Carolina Tar Heels then squeaked out a win over Clemson in a nail biter L (6-11). The Tar Heels handed Clemson its only loss of the season. Carolina's Newton scored first, with a bloody nose. He also scored the second touchdown. Clemson had one touchdown by Johnny Maxwell called back due to an offside penalty.

The Tigers came back on November 21 against Davidson at Latta Park, Charlotte NC for a nice win W (24-0). Charlotte, NC Clemson won easily over Davidson 24–0. One writer noted "Clemson playing against eleven wooden men, would attract more attention. "Then in the SIAA Championship game on November 26, the Clemson Tigers were tied by the Cumberland Phoenix T 11-11) in Montgomery Alabama to become co-champions of the conference.

In this game billed as the "SIAA Championship Game." Cumberland rushed out to an early 11–0 lead. Wiley Lee Umphlett in Creating the Big Game: John W. Heisman and the Invention of American Football writes, "During the first half, Clemson was never really in the game due mainly to formidable line play of the Bridges brothers– giants in their day at 6 feet 4 inches–and a big center named "Red" Smith, was all over the field backing up the Cumberland line on defense. Clemson had been outweighed before, but certainly not like this."

Quarterback John Maxwell, 1903

Quarterback John Maxwell returned a kickoff for a touchdown. A contemporary account reads "The Clemson players seemed mere dwarfs as they lined up for the kickoff. To the crowd on the sidelines it didn't seem that Heisman's charges could possibly do more than give a gallant account of themselves in a losing battle."

A touchdown was scored by fullback E. L. Minton (touchdowns were worth 5 points). Guard M. O. Bridges kicked the extra point. Halfback J. A. Head made another touchdown, but Bridges missed the try. After halftime, Clemson quarterback John Maxwell raced 100 yards for a touchdown. Clemson missed the try. Cumberland fumbled a punt and Clemson recovered. Cumberland expected a trick play when Fritz Furtick simply ran up the middle and scored.

One account of the play reads "Heisman saw his chance to exploit a weakness in the Cumberland defense: run the ball where the ubiquitous Red Smith wasn't. So, the next time Sitton started out on one of his slashing end runs, at the last second he tossed the ball back to the fullback who charged straight over center (where Smith would have been except that he was zeroing in on the elusive Sitton) and went all the way for the tying touchdown." Jock Hanvey kicked the extra point and the game ended in an 11–11 tie.

<<< Captain Hope Sadler 1903 The winning team was to be awarded the ball. Captain W. W. Suddarth of Cumberland wanted captain Hope Sadler of Clemson to get the ball, and Sadler insisted Suddarth should have it. Some ten minutes of bickering was resolved when the ball was given to patrolman Patrick J. Sweeney, for warning the media and fans to stay down in front and allow spectators to see the game.

The school claims a share of the title. Heisman pushed for Cumberland to be named SIAA champions at year's end. It was Heisman's last game as Clemson head coach, who was hired at Georgia Tech for $450 more per year. After getting married and being offered a 25% pay increase, Heisman could not say no. Too bad Clemson was not able to pay Heisman what he was worth.

Chapter 7 Shack Shealy and Eddie Cochems Era 1904-1905

Coach # 5 Shack Shealy
Coach # 6 Eddie Cochems

Year	Coach	Record	Conference	Record
1904	Shack Shealy	3-3-1	SIAA	3-2-1
1905	Eddie Cochems	3-2-1	SIAA	3-2-1

1904 Coach Shack Shealy

1904 Clemson Tigers Football Coach Shack Shealy

The 1904 Clemson Tigers football team represented the Clemson Agricultural College during the 1904 college football season as a member of the SIAA. Shack Shealy, formerly a team captain, was the head football coach in his first and only season at Clemson. The Tigers completed their ninth season overall and also their ninth in the SIAA with a record of 3-3-1 overall and 3-2-1 in the SIAA. They gained ninth place of 19 teams in the SIAA. Joe Holland was the captain

1905 Clemson Tigers Football Coach Eddie Cochems

The 1905 Clemson Tigers football team represented the Clemson Agricultural College during the 1905 college football season as a member of the SIAA. Eddie Cochems, one of the immortals and early tradesmen in football strategies was the head football coach in his first and only season at Clemson. Eddie Cochems was just getting started but he would become well known in College football. He was a future innovator of the forward pass. Clemson was not his first choice. He had just lost out to Phil King for the Wisconsin job, when he accepted to coach Clemson's 1905 team. A fine coach, Cochems left after just one year.

The Tigers completed their tenth season overall and also their tenth in the SIAA with a record of 3-2-1 overall and 3-2-1 in the SIAA. They gained fifth place of 169 teams in the SIAA. Puss Derrick was the captain. Though the team finished fifth in the SIAA, they did not play all teams. Sports pundit John de Saulles rated Clemson as the third best team in the SIAA.

1905 Clemson Coach Eddie Cochems

1905 Clemson Tigers Football team

<<< Puss Derrick, Clemson Captain
On Oct 14, in the season home opener, Tennessee marched into Bowman Field to play Eddie Cochems' Tigers and the tough Volunteers came away with a tie T (5-5). On the road the next week, Oct 21 at Georgia, the Tigers laid a wallop to the Georgia Bulldogs W (35-0). On Oct 25 at the State Fairgrounds in Columbia SC, The Fighting Tigers got the best of Alabama W (25-0).

On November 11, at Auburn, an inspired Clemson team triumphed v these Tiger rivals W (26-0). So far, there were no losses but that would not last more than one week. On November 11, the Clemson Tigers traveled to Dudley Field in Nashville Tennessee and they were shut out badly by a tough Vanderbilt team L (0-41). By November 30, the next game, the Tigers had regained composure and they played a tough game in Grant Field Atlanta GA but it was not tough enough to defeat Georgia Tech's Yellow Jackets who stung the Tigers L (10-17)

Chapter 8 Bob Williams & Frank Shaughnessy Era 1906-1907

Coach # 7 Bob Williams
Coach # 8 Frank Shaughnessy

Year	Coach	Record	Conf	Record
1906	Bob Williams	3-3-1	SIAA	4-0-1
1907	Frank Shaughnessy	4-4-0	SIAA	1-3-0

1906 Clemson Tigers Football Coach Bob Williams (Championship caliber)

<<< Coach Bob Williams

The 1906 Clemson Tigers football team represented the Clemson Agricultural College during the 1906 college football season as a member of the SIAA.

Bob Williams, a coach who would be at the Clemson helm for six years at various times, but none longer than two years, was the head football coach in his first of six seasons at Clemson and his only year in a row this time.

he Tigers completed their eleventh season overall and also their eleventh in the SIAA with a record of 4-0-3 overall and 4-0-1 in the SIAA. Fritz Furtick was the captain. The team finished tied for first place in the SIAA.

Heralding one of the best defenses in the South for the season, the Tigers allowed no touchdowns scored by their opponents in seven games, and only 4 points scored overall. The team tied with Vanderbilt for the SIAA title, but few writers chose them over the vaunted Commodores.

On Oct 13, the Tigers tied VPI T (0-0) at home. On Oct 20, Clemson beat Georgia at home W (6-0). The it was North Carolina A &M at Columbia SC in the second scoreless tie of the season T (0-0). This was followed by a repeat no-score tie v Davidson at Davidson, NC T 0-0).

In a nail biter v Auburn on Nov 10 at home in Bowman Field, The Clemson Tigers beat the Auburn Tigers W (6-4). Next was Tennessee at Bowman Field on Nov 19 W (10-0). In the season finale, Bob Williams' Tigers put it all together and beat Georgia Tech on November 29 at Grant Field in Atlanta, GA W (10–0)

The GA Tech game was sweeter than usual because John Heisman was the Tech Coach. In this 10–0 victory over John Heisman's Georgia Tech team, Captain Fritz Furtick scored Clemson's first touchdown. An onside kick set up the second TD.

Clemson's first forward pass ever took place during the game. Left end Powell Lykes, dropped back to kick, but lobbed a 30-yard pass to George Warren instead. Baseball star Ty Cobb was in attendance at this game.

The starting lineup was Coagman (left end), Lykes (left tackle), Gaston (left guard), Clark (center), Carter (right guard), McLaurin (right tackle), Coles (right end), Warren (quarterback), Allen (left halfback), Furtick (right halfback).

Bob Williams coached just one year in this stint, his first of four separate times being named the Clemson head football coach. He would be back in 1909 for another one-year stint.

1907 Clemson Tigers Football Coach Frank Shaughnessy

<<< Coach Shaughnessy

The 1907 Clemson Tigers football team represented the Clemson Agricultural College during the 1907 college football season as a member of the SIAA. Frank Shaughnessy was the head football coach. The Tigers completed their twelfth season overall and also their twelfth in the SIAA with a record of 4-4 overall and 1-3-0 in the SIAA. They gained tenth place of 13 teams in the SIAA. Mac McLaurin was the captain.

The Clemson Fighting Tigers began the 1907 with a new coach, Frank Shaughnessy and they played their first three games at home at Bowman Field. They opened the season with Gordon State, a small Institute that had some tough players. They won the game on Sept 28 by a touchdown, with five points at the time W (5-0). On Oct 9, the Tigers beat Maryville W (35-0) and then Tennessee gave Clemson its first loss in a tight match L (0-4). On Oct 31, the Tigers came back ten days later against North Carolina in Columbia SC for the win W (15-6).

On Nov 4, the Tigers traveled to Auburn and were beaten by the Auburn Tigers L (0-12). Next it was Georgia on Nov 9 in Augusta L (0-8). On Nov 9, Davidson beat the Tigers at Bowman Field L (6-10). The Tigers won the last game of the season v Georgia Tech at Grant Field in Atlanta GA 6-5) with John Heisman as the GA Tech coach.

Chapter 9 Stein Stone, Frank Dobson & Bob Williams Era 1908-1915

Coach #7 Bob Williams
Coach #9 Stein Stone
Coach #10 Frank Dobson

Year	Coach	Record	Conference	Record
1908	Stein Stone	1-6-0	SIAA	0-4-0
1909	Bob Williams	6–3-0	SIAA	1-2-0
1910	Frank Dobson	4-3-1	SIAA	2-3-1
1911	Frank Dobson	3-5-0	SIAA	3-5-0
1912	Frank Dobson	4-4-0	SIAA	3-3-0
1913	Bob Williams	4-4-0	SIAA	2-4-0
1914	Bob Williams	5-3-1	SIAA	2-2-0
1915	Bob Williams	2-4-2	SIAA	2-2-0

1908 Clemson Tigers Football Team Picture

1908 Clemson Tigers Football Coach Stein Stone

<<< Coach Stein Stone

The 1908 Clemson Tigers football team represented the Clemson Agricultural College during the 1908 college football season as a member of the SIAA. Stein Stone was the head football coach in his first and only year. The Tigers completed their thirteenth season overall and also their thirteenth in the SIAA with a record of 1-6 overall and 0-4-0 in the SIAA.

They finished in last place out of twelve active SIAA teams. Sticker Coles was the captain.

The Tigers opened the season at home in Bowman Field on Sept 26 at home with a win against Gordon W (15-0). It would be the only win of the season. The losses for the season were as follows:

Oct 10, Home, VPI, L (0-6)
Oct 17, Dudley Field Nashville, Vanderbilt, L (0-41)
Oct 28, Columbia SC, Davidson, L (0-31)
Nov 5, Augusta Ga., Georgia, L (0-6)

Nov 14, 15th & Cumberland Field Knoxville, Tennessee L (5-6)
Nov 26, Grant Field Atlanta GA, L (6-30)

It was the Fighting Tigers worse season ever and something had to be done. 1906 Coach Bob Williams was asked to come back and give it a try.

1909 Clemson Tigers Football Coach Bob Williams

The 1909 Clemson Tigers football team represented the Clemson Agricultural College during the 1909 college football season as a member of the SIAA. Bob Williams was the head football coach for the second time for another one year stint. The Tigers completed their fourteenth season overall and also their fourteenth in the SIAA with a record of 6-3 overall and 1-2 in the SIAA. They finished in ninth place out of fourteen active SIAA teams. C. M. Robbs was the captain.

Clemson 1909 Football Team Coach Bob Williams

1910 Clemson Tigers Football Coach Frank Dobson

The 1910 Clemson Tigers football team represented the Clemson Agricultural College during the 1910 college football season as a member of the SIAA. Frank Dobson was the head football coach for year one of a three-year stint. The Tigers completed their fifteenth season overall and also their fifteenth in the SIAA with a record of 4-3-1 overall and 2-3-1 in the SIAA. They again finished in ninth place out of fourteen active SIAA teams. W. H. Hanke was the captain. In 2016, Clemson placed its membership in the SIAA during this season in dispute.

Opening the season on Sept 24, the Tigers crushed Gordon W (26-0) at home at Bowman Field, On Oct1, the Tigers played their first game against Mercer at home and were beaten in a very close match L (0-3). Howard was another first. They invited the Tigers to play in Homewood AL, and the Clemson obliged with a nice win W (24-0). Clemson then traveled to College Park Stadium on Oct 15 to beat the Citadel W (32-0).

In the Auburn rivalry, played in Auburn AL this particular year, the Tigers lost L (0-17). On Nov 3, at Columbia SC on Big Thursday, the Clemson Fighting Tigers defeated the Gamecocks W (24-0). Then came the first tie of the season on Nov 10 against Georgia in Augusta, T (0-0). Meanwhile John Heisman was fine tuning his Yellow Jacket Team to be contenders. Georgia Tech shut out the Tigers on Nov 24 at Grant Field in Atlanta L (0-34).

Clemson's 10th Football Coach 1910 -1912 Frank Dobson

1911 Clemson Tigers Football Coach Frank Dobson

The 1911 Clemson Tigers football team represented the Clemson Agricultural College during the 1911 college football season as a member of the SIAA. Frank Dobson was the head football coach for the second year of a three-year stint. The Tigers completed their sixteenth season overall and also their sixteenth in the SIAA with a record of 3-5 overall and 3-5 in the SIAA. They again finished in eleventh place out of eighteen active SIAA teams. Paul Bissell was the captain.

1911 Clemson Football Team Frank Dobson Coach

1912 Clemson Tigers Football Coach Frank Dobson

For the 1912 season, the value of a touchdown was increased to six points. The end-zone area was also added. Before the addition of the end zone, forward passes caught beyond the goal line resulted in a loss of possession and a touchback. The increase from five points to six did not come until much later in Canada, and the touchdown remained only five points there until 1956.

The 1912 Clemson Tigers football team represented the Clemson Agricultural College during the 1912 college football season as a member of the SIAA. Frank Dobson was the head football coach for the third year of a three-year stint. The Tigers completed their seventeenth season overall and also their seventeenth in the SIAA with a record of 4-4-0 overall and 3-3-0 in the SIAA. They finished in twelfth out of twenty active SIAA teams. W. B. Britt was the captain.

1912 Clemson Football Team

A pattern seemed to be developing in the past few seasons which were captured in this chapter. Clemson was not beating the better teams; was walloping the smaller teams; and sometimes was having trouble with the teams in the mid-size group. This was not the recipe of success for a team that would one day win the National Championship. Change was coming as Bob Williams was about to come back the following year for his third stint of four as a Clemson Head Coach.

1913 Clemson Tigers Football Coach Bob Williams

The 1913 Clemson Tigers football team represented the Clemson Agricultural College during the 1913 college football season as a member of the SIAA. Bob Williams was the head football coach for the first year of his third stint as Clemson head coach. The Tigers completed their eighteenth season overall and also their eighteenth in the SIAA with a record of 4-4-0 overall and 2-4-0 in the SIAA. They finished in tenth out of eighteen active SIAA teams. The SIAA membership was in flux at the time. A. P. Gandy was the captain.

1914 Clemson Tigers Football Coach Bob Williams

In 1914, the founder of Clemson football, Walter Riggs, as College President was working behind the scenes to give the football team a big boost. His plan was to build a nice stadium on campus for Clemson to host its football games. This would not come in 2014, however.

The 1914 Clemson Tigers football team represented the Clemson Agricultural College during the 1914 college football season as a member of the SIAA. Bob Williams was the head football coach for the second year of a four-year stint. The Tigers completed their nineteenth season overall and also their nineteenth in the SIAA with a record of 5-3-1 overall and 2-2-0 in the SIAA. They finished in eighth out of nineteen active SIAA teams. William Schilletter was the captain.

Clemson 1914 Football Team Bob Williams Coach

CU was looking good this season, knowing they could score. On what was called Big Thursday, Oct 29 at Columbia SC, they whooped South Carolina W (29-6). The Citadel played tough against CU at College Park Stadium in Charleston, SC, but were defeated W (14-0). The next game against Georgia was a big one because Georgia had been beating the Tigers regularly for a number of years. Not this year, as Clemson defeated Georgia at Sanford Field on Nov 7 in Athens GA W (35-13). The next week the Tigers showed they were back by beating a tough VMI team in a nail-biter W (27-23). Could they beat John Heisman's Georgia Tech Yellow Jackets? That answer came on November 26 as the margin of victory for the Yellow Jackets triumph over the Tigers was smaller but Heisman's team won another one L (6-26).

1915 Clemson Tigers Football Coach Bob Williams

In 1915, Walter Riggs, College President was able to pull it off and the Clemson Tigers began to play games on the newly constructed Riggs Field. It was Clemson's new home stadium. Riggs Field would host the football team until Memorial Stadium was built in 1942.

The 1915 Clemson Tigers football team represented the Clemson Agricultural College during the 1915 college football season as a member of the SIAA. Bob Williams was the head football coach for the third year of a four-year stint. The Tigers completed their twentieth season overall and also their twentieth in the SIAA with a record of 2-4-2 overall and 2-2-0 in the SIAA. They finished in twelfth out of twenty-three active SIAA teams. W. K. McGill was the captain.

Looking at just the record, one would conclude that Bob Williams' Tigers did not play as well as in 1914. However, when you look closely at the scores you find a story of a fine defense without a corresponding offense to match. The tough games lost in this season, and there were twice as many as those won, were by margins of two touchdowns or less. Many games were decided by two or three points.

Coach Bob Williams left Clemson and quit coaching after the 1915 season. However, Clemson brought him back one mere time in 1929 for five games to finish the season so there was a deep fondness for coach Williams. He was a great coach. Between 1915 and 1926, Williams practiced law in Roanoke, Virginia, and was the city's mayor.

He returned to coach Clemson for the final 5 games of 1926. He died after a stroke in Deland, Florida in 1957. He goes down in history as one of the great pioneer coaches of the early football era. It helps to recall that in the 1902 season when Williams was coaching South Carolina, his Gamecocks beat John Heisman's Clemson Tigers ruining Heisman's undefeated season. That alone gives Williams some great credentials.

Games of the Season

On Oct 2, CU began the 2015 season at home in Riggs Field, the first game ever played there, with a tie against Davidson T (6-6). The Tigers then traveled to Tennessee on Oct 9 and beat a tough Volunteers team in a very close match W (3-0). The Oct 16 Auburn game was played in Anderson SC and Auburn won in a close game W (14-0). On Big Thursday in Columbia SC, Oct 28, The Gamecocks and Tigers played to a scoreless tie T (0-0)

Riggs Field – The First Game Oct 2, 1915 v Davidson

On Nov 6, CU traveled to Greeneville, SC to play North Carolina in a losing effort that was very close L (7-9). Next came a tough VMI team in a game played at Richmond VA. It was another close call but the Tigers were on the underside of the score L (3-6). It had to be getting frustrating for the team to be losing such close ones. Georgia was another loss on Nov 25 at Sanford Field in Athens GA, L (0-13). This year, there was no Georgia Tech game scheduled. The Tigers were glad to get this strange season behind them.

Tell me more about **Riggs Field**

April 3, 2002
🐾Welcome to Historic Riggs Field
by Sam Blackman

Author's Note. This well-written tribute piece by *Sam Blackman* of the Tigers staff puts the importance of Walter Riggs and Riggs Field in perspective. Both were major building blocks to the ultimate success of Clemson University and its College Championship Football Team.

t

Riggs Field Today – Used for various purposes

Welcome to Historic Riggs Field!

Saturday will be a special occasion as a Clemson varsity football team will return to Riggs Field for a football game for the first time since 1941. The varsity's last game here was on November 15, 1941, a 29-0 victory over Wake Forest.

This facility was the home of Clemson football from 1915-41 and it saw many landmark accomplishments for the Clemson program. It is being used today because Frank Howard field and surrounding facilities are undergoing renovations.

Perhaps one of the first big "stepping stones" in helping make Clemson successful in football and other areas of athletics even today was the construction of Riggs Field. Named after one of the most beloved leaders of the early years, Riggs Field is in its 88th year of service to Clemson University.

What made Riggs Field so significant to the school at the time it was first built in 1915? It was the first major facility on the Clemson University campus dedicated to intercollegiate athletics. Prior to Riggs Field, Clemson's teams played on Bowman Field in front of Tillman Hall. This field was used as the parade grounds for the corps of cadets, and served as the home of the football, track, baseball and yes, even the basketball team-one could imagine the overuse of Bowman field.

Riggs Field gave the football team a place to play and practice on its adjunct fields. The baseball field was constructed where the tennis courts are now and the track encircled the football field.

Construction of Riggs Field started in the early summer of 1914. Approximately $10,000 was appropriated for the construction of the facility that covered almost nine acres. Before its completion the Clemson Board of Trustees unanimously agreed to name the new athletic complex, Riggs Field in honor of Clemson's first football coach and originator of the Clemson Athletic Association, Dr. Walter M. Riggs.

Riggs was the first football coach at Clemson in 1896. He stepped down as head coach in 1897 to devote full time to academics, as he was also an engineering professor. He also coached the team in 1899 because the athletic association was low on funds. However, in 1900, the search for a new coach must have become serious, as Riggs hired John Heisman to coach the Tigers.

Although no longer the head coach, Clemson athletics and Riggs could not be split. Riggs also was the equivalent of an athletic director, managing the money and making contracts with other teams. The well-respected Riggs was also president of the Southern Intercollegiate Athletic Association (SIAA) an early conference presiding the Southern Conference. Riggs later became president of Clemson on March 7, 1911. He served in this capacity until his death in 1924.

Riggs Field was dedicated in grand fashion on October 6, 1915. The band, corps of cadets, along with faculty and alumni marched from Tillman Hall to the new field. According to The Tiger, the group formed a "C" formation on the field and poured forth a thrilling volume of patriotic Tiger yells and songs. Professor J.W. Gantt, President of the Athletic Association, introduced Dr. Riggs as, "the man who has done more for the athletics at Clemson and probably more for southern athletics than any other man."

In presenting the field to the corps of cadets, Dr. Riggs said, "This magnificent field is a token of recognition by the Trustees of Clemson College of the importance of military and athletic training for the cadets. It is to be a place for the teaching of the principles of teamwork and fair play. This large and beautiful athletic field is to stand for the development of the physical man and whether in real work or in play, it is hoped that this field will be used as an agency in the development of high and honorable men. "Whether victorious or defeated, may the men of this field always be gentlemen of the highest type. A few minutes later, Dr. Riggs made the initial kickoff in the first football game played on the new field. While on the field, he wore a new orange and blue sweater he had just received from Auburn, his alma mater, as they too wanted to congratulate Clemson and Dr. Riggs for their accomplishments. Clemson and Davidson played to a 6-6 tie that day.

While looking at the well-manicured surface today, many other facets about this historic place come to mind.

This ground is where Clemson's first All-American played, O.K. Pressley in the late 20s. He was a center and a linebacker for the Tigers in 1926-28. Another incredible feat that is still a Clemson record occurred when Maxcey Welch scored five touchdowns in Clemson's 75-0 win over Newberry on October 17, 1930.

It was also home to Clemson's most versatile athlete, Banks McFadden (see front cover of this program). McFadden was an All-American in both football and basketball in the same calendar year in 1939. He was named the nation's most versatile athlete for 1939-40. He was a record setter on the field as a runner, passer and punter. He led the Tigers to state championships in track twice in his three years on the team. He was also the star player who led Clemson to a surprise 6-3 win over Boston College in the 1940 Cotton Bowl, the Tigers first ever bowl appearance.

Head Football Coach Frank Howard coached his first game, a 38-0 win over Presbyterian on September 21, 1940. In Howard's first game as head coach, Clemson scored on the first offensive play as George Floyd reversed around left end and raced 18 yards untouched for a Clemson touchdown.

In1940, Clemson won the Southern Conference football title while calling Riggs Field Home. It was the first of eight conference championships for the Tigers under Frank Howard.

Clemson' football teams compiled a 57-16-6 record during their 27 years at Riggs field and that .759 winning percentage is actually better than the winning percentage the Tigers have earned in Death Valley (72 percent). The baseball team won over 70 percent of its games there when the diamond was part of the complex.

Riggs Field today is considered to be one of the top if not top soccer facilities in the nation. It has been the home of Clemson's soccer program since 1980 and the men's team has compiled a 283-53-20 record there. The1987 NCAA Men's Soccer Final Four was contested here and Clemson won the National Championship before a crowd of 8,332, then an all-time record crowd for a NCAA Championship soccer match. Since 1996, the Clemson Lady Tiger soccer team has an impressive 82-12-4 record at Riggs Field.

As one looks from Riggs Field and sees the grand clock tower of Tillman Hall guarding campus, it is only appropriate that these two symbols of the university are so close in proximately as both have played such a significant role in Clemson history.

Chapter 10 Wayne Hart & Edward Donahue Era 1916-1918

Coach # 11 Wayne Hart
Coach # 12 Edward Donahue

Year	Coach	Record	Conference	Record
1916	Wayne Hart	3-6-0	SIAA	2-4-0
1917	Edward Donahue	6-2-0	SIAA	4-1-0
1918	Edward Donahue	5-2-0	SIAA	3-1-0
1919	Edward Donahue	6-2-2	SIAA	2-2-2
1920	Edward Donahue	4-6-1	SIAA	2-6-0

This five year period showed no championships and no almost championships. Besides, coaches were not staying around a long time in this period to build great teams.

1916 Clemson Tigers Football Coach Wayne Hart

<<< Coach Wayne Hart 1916

The 1916 Clemson Tigers football team represented the Clemson Agricultural College during the 1916 college football season as a member of the SIAA. Wayne Hart was the head football coach for his first and only year The Tigers completed their twenty-first season overall and also their twenty-first in the SIAA with a record of 3-6-0 overall and 2-4-0 in the SIAA. They finished in fifteenth out of twenty-five active SIAA teams. S. S. Major was the captain. Stumpy Banks caught two touchdowns against rival South Carolina.

1917 Clemson Tigers Football Coach Edward Donahue

<<< Edward Jiggs Donahue

The 1917 Clemson Tigers football team represented the Clemson Agricultural College during the 1917 college football season as a member of the SIAA. Edward Donahue was the head football coach for his first of four seasons.

The Tigers completed their twenty-second season overall and also their twenty-second in the SIAA with a record of 6-2-0 overall and 4-1-0 in the SIAA. They finished in third out of sixteen active SIAA teams. F. L. Witsel was the captain. Stumpy Banks scored five touchdowns against Furman for a school record. caught two touchdowns against rival South Carolina. John Heisman ranked Clemson fourth in the south, or third in the Southern Intercollegiate Athletic Association.

1918 Clemson Tigers Football Coach Edward Donahue

World War I caused many colleges to skip the 1917 football season. In 1918 about thirty major colleges across the country dropped the sport either temporarily or permanently as getting players had become a major difficulty. Each of the major services has football teams during the war as a source of recreation and camaraderie. Some were very, very good because the Army, Navy, etc. had a lot of former college players in the camps with which to form teams. Colleges were very agreeable in playing the service camps.

The 1918 Clemson Tigers football team represented the Clemson Agricultural College during the 1918 college football season as a member of the SIAA. Edward Donahue was the head football coach for his second of four seasons. The Tigers completed their twenty-third season overall and also their twenty-third in the SIAA with a record of 5-2-0 overall and 3-1-0 in the SIAA. They finished in fourth out of ten active SIAA teams. Stumpy Banks was the captain.

Coach Donahue was a busy guy as WWI came to an end in 1918. He was a great athlete and a great coach. In the Academic Year 1918-1919, he not only coached football, but also basketball, baseball, and track teams to enable their seasons.

On Nov. 9, Camp Hancock came to Riggs Field to play the Tigers and this well-staffed service team shellacked the Tigers L (13-66). The team finished well with three wins. On Nov 16, CU defeated the Citadel in Columbia SC W (7-0). On November 23, the Tigers walloped Furman at home W (67-7). To close the 1918 season at home, CU defeated Davidson W (7-0).

1919 Clemson Tigers Football Coach Edward Donahue

The 1919 Clemson Tigers football team represented the Clemson Agricultural College during the 1919 college football season as a member of the SIAA. Edward Donahue was the head football coach for his third of four seasons. The Tigers completed their twenty-fourth season overall and also their twenty-fourth in the SIAA with a record of 6-2-2 overall and 2-2-2 in the SIAA. They finished in tenth out of twenty-three active SIAA teams. Stumpy Banks was the captain.

1920 Clemson Tigers Football Coach Edward Donahue

The 1920 Clemson Tigers football team represented the Clemson Agricultural College during the 1920 college football season as a member of the SIAA. Edward Donahue was the head football coach for his fourth (last) of four seasons. It was Donahue's worst record. The Tigers completed their twenty-fifth season overall and also their twenty-fifth in the SIAA with a record of 4-6-1 overall and 2-6-0 in the SIAA. They finished fifteenth out of twenty-four active SIAA teams. Boo Armstrong was the captain.

Chapter 11 E J Stewart & Bud Saunders Era 1921-1926

Coach # 13 E J Stewart
Coach # 14 Bud Saunders

Year	Coach	Record	Conference	Record
1921	E J Stewart	1-6-2	SIAA	0-4-2
1922	E J Stewart	5-4-0	SIAA/SoCon	2–2-1
1923	Bud Saunders	5-2-1	SoCon	1–1-1
1924	Bud Saunders	2-6-0	SoCon	0-3-0
1925	Bud Saunders	1-7-0	SoCon	0-4-0
1926	Bud Saunders	2-2-0	SoCon	1-1-0
1926	Bob Williams	0-5	SoCon	0-2-0

1921 Clemson Tigers Football Coach E J Stewart

This seven year period showed no championships and no "almost championships." Besides, coaches still were not staying around a long time in this period to help build great teams.

1921 Clemson Coach EJ Stewart

The 1921 Clemson Tigers football team represented the Clemson Agricultural College during the 1921 college football season as a member of the SIAA. E. J. Stewart was the head football coach for his first of two seasons. So far, no coach for Clemson has stayed more than four years. It is surprising that the team has done so well without such consistency in coaching.

The Tigers completed their twenty-sixth season overall and also their twenty-sixth in the SIAA with a record of **1-6-2** overall and 0-4-2 in the SIAA. They finished twenty fifth out of twenty-six active SIAA teams. J. H. Spearman was the captain.

1922 Clemson Tigers Football Coach E J Stewart

The 1922 Clemson Tigers football team represented the Clemson Agricultural College during the 1922 college football season as a member of the SoCon. E. J. Stewart was the head football coach for his second of two seasons. The Tigers completed their twenty-seventh season overall and their first in the Southern Conference with a record of 5-4-0 overall, 2-4 in SIAA, and 1-2 in the SoCon. They finished twelfth out of twenty active SoCon teams. E. H. Emanuel was the captain.

This year, after 26 years as part of the SIAA, Clemson made a big switch to the Southern Conference. The SIAA was more or less going away and most of the bigger teams were moving to the Southern Conference. In this transition year, Clemson played as members of both the Southern Intercollegiate Athletic Association and newly formed Southern Conference. SIAA only games were matchups with Centre, The Citadel, and Furman.

1923 Clemson Tigers Football Coach Bud Saunders

The 1923 Clemson Tigers football team represented Clemson College during the 1923 college football season as a member of the SoCon. Bud Saunders was the head football coach for his first of four seasons. The Tigers completed their twenty-eighth season overall and their second in the Southern Conference with a record of 5-2-1 overall, 1-1-1 in the SoCon. They finished twelfth out of twenty active SoCon teams. Butch Holohan was the captain.

1924 Clemson Tigers Football Coach Bud Saunders

<<< Coach Bud Saunders

The 1924 Clemson Tigers football team represented Clemson College during the 1924 college football season as a member of the SoCon. Bud Saunders was the head football coach for his second of four seasons. The Tigers completed their twenty-ninth season overall and their third in the Southern Conference with a record of 2-6-0 overall, 0-3-0 in the SoCon. They finished twenty-first of twenty-three active SoCon teams. Charlie Robinson was the captain.

Every now and then, there is a winter so bad, if you were asked in the beginning by God if you would give up those three or so months of your life so that you could be in the springtime the next day, there are times, when you are young that you might consider saying "yes."

There are probably sometimes when if you really knew how bad it would be, you would definitely say yes. Every now and then a football year comes by in which we wish we could skip it, and move on to the next year. If we never had to face such a year, and we could change history, we might even X it from the record. Maybe???

The 1924 Clemson Tigers football team, which represented Clemson College during the 1924 college football season was a very poor team record wise and there is little happiness for any of us in recounting all of the foibles. So, let's talk about the two positives first.

On September 12 in the home opener at Riggs Field in Calhoun GA, Clemson whipped Elon, a new team on the schedule, into complete oblivion, with a 60-0 trouncing. It was a game just a step above playing against the practice tackling dummies. My apologies to the Elon fans. But, this Clemson group was not tough—even against Presbyterian who they would typically take to the woodshed and clean their clocks. Presbyterian had a chance of winning this year in a home game shutout with a low score of W (14-0) There were no more W's this year. Believe me, I regret to report that.

So, rather than lament any more, I will simply report the rest of this season which consisted of all losses as follows:

Oct 4 at Auburn	Drake Field, Auburn, AL	L (0–13)
Oct 23 at SC	(Big Thursday)	L (0–3)
Nov 1 VPI	Riggs Field, Calhoun, SC	L (6–50)
Nov 8 at Davidson	Charlotte, NC	L (0–7)
Nov 11 at Citadel	Anderson, SC	L (0–20)
Nov 27 Furman	Riggs Field, Calhoun, SC	L (0–3)

1925 Clemson Tigers Football Coach Bud Saunders

The 1925 Clemson Tigers football team represented the Clemson College during the 1925 college football season as a member of the SoCon. Bud Saunders was the head football coach for his third of four seasons. The Tigers completed their thirtieth season overall and their fourth in the Southern Conference with a record of 1-7-0 overall, 0-4-0 in the SoCon. They were tied for twenty-first with Maryland which was also last of 22 active SoCon teams. G. I. Finklea was the captain.

1926 Clemson Tigers Football Coach Bud Saunders

The 1926 Clemson Tigers football team represented the Clemson College during the 1926 college football season as a member of the SoCon. Bud Saunders was the head football coach for his fourth of four seasons. Saunders resigned after the first four games of the 1926 season. Bob Williams, who had previously served as Clemson's head coach in 1906, 1909, and from 1913 to 1915, led the team for the final five games of the season. The Tigers completed their thirty-first season overall and their fifth in the Southern Conference with a record of 2-7-0 overall, 1-3-0 in the SoCon. They were ranked 18th out of 22 active SoCon teams. B. C. Harvey was the captain. No chance for a championship.

Chapter 12 Josh Cody Era 1927-1930

Coach #15 Josh Cody

Year	Coach	Record	Conference	Record
1927	Josh Cody	5-3-1	SoCon	2-2-0
1928	Josh Cody	8-3-0	SoCon	4-2-0
1929	Josh Cody	8-3-0	SoCon	3-3-0
1930	Josh Cody	8-2-0	SoCon	3-2-0

This four year period with Josh Cody at the helm showed no championships but there were "almost" championships. Though Cody stayed just four years which was typical, he reaslly got the Fighting Tigers back to playing John Heisman's type of football and set the stage for grooming son great teams.

1927 Clemson Tigers Football Coach Josh Cody

The 1927 Clemson Tigers football team represented Clemson College during the 1927 college football season as a member of the SoCon.

Josh Cody was the head football coach for his first of four seasons. The Tigers completed their thirty-second season overall and their sixth in the Southern Conference with a record of 5-3-1 overall, 2-2-0 in the SoCon. They were ranked 9th out of 22 active SoCon teams. Bud Eskew was the captain.

The 1926 season was strange to say the least. Though Bob Williams was a fine coach, he had not coached anywhere in over ten years and was not familiar with the team, nor the team with him. It was a relief for Clemson to have such a year behind them. Josh Cody was a fine coach wherever he coached and so the Tigers were pleased to begin a season with him as their head coach.

1928 Clemson Tigers Football Coach Josh Cody

The 1928 Clemson Tigers football team represented Clemson College during the 1928 college football season as a member of the Southern Conference (SoCon.) Josh Cody was the head football coach for his second of four seasons. The Tigers completed their thirty-third season overall and their seventh in the Southern Conference with a record of 8-3-0 overall, 4-2-0 in the SoCon. They were ranked 7th out of 22 active SoCon teams. O.K. Pressley was the captain.

The season began well at home in Riggs Field, on the Clemson campus at Calhoun SC with a nice win over Newberry on Sept 22 W (30-0). The next win came against Davidson the following week on Sept 29. W (6-0). Auburn was next at Drake Field in Auburn Al in another W (6-0) victory. On Oct 12, the winning score was about the same W (7-0) as the Textile Bowl was played game in Florence SC. The extra point was the only scoring difference.

The Clemson offensive drought was about to change on Oct 19 when Erskine was shellacked by the Tigers W (52-0). On Oct 25, on Big Thursday, the Tigers whooped the Gamecocks W (32-0) in Columbia SC.

Captain O.K. Pressley starred in this rivalry game with South Carolina, recording four tackles for a loss in a row despite a hand injury. He was the first Clemson Tiger to make any All-America team when he was selected third-team All-America at season's end.

On Nov 3, Ole Miss defeated the Tigers in the first game ever played between the two L (7-26) The game was played at Hemingway Stadium in Oxford, MS. On Nov 10, Clemson traveled to

Lynchburg. The Gators played the Tigers on Nov 17 at Jacksonville FL and prevailed against CU L (6-27). On Nov 29, the Tigers beat Furman at Greenville, SC   W 27–12. In the season finale on Dec 8, the Citadel got the best of Clemson at Johnson Hagood Stadium in Charleston, SC L (7–12).

Great Player O.K. Pressley C 1926-28

In 1928, Pressley was voted Third-team All-American by Newspaper Enterprise of America, John Heisman, and Walter Trumbull. He was the first Tiger named to any All-America team. Pressley was the starting center from 1926-28. He was honored by being captain as a senior in 1928.

Center / Captain O. K. Pressley Ready to snap the ball

Pressley was rugged and durable. He started 25 games at center in his three years out of a possible 29 games Clemson had a school-record eight wins his senior year...O.K. Pressley was All-Southern in 1928.

1929 Clemson Tigers Football Coach Josh Cody

The 1929 Clemson Tigers football team represented Clemson College during the 1929 college football season as a member of the Southern Conference (SoCon). Josh Cody was the head football coach for his third of four seasons. The Tigers completed their thirty-fourth season overall and their eighth in the Southern Conference with a record of 8-3-0 overall, 3-3 in the SoCon. They were ranked twelfth out of 23 active SoCon teams. O.D. Padgett was the captain.

1930 Clemson Tigers Football Coach Josh Cody

The 1930 Clemson Tigers football team represented Clemson College during the 1930 college football season as a member of the Southern Conference (SoCon). Josh Cody was the head football coach for his fourth and last of four seasons. This would be Cody's best season. The Tigers completed their thirty-fifth season overall and their ninth in the Southern Conference with a record of 8-2-0 overall, 3-2 in the SoCon. They were ranked ninth out of 23 active SoCon teams. Johnnie Justus was the captain.

Unidentified Clemson Game at Riggs Field from Depression Era

Chapter 13 Jess Neely Era 1931-1939

Coach # 16 Jess Neely

Year	Coach	Record	Conference	Record
1931	Jess Neely	1-6-2	SoCon	
1932	Jess Neely	3-5-1	SoCon	
1933	Jess Neely	3-6-2	SoCon	
1934	Jess Neely	5-4-0	SoCon	
1935	Jess Neely	6-3-0	SoCon	
1936	Jess Neely	5-5-0	SoCon	
1937	Jess Neely	4-4-1	SoCon	
1938	Jess Neely	7-1-1	SoCon	
1939	Jess Neely	9-1-0	SoCon	

Jess Neely started his rebuilding slow but by the end of the Neely era his one-loss seasons were the best so far in Clemson history.

t

Coach Jess Neely

Jess Neely

Jess Neely was the first Clemson head coach to stay more than four consecutive years at Clemson. He added needed stability to a program that was just waiting to break out. Nothing worth having is easy. Jess Neely knew that his team needed to be financed properly in order to survive and be able to win in the Southern Conference. After his 1-6-2 season his first year, at other institutions that were well endowed and had a lot of rich alums, they would be calling for his head.

In the article that I selected, we all get introduced to this great coach and great man, Jess Neely. You will learn that he was more about goodness and reality than anything else. Sure, winning mattered, but the college could not expect the students to pay for their uniforms during the great depression and it was tough to get anybody to give up a dime even if the cause was worthwhile.

Neely kept at it and succeeded and he eventually had a great four-year record, capped by one of the finest bowl game victories over a coach who would soon have four national championships to his credit. Who knows if Clemson would have made it through the war years without the boost that the programs created by Jess Neely gave to the Clemson Tigers. We'll never have to answer that because Jess Neely was there at the right time and Clemson continues as the beneficiary.

The first piece is from the Clemson Media Guide and the second is from an author who wrote a nice book about Clemson's great coaches.

Jess Neely
Head Coach Years: 1931-1939
Record at Clemson: 43-35-7
Winning Percentage: .547

Perhaps one of Clemson's most beloved coaches was Jess Neely. Neely influence and inspiration is still present today as the IPTAY Scholarship Club was founded during his coaching Tenure. IPTAY is the lifeblood of the Clemson Athletic Department. It provides funds for athletic scholarships and capital improvements.

Thousands of athletes have benefited through the IPTAY Scholarship fund since its inception in 1934. That first year of IPTAY, Neely and his staff convinced 160 people to pay $10.00 a year to Clemson, for a grand total of $1,600 the first year, (not bad during the middle of the great depression.)

Neely was head coach at Clemson from 1931 through 1939 and spent the next 26 years at Rice University in Houston.

Neely coached Clemson to its first bowl game, the 1940 Cotton Bowl, where the Tigers capped a 9-1-0 season by beating Boston College 6-3. Clemson ended the season ranked l2th in the final Associated Press poll, its first top 20 season in history. Boston College was ranked 11th going into the game and it was Clemson's first win over a top 20 team in its history. The team featured the play of Banks McFadden Clemson's first Associated Press All American. Clemson had a 43-35-7 record during Neely's tenure.

Neely coached Rice to four Southwest Conference Championships and six bowl appearances, the last being a trip to the Bluebonnet Bowl in 1961.

During 40 years of college coaching he compiled a record of 207-99-14. Neely is eighth in college football history in victories by a Division I-A coach when heading into the 1995 season. For his accomplishments, he was inducted into the College Football Hall of Fame in 1971.

Neely graduated from Vanderbilt in 1924, after lettering three years in football and serving as captain of the 1922 team. He coached a year of high school football before returning to his alma mater to obtain a law degree. But he never practiced.

He coached four years at Southwestern college in Clarksville, Tenn. and then went to the University of Alabama in 1928. It was there that he met Frank Howard. Neely brought Howard to Clemson as line coach in 1931. Howard replaced him in 1940 and remained as head coach for 30 years. In 1967, Neely returned to his alma mater as athletic director. He officially retired in 1971, but continued to coach golf until 1981, when he moved back to Texas.

"If I didn't look in the mirror every day, I wouldn't know how old I am, "Neely once said. "Working with the boys makes you feel young, I feel that in athletics the boys learn a sense of loyalty and sacrifice and values they don't learn anywhere else.

"They learn to compete," he said, "and that is what life is all about-its competition.

"If they make good in football, chances are they'll be successful elsewhere. I like to see that those boys make something of themselves. That is my reward.

"The boys go to college to study and get that degree. Playing football is a side activity. When fellows go to a school first to play football they get an entirely wrong sense of values.

"And when you start them off with the wrong sense, it isn't difficult for them to go astray."

"He was a cool, southern gentlemen, but he worked us like dogs. The work- outs were always twice as hard as the games, "said Dick Maegle. "There were no superstars, no victory that was better than all the other victories. To him football was a team game and we were all team players." Maegle was the player tackled in a famous episode in the 1954 Cotton Bowl, when frustrated Tommy Lewis came off the bench to stop a certain touchdown. Rice won that game, 28-6.

Neely died at the age of 85 in 1983, but his landmark accomplishments in the 1930s at Clemson contributed significantly to Clemson's outstanding football tradition.

The numbers and the names have changed since 1995 but the idea has not. Jess Neely, whose first Clemson season at 1-6-2 season will be explored shortly, is on the 1995 list on the next page. That is something.

Neely was great at Clemson and after Clemson.

All-Time I-A Coaching Victories (Not Including Wins Since 1995)

Paul 'Bear' Bryant	Maryland, Kentucky, Texas A&M, Alabama	323
Amos Alonzo Stagg	Springfield, Chicago, Pacific	314
Glenn 'Pop' Warner	Georgia, Cornell, Carlisle, Pittsburgh, Stanford, Temple	313
Joe Paterno	Penn State	268
Bobby Bowden	Samford, West Virginia, Florida State	250
Woody Hayes	Denison, Miami (OH), Ohio State	238
Bo Schembechler	Miami (OH), Michigan	234
Jess Neely	Rhodes, Clemson, Rice	207

Source: 1996 Clemson Football Media Guide

End of piece

Great Clemson Player Banks McFadden CB 1936-40

No book about Clemson greats could be written without discussing Banks McFadden.

<< *Banks McFadden*

To repeat, in any book such as this that honors great Clemson players, we could not leave off an athletic legend like Banks McFadden, who is without a doubt one of the greatest Clemson athletes of all time. Pulling full-time duty with football, basketball, and baseball, McFadden excelled as a defensive back thanks to his great athleticism that few could match. He is one of just three Football Tigers to have his jersey and number retired.

Check out the years in which McFadden played and then please remember we already declared that McFadden is widely considered to be the greatest athlete in Clemson University history, after lettering in three sports (football, basketball and track).

McFadden was All-American in both football and basketball in the same calendar year (1939), He is the only Clemson athlete to do that. In 1939-40, he was named the nation's most versatile athlete. He was also Clemson's first wire-service AP All-American.

Banks was a record setter on the field as a runner, passer, and punter. A born athlete, he kept busy in all sports seasons. For example, he led the Tigers to state championship in track twice in his three years...

He was elected to National Football Hall of Fame in 1959 and he received the Distinguished Alumni Award from Clemson in 1966. He is a charter member of the Clemson Athletic Hall of Fame and the state of South Carolina Athletic Hall of Fame.

As noted above but worthy of mention again, McFadden is the only Tiger to have his jersey retired in two sports.

He was a great football player and had options after college. He was the #4 pick of the Brooklyn Dodgers (football) after the 1939 season, that is still the highest draft pick ever by a Clemson player. It took eleven passes to get to DeShaun Watson this year.

As noted, Banks played one year in the NFL and led the league in yards per rush...coached the defensive backs at Clemson for 26 years, he was also the head basketball coach from 1947-56...Clemson's McFadden Building, dedicated in 1995, is in his honor...named to Clemson's Centennial team in April, 1996...ranked as Clemson's #1 football player of all-time by a panel of Clemson historians in 1999. That is how good he was.

In 1939, McFadden was voted the Associated Press' "Athlete of the Year". McFadden was also a two-time All-American in basketball (1938 and 1939) and lead the Tigers basketball team to a Southern Conference championship in 1939.

McFadden also played halfback and punter on the football team and was named Clemson's first Associated Press All-American in football in 1939, which saw the Tigers play and win their 1st bowl game (1940 Cotton Bowl Classic).

Upon graduating, McFadden played football for the National Football League's Brooklyn Dodgers. He was the #4 overall NFL draft pick in 1940. In his first, and only, year as a professional he played in 11 games. He had the longest rush in the NFL that year - 75 yards. He was tied for second for most yards per attempt with a 4.8 yards per carry average.

He was also fifth in the league for most rushing yards per game. Defensively he had two interceptions. Despite his success, McFadden preferred the small-town life and the family atmosphere of Clemson. He returned to the state of South Carolina to coach at his alma mater. A great Clemson Tiger for sure.

Neely always fought adversity at Clemson with slow and well thought out solutions. How many coaches today could win 36 games in six seasons with only 14 of those 56 games played at home?

Only once did Clemson play as many as four games at home in a year during Neely's stay, and only twice were there three home games in a year. Thirteen of the 56 games were played on neutral sites. Even his 1939 team—his best at Clemson—only played two games at home, opening the season with an 18-0 win over Presbyterian and then in the seventh game, a 20-7 victory over Wake Forest.

The 1939 team was called "Road Clemson" because of this. But despite the tough road schedule, the Tigers stayed strong. With the exception of the Tulane loss, they were only behind twice in their nine wins. And though players went both ways in those days, Clemson only gave up 45 points in 10 games.

The Tigers suddenly found themselves—a group of players from small town environments—playing big-time football. Neely rewarded the team for its efforts by taking all 51 players to Dallas for the Cotton Bowl game.

While in Dallas for the bowl game, talk was rampant that Neely might leave Clemson for the head coaching job at Rice. Bill Sullivan was the publicity man for Frank Leahy and Boston College, and he said he was in the hotel room in Dallas when Neely told a small group that he would definitely take the Rice offer.

Frank Howard, who was Neely's line coach, spoke up and said: "Well, I'm not going with you." And according to Sullivan, Neely said: "I hadn't planned to ask you."

When Howard was confronted with this, he denied it and said that J.C. Littlejohn, Clemson's business manager, had promised him the Clemson head coaching job if Neely left.

Neely is still known today as one Clemson's most beloved coaches. His influence and inspiration is still present thanks to the IPTAY Scholarship Club as it is the lifeblood of the Clemson Athletic Department.

From 1931-'39, Clemson had a 43-35-7 record during Neely's tenure. After the Tigers' Cotton Bowl win over Boston College, Neely spent the next 26 years at Rice University in Houston.

During 40 years of college coaching he compiled a record of 207-99-14. For his accomplishments, he was inducted into the College Football Hall of Fame.

Article Editor's note: *This story was an insert from the book I co-authored last summer called* Clemson: Where the Tigers Play, *which you can buy on amazon.com. This is the third story in a series of stories that chronicles how these coaches turned Clemson into the football power it has come to be over the years*

1931 Clemson Tigers Football Coach Jess Neely

The 1931 Clemson Tigers football team represented Clemson College during the 1931 college football season as a member of the Southern Conference (SoCon). Jess Neely was the head football coach for his first of nine seasons. The Tigers completed their thirty-sixth season overall and their tenth in the Southern Conference with a record of 1-6-2 overall, 1-4-0 in the SoCon. They were ranked ninth out of 23 active SoCon teams. A. D. Fordham was the captain. In most schools a new coach does not do well while adjusting the team to new winning ways. Some might say that if God switched to coaching at a new school, Ge too would find it a deep challenge. i

Alabama was beginning to flex its muscles in the Southern Conference and on Nov 14, the Crimson Tide flattened Clemson L (7-74). Clemson remembers such run up scores. Clemson was having a very bad season. On Nov 26, The Tigers managed a pride saving scoreless tie v Furman in Greenville SC T (0-0).

1932 Clemson Tigers Football Coach Jess Neely

The 1932 Clemson Tigers football team represented Clemson College during the 1932 college football season as a member of the Southern Conference (SoCon). Jess Neely was the head football coach for his second of nine seasons. The Tigers completed their thirty-seventh season overall and their eleventh in the Southern Conference with a record of 3-5-1; 0-4-0 in the SoCon. They were ranked twenty-first, tied with Mississippi State out of 23 active SoCon teams. Bob Miller was the captain.

1933 Clemson Tigers Football Coach Jess Neely

The 1933 Clemson Tigers football team represented Clemson College during the 1933 college football season as a member of the Southern Conference (SoCon). Jess Neely was the head football coach for his third of nine seasons. The Tigers completed their thirty-eighth season overall and their twelfth in the Southern Conference with a record of 3-6-2; 0-3-0 in the SoCon. They were ranked twenty-first, tied with Mississippi State out of 10 active SoCon teams. John Heinemann was the captain.

You may have noticed that instead of twenty-three teams as in 1932, the 1933 Southern Conference (SoCon) consisted of just ten teams. Saturday Down South (saturdaydownsouth.com) describes what happened in 1933 as follows:

"The unwieldy Southern Conference has split along geographical lines and out of the break today emerged a new group of thirteen schools, mostly of the deep South, to be known as the Southeastern Conference." This group included the core of today's SEC —Alabama, Auburn, Georgia, Florida, LSU, Ole Miss,

Mississippi State, Kentucky, Tennessee and Vanderbilt —along with Georgia Tech, Tulane, and Sewanee (also known as the University of the South). The remaining Southern Conference schools were all located in Maryland, Virginia or the Carolinas: Virginia, Virginia Tech, Virginia Military Institute, Washington & Lee, Maryland, North Carolina, North Carolina State, Duke, South Carolina and Clemson; seven of those schools —along with Wake Forest, which joined the Southern Conference in 1936 — left in 1953 to form the Atlantic Coast Conference.

This was the third losing season of the period of years known as the seven lean years. The biblical connotation is clear but most Clemson fans were looking for seven or more years of plenty. The next season would mark the midpoint of the seven lean years.

1934 Clemson Tigers Football Coach Jess Neely

The 1934 Clemson Tigers football team represented Clemson College during the 1934 college football season as a member of the Southern Conference (SoCon). Jess Neely was the head football coach for his fourth of nine seasons. The Tigers completed their thirty-ninth season overall and their thirteenth in the Southern Conference with a record of 5-4-0; 2-2-0 in the SoCon. They were ranked fifth out of 10 active SoCon teams. Henry Woodward was the captain. It is always nice to have more wins than losses.

Clemson at the time, was playing good football but in many cases, were outmanned by the financial resources of their opponents. Neely was a far better coach than his record.

1935 Clemson Tigers Football Coach Jess Neely "Almost" Championship

The 1935 Clemson Tigers football team represented Clemson College during the 1935 college football season as a member of the Southern Conference (SoCon). Jess Neely was the head football coach for his fifth of nine seasons. The Tigers completed their fortieth season overall and their fourteenth in the Southern Conference with a record of 6-3-0; 2-1-0 in the SoCon. They were ranked fourth out of 10 active SoCon teams. Henry Shore was the captain. Clemson was gettng close to a championship season.

Presbyterian was first on the schedule for 1935 again at home in Riggs Field on the Clemson Campus in Clemson SC. Clemson won the game on Sept 21, W (25–6). Next was VPI at Miles Stadium in Blacksburg, VA for a nice Clemson win W (28-7) September 28 at VPI's Miles Stadium, Blacksburg, VA. On Oct 5, Wake Forest came to Clemson and were defeated W (13-7). Sitting undefeated after three games, things were going good for Neely's Tigers before they traveled to Duke on Oct 12, and were beaten convincingly by the Blue Devils L (12-38)

On Oct 24 at Columbia Municipal Stadium in Columbia, SC, on Big Thursday, the Tigers overwhelmed the Gamecocks in a big shutout win W (44-0). Life was showing signs of life.

1936 Clemson Tigers Football Coach Jess Neely

The 1936 Clemson Tigers football team represented Clemson College during the 1936 college football season as a member of the Southern Conference (SoCon). Jess Neely was the head football coach for his sixth of nine seasons. The Tigers completed their forty-first season overall and their fifteenth in the Southern Conference with a record of 5-5-0; 3-2-0 in the SoCon. They were ranked fourth out of 15 active SoCon teams. Net Barry was the captain.

Clemson needed to shake out all its bad seasons out this season. On Nov 14, at Kentucky, the Tigers lost a close match to the Wildcats, L (6-7). Finishing the season up at home, the Tigers were shut out by the Furman Paladins L (0-12). The Fighting Tigers would remember not being able to compete and it was a motivator.

1937 Clemson Tigers Football Coach Jess Neely

The 1937 Clemson Tigers football team represented Clemson College during the 1937 college football season as a member of the Southern Conference (SoCon). Jess Neely was the head football coach for his seventh of nine seasons. The Tigers completed their forty-second season overall and their sixteenth in the Southern Conference with a record of 4-4-1; 2-0-1 in the SoCon. They were ranked third out of 15 active SoCon teams. H. D. Lewis was the captain.

Jess Neely's work in getting donations and financing for the team was finally beginning to pay off and the next two years would show a marked improvement before Frank Howard came in to guide the Tigers for the next thirty years. You may recall Jess Neely was the coach who suggested not to build the Death Valley Stadium because about 10,000 seats by the old YMCA was all the Tigers needed. During the next two tears from this, Neely had his opportunity to shine a lot better than his stadium prediction.

1938 Clemson Tigers Football Coach Jess Neely "Almost" Championship

The 1938 Clemson Tigers football team represented Clemson College during the 1938 college football season as a member of the Southern Conference (SoCon). Jess Neely was the head football coach for his eighth of nine seasons. The Tigers completed their forty third season overall and their seventeenth in the Southern Conference with a record of 7-1-1; 3-0-1 in the SoCon. They were ranked second out of 15 active SoCon teams. Charlie Woods was the captain. They were very good.

Presbyterian was at Riggs Field again on the Clemson campus in Clemson NC to kick off the football season against the Tigers. They were shut out w (26-0) on Sept 17. A week later, on Sept 24 at Tulane Stadium in New Orleans, Clemson beat Tulane W (13-10). On Oct 1, #2 ranked Tennessee beat the Tigers for their only loss of the season at Shields Watkins Field in Knoxville L (7-20). On Oct 8. VMI tied the Tigers at Memorial Stadium in Charlotte NC T (7-7). Then, for Big Thursday on Oct 20, in Columbia Municipal Stadium, Columbia SC, the Tigers beat the SC Gamecocks w (34-12)

On Oct28, at Wake Forest, Clemson won W (7-0) The following week on Nov 5, Clemson traveled to George Washington at Greenville NC and won the game via shutout W (27-0). The Tigers grabbed another shutout the following week Nov 12 at Kentucky's McLean Stadium in Lexington KY, W (14-0). Wrapping up the season again v a tough Furman team, the Tigers prevailed W (10-7).

1939 Clemson Tigers Football Coach Jess Neely Championship

The 1939 Clemson Tigers football team represented Clemson College during the 1939 college football season as a member of the Southern Conference (SoCon). Jess Neely was the head football coach for his ninth (last) of nine seasons. The Tigers completed their forty fourth season overall and their eighteenth in the Southern Conference with a record of 9-1-0; 4-0 in the SoCon. Wow! What a season!!!

They were listed along with Duke at the top of the SoCon standings for 1939 out of 15 active SoCon teams. Joe Payne was the captain. Clemson participated in its first bowl game, beating a tough Boston College coached by the immortal Frank Leahy in the 1940 Cotton Bowl Classic. It was a great season changer for the Tigers. The seven lean years were officially over.

On Sept 23, the season began again with Presbyterian at home at Riggs Field on the campus of Clemson University in Clemson SC. Clemson shut out the Blue Hose W (18-0. Just a week later on Sept 30 at Tulane, the Tigers lost a tight one in Tulane Stadium, New Orleans, LA L (6–7). Then, on Oct 7 v NC State in the Textile Bowl in Charlotte, NC, W (25–6). On Big Thursday at Columbia Municipal Stadium in Columbia, SC, the Tigers shut out the Gamecocks of SC W (27–0)

Navy played the Tigers for the first time on Oct 28 at Thompson Stadium in Annapolis, MD. Clemson had a tough time but won W (15–7). Then in Washington DC at on Nov 3 at George Washington, the tigers won another close one W (13–6). Coming back home on Nov 11, the Tigers beat Wake Forest at Riggs Field W (20–7). Getting close to the season finale, on Nov 18, at Southwestern Presbyterian, the #16 ranked Tigers won at Memphis, TN W (21–6). As the season closed on Nov 25, Furman always was there for the last game at Sirrine Stadium in Greenville, SC, The Tigers triumphed W 10–7.

Not typically being a bowl contender, the Clemson Fighting Tigers were unaccustomed to the great accolades as brought forth during the 1939 season. The year was so good the team was invited to the Cotton Bowl Classic. The participants in the January 1, 1940 Cotton Bowl game were the #11 Boston College Eagles vs the #12 Clemson Tigers. The great Cotton Bowl classic game was played at Dallas Texas and though the well-known Frank Leahy coached the Eagles and Jess Neely, known for his great work at Clemson coached the Tigers. In this highly publicized game. Neely beat Leahy but not much by more than a nudge W (6-3) What a win for Clemson and what a loss for Boston College.

Chapter 14 Frank Howard Era 1940-1964

Coach # 17 Frank Howard

Year	Coach	Record	Conference	Record
1940*	Frank Howard	6-2-1	SoCon	4-0-0
1941	Frank Howard	7-2-0	SoCon	5-1-0
1942	Frank Howard	3-6-1	SoCon	2-3-1
1943	Frank Howard	2-6-0	SoCon	2-3-0
1944	Frank Howard	4-5-0	SoCon	3-1-0
1945	Frank Howard	6-3-1	SoCon	2-1-1
1946	Frank Howard	4-5-0	SoCon	2-3-0
1947	Frank Howard	4-5-0	SoCon	1-3-0
1948*	Frank Howard	11-0-0	SoCon	5-0-0
1949	Frank Howard	4-4-2	SoCon	2-2-0
1950	Frank Howard	9-0-1	SoCon	3-0-1
1951	Frank Howard	7-3-0	SoCon	0-1-0
1953	Frank Howard	3-5-1	ACC	1-2-0
1954	Frank Howard	5-5-0	ACC	1-2-0

As you can see from the Howard record listed above,there are a lot of almost championships and championships in the record. Plus lots of conference championships. There would be no more lean years for Clemson. Bravo!

Frank Howard 1940-1969 Longest Seving Clemson Coach

1940 Clemson Tigers Football Coach Frank Howard <u>Championship SoCon</u>

The 1940 Clemson Tigers football team represented Clemson College during the 1940 college football season as a member of the Southern Conference (SoCon). Frank Howard was the head football coach for his first of thirty seasons. The Tigers completed their forty-fifth season overall and their nineteenth in the Southern Conference with a record of 6-2-1; 4-0-0 in the SoCon. The Tigers came in first in the SoCon out of 15 active SoCon teams. Red Sharpe was the captain. Coach Frank Howard got the Tigers off to a great start in his first year at the helm

On Sept 21, the home opener was again against Presbyterian at Riggs Field on the campus of Clemson University in Clemson, SC. The Tigers shut out the Blue Hose W (38-0). On Sept 28, the Tigers played Wofford at home and beat the Terriers W (26-0). The next game was at American Legion Memorial Stadium in Charlotte NC. It was the annual Textile Bowl on Oct 5 with NC State. The Tigers beat the Tar Heels W (26-0). Wake forest gave the Tigers their fourth win in a row in a home game on Oct 12 W (39-0) and so far, the Tigers were competing in an undefeated season. On Big Thursday Oct 24 at Columbia SC, the Tigers beat the Gamecocks W 21-13).

On Nov 2, the Tigers traveled to Tulane Stadium in New Orleans Tulane at and were beaten in s shutout by the Green Wave for the first loss of the season. Then the Auburn Tigers beat the beat the Clemson Tigers on Nov 9 at Auburn Stadium in AL, L (7-21). The Tigers came back for a tie at Southwestern Presbyterian at Crump Stadium in Memphis TN on Nov 16 T (12-12). Then, on Nov 23the Tigers played Furman at Sirrine Stadium in Greenville, SC on the way to a nice victory W 13–7.

1941 Clemson Tigers Football Coach Frank Howard <u>Championship</u>

The 1941 Clemson Tigers football team represented Clemson College during the 1941 college football season as a member of the Southern Conference (SoCon). Frank Howard was the head football coach for his second of thirty seasons. The Tigers completed their forty sixth season overall and their twentieth in the Southern Conference with a record of 7-2-0; 5-1-0 in the SoCon. The Tigers came in third in the SoCon out of 15 active SoCon teams. Duke was again # 1. Wade Padgett was the captain.

Player Great Joe Blalock WR 1938-41

In these early days of football, there were lots of opportunities for firsts. For example, Joe Blalock was Clemson's first two-time All-American. He was a starter as a sophomore when real Freshman were prohibited from playing in the 1940's.

He started on the 1940 Cotton Bowl team. He led the Tiger receiver squad for three straight years. For many years, he was tied for seventh in Tiger history in career touchdown catches (11). He averaged 20.3 yards per catch in his career, still the school record on a yards per catch basis...

When he graduated, he was a fifth-round pick of the Lions after the 1941 season. To keep in shape and because he loved Sports, Blalock also played Clemson basketball in 1940-41. He is a charter member of the Clemson Athletic Hall of Fame being inducted in 1973. He has many accolades and awards such as being inducted into the state of South Carolina Hall of Fame and being named to Clemson's Centennial team in 1996. Blalock died August 21, 1974. In 1999, an esteemed panel of historians slotted Joe Blalock as Clemson's #16 gridder of all-time.

The season began at home on Sept 20 v Presbyterian at Riggs Field on the campus of Clemson University in Clemson SC. The Tigers beat the Blue Hose W (41-12) On Sept 27, Clemson traveled to Lynchburg, VA and played VIMI at City Stadium for the win W (36-7). On Oct 4, in the Textile Bowl at American Legion Stadium in

Charlotte NC, the Tigers beat the Wolfpack W (27-6). On Oct 11, the Tigers got the rare treat of traveling to Boston to play in Fenway Park against Boston College. They had beaten BC, coached at the time by the immortal Frank Leahy in their first outing in the Cotton Bowl in 1939; They beat the Eagles again W (26-13). Denny Myers had taken over for Leahy at BC.

On Oct 23 at South Carolina, on Big Thursday, the Tigers suffered a rare loss while nationally ranked at #14 to the unranked Gamecocks in a close match L (14-18). Then next venue was Griffith Stadium in Washington DC v George Washington. The Tigers picked up a nice 1in W (19-0). On Nov 15, at home, the Tigers shut out Wake Forest W (29-0). The next week Nov 22 at Sirrine Stadium in Greenville SC, the #18 ranked Tigers beat Furman W (34-6). In the season finale on Nov 29 at Auburn, the Tigers were ranked #16 going in but were nonetheless beaten by the Auburn Tigers L (7-28).

1942 Clemson Tigers Football Coach Frank Howard

The 1942 Clemson Tigers football team represented Clemson College during the 1942 college football season as a member of the Southern Conference (SoCon). Frank Howard was the head football coach for his third of thirty seasons. The Tigers completed their forty seventh season overall and their twenty-first in the Southern Conference with a record of 3-6-1; 2-3-1 in the SoCon.

It was a poor season for sure. The Tigers came in ninth in the SoCon out of 16 active SoCon teams. WM & Mary were #1 in the Conference. Charlie Wright was the captain. The new Memorial Stadium was inaugurated September 19 with a win against Presbyterian. Clemson's 200th win came on Big Thursday against South Carolina. From that point on Riggs Stadium was for special events and other sports than football.

1943 Clemson Tigers Football Coach Frank Howard

The 1943 Clemson Tigers football team represented Clemson College during the 1943 college football season as a member of the Southern Conference (SoCon). Frank Howard was the head football coach for his fourth of thirty seasons. The Tigers completed their forty eighth season overall and their twenty-second in the Southern Conference with a record of 2-6-0; 2-3-0 in the SoCon. It was an even poorer season than the poor Clemson season before. Frank Howard of course did not get his many Clemson accolades and his many uniform Chevrons for seasons such as this.

The Tigers came in seventh in the SoCon out of 10 active SoCon teams. Duke was again at the top of the Southern Conference. The conference itself was being depleted and was down to ten members. Ralph Jenkins was the Clemson Captain for 1943. The new Memorial Stadium had been inaugurated September 19 of the prior year with a close win against Presbyterian. This year, Clemson would not be so fortunate.

On Sept 25, Presbyterian noticed that Clemson for its own reasons was not playing its best football. Frank Howard had yet to set his eternal pattern to become an immortal coach in motion and the Clemson teams under his tutelage were not improving. Or if they were improving it was not noticeable to the discerning eyes of the general public—especially those who rooted exclusively for Clemson.

And, so just like every other year for many years, Clemson chose to kick off its home season at the home Ball Park, Memorial Stadium in Clemson, SC against a team that was willing to play an away game every year at Clemson, Presbyterian. Now the Blue Hose were never push-overs and they were always hoping to place a lick on Clemson but had yet to be able to do so. Well, until this year. Clemson seemed to have a problem getting that extra point after a touchdown when it was one point no matter how ya got it. This was another one of those years. Both teams scored two touchdowns but only one team was able to squeeze an extra point into the score and that team unfortunately for Tigers Fans was not Clemson.

And, so, Presbyterian licked Clemson at home in the season opener for the first time ever L (12–13). I already told you all this was a bad year so we won't spend a lot of words talking about the exact hurts of the season.

1944 Clemson Tigers Football Coach Frank Howard

The 1944 Clemson Tigers football team represented Clemson College during the 1944 college football season as a member of the Southern Conference (SoCon). Frank Howard was the head football coach for his fifth of thirty seasons. The Tigers completed their forty ninth season overall and their twenty-third in the Southern Conference with a record of 4-5; 3-1 in the SoCon. It was a much better season than the two poor Clemson seasons before. But, it was not a Cigar Season. The Tigers came in third in the SoCon out of 10 active SoCon teams. Duke was again at the top of the Southern Conference. The conference itself was not depleted this year as it held steady at ten members. Ralph Jenkins was again the Clemson Captain for 1944

1945 Clemson Tigers Football Coach Frank Howard

The 1945 Clemson Tigers football team represented Clemson College during the 1945 college football season as a member of the Southern Conference (SoCon). Frank Howard was the head football coach for his sixth of thirty seasons. The Tigers completed their fiftieth season overall and their twenty-fourth in the Southern Conference with a record of 6-3-1; 2-1-1 in the SoCon. The Tigers came in fourth in the SoCon out of 11 active SoCon teams. Duke was again at the top of the Southern Conference. Ralph Jenkins was captain for the third year in a row in 1945

Frank Howard's Clemson Players Taking a Water Break

1946 Clemson Tigers Football Coach Frank Howard

The 1946 Clemson Tigers football team represented Clemson College during the 1946 college football season as a member of the Southern Conference (SoCon). Frank Howard was the head football coach for his seventh of thirty seasons. The Tigers completed their fifty-first season overall and their twenty-fifth in the Southern Conference with a record of 4-5-; 2-3 in the SoCon. The Tigers came in tenth in the SoCon out of 16 active SoCon teams. Duke was again at the top of the Southern Conference. Chip Clark was the captain.

1947 Clemson Tigers Football Coach Frank Howard

The 1947 Clemson Tigers football team represented Clemson College during the 1947 college football season as a member of the Southern Conference (SoCon). Frank Howard was the head football coach for his eighth of thirty seasons. The Tigers completed their fifty-second season overall and their twenty-sixth in the Southern Conference with a record of 4-5-; 1-3 in the SoCon. The Tigers came in twelfth in the SoCon out of 16 active SoCon teams. WM & Mary won the Southern Conference in 1947. Cary Cox was the Clemson team captain.

There was a time or so it seemed that Clemson never lost to South Carolina. Those days were in the past. On Oct 23 at South Carolina in Carolina Stadium, Columbia, on Big Thursday, the Gamecocks had their fill and beat the Tigers L (19–21). On Oct 31, it was another loss – this time at Georgia in Sanford Stadium, Athens, GA. L (6-21). On Nov 22, Auburn played the Tigers at home and were defeated by the other Tigers W (34–18). The record was mixed but never bad in the Frank Howard years.

1948 Clemson Tigers Football Coach Frank Howard Championship SoCon

The 1948 Clemson Tigers football team represented Clemson College during the 1948 college football season as a member of the Southern Conference (SoCon). Frank Howard was the head football coach for his ninth of thirty seasons. The Tigers completed their fifty-third season overall and their twenty-seventh in the Southern Conference with a record of 11-0; 5-0 in the SoCon. The Tigers came in a clean first in the SoCon out of 16 active SoCon teams in 1947. Bob Martin

& Phil Prince were co-captains for the 1948 Clemson team. It was Clemsons best year ever. Wow!'

Bobby Gage was a great player (1945-48)

BOBBY GAGE

Nobody contests that Bobby Gage was one of the finest all-around football players in Clemson history. He played in the two-platoon era and he really had an effect on three platoons because he changed the course of games with his punt and kickoff returns. Gage played everywhere and he was great.

Looking closely ag his stats in 1948 shows a season in which he had a 100-yard rushing game (12-104 vs. Furman), a 172-yard passing game (against Mississippi State), a two-interception game on defense (also against Mississippi State) and a 100-yard punt return game (101 on three returns against NC State). His 90-yard punt return in that game proved to be the game winner and is still the longest punt return by a Clemson player in the history of Death Valley.

Bobby Gage was the true triple threat football player of the 1940s. He ended his career with 35 touchdowns--eight on rushes; 24 touchdown passes, one via punt return, one via kickoff return and even one on a reception. He still ranks in the top 10 in Clemson history in total offense and interceptions defensively. That is success on both sides of the ball, something you don't see today. His raw talent was a motivator for all Celmson athletes.

For his accomplishments in 1948, Gage was named a first-team All-American. He was a first-round draft choice of the Pittsburgh Steelers after the season. There were many great young men on Clemson's 1948 team that posted a perfect 11-0 record, the first perfect season at Clemson in 48 seasons. But, Gage might have been the top all-around player and senior leader. He had the stats to back it up.

It was not easy to become an All-American yet in his senior-year, he crossed the All-American threshold as a QB after leading Clemson to an 11-0 season and a 24-23 Gator Bowl win over Missouri. He was a unanimous choice as MVP in the 1949 Gator Bowl...

Gage was in the top 10 in career total offense at Clemson with 3,757 yards. When the greats were reported, he was tied for seventh in Tiger history in career interceptions (10). He also had perhaps the best all-around passing game in Tiger history when he completed 9-11 for 245 yards and two scores versus Furman in 1947. Gage knew the game and played it very well.

Bobby had four touchdown passes against Auburn in 1947, He was the first Tiger to do that. He was even better. He was called on the first-round of the NFL draft pick as the sixth selection of the Steelers. He played with the Steelers for two years.

He was inducted into the 1976 Clemson Athletic Hall of Fame. He was an inductee also to the state of South Carolina Hall of Fame in 1978. Gage was also named to the Gator Bowl Hall of Fame in 1990. After leaving the pros, he worked in the south in a big industry -- textiles at Chemurgy Products, Inc.

He was ranked as Clemson's #5 gridder of all-time by a panel of historians in 1999...At the time, he resided in Greenville, SC. The South Carolina gridders love South Carolina as their home. What is there not to love?

Great Player Fred Cone (1948-50)

Every coach has a great recruiting story but there is no question that Coach Frank Howard had one of the best. The most unusual recruiting story that you can find at Clemson was the case of Fred Cone. In the summer of 1947, Coach Frank Howard was informed by his sister, who lived in Mississippi, that there was a terrific athlete related to her next-door neighbor. When Howard turned in the names of his scholarship players for the fall of 1947, he had one spot left, so he added Fred Cone to the list, sight unseen. How's that for a guided light?

Clemson®

FRED CONE

Had he wanted to watch Cone play high school football he could not have done it. Cone did not play football in high school. Howard's sister was simply impressed with is athletic ability diving into the neighbor's pool.

By his sophomore year, 1948, Cone was leading the Tigers to an undefeated season, Clemson's first perfect year since 1900. Cone had 635 yards rushing and seven TDs, leading Clemson to the Gator Bowl, where Clemson downed Missouri 24-23. His second-effort run on fourth-and-three for a first down in the final minutes allowed Clemson to run out the clock and claim the landmark victory. Clemson has many great championships, even some seventy years ago. .

Two years later, Cone was leading Clemson to another undefeated season and he garnered first-team All-Southern honors. He scored 15 touchdowns and gained 845 yards in 1950 and concluded his career with 31 touchdowns, a record. After his Hall of Fame career at

Clemson, Cone went on to a Hall of Fame career with the Green Bay Packers. He led the NFL in field goals in 1955.

In 1997 he was inducted into the Clemson Ring of Honor—a distinction he richly deserves. Not a bad record for someone who never played high school football. I never played in a varsity game though I was on the Freshman team. Am I still eligible? I joke sometimes that I have foru years of elegiblity left. Any chance at 71 years of age that I can get a second masters on a scholarship. At 310 pounds perhaps the golf cart can teake me out just for goal line stands. OK, the dream is over, back to the Clemson book.

Why Clemson was ignored for the national championship?

I was born in January 1948 and so when I write one of these special Great Championship books highlighting any college team , it is always a great moment when I hit the events in the football season of 1948. I do not read ahead so I am always surprised to see how it goes in my year of birth. Clemson was as good as any other team in the country in the year of my birth but, nonethless, the Southern Conference had been the Conference from which the better teams were leaving for many years.

The SEC was grabbing the really tough teams for its conference at the time. When we look around the country at college football in 1948, if Clemson, undefeated at 11-0, was not close enough in the AP or Coach's polls to win the National Championship, then we all are asking, then who?

Well, it isn't as easy as it looks to figure out the sentimetality from the reality. Though playing top caliber football, Clemson and its opponents were reasonably unknown to the rest of the voting country especially the Associated Press. Hey, who trusts the press about anything today anyway. Anyway these polls were all we had to go by back in 1948.

So, I dug into the many archives, many of which are slanted to see what was going on that would preclude Clemson from being declared National Champions with an 11-0 record, undefeated and untied.

After an undefeated season and being a unanimous # 1 team in the Southern Conference, why not?

Here is what they say in a nutshell: Lots has been written. Michigan won it all in 1948. Unlike Clemson which went 11-0, the Wolverines went 9-0 and they had enough "press and pundit" clout to claim the #1 spot in the final AP poll over 9-0 Notre Dame. Michigan felt this season made up for the 1947 season when Notre Dame got the crown. It made up up for 1947, when Michigan had also gone 9-0, but finished #2 to Frank Leahy's 9-0 Notre Dame. The pundits had not figured out how to get the rest of the country in on the declared championships. Too bad!

They used this as an excuse: Michigan had capped the 1947 season with a huge 49-0 rout of Southern Cal in the Rose Bowl, and the AP conducted a post-bowl poll that went with Michigan at #1 over Notre Dame, but the AP had declared that the post-bowl poll was not "official." This season, it was Notre Dame that played a game against Southern Cal after the final AP poll. That's because the AP poll ended before their December 4th trip to Southern Cal, where Notre Dame was tripped up by a 14-14 tie to 6-3-1 USC, finishing the Irish at 9-0-1.

Because of that upset, there were no apparent contenders to Michigan's crown this season, since they did not even look at the Southern Conference. Thus, all the reporters who live around the big colleges declared Michigan as the unanimous choice for 1948 mythical national champion (MNC) amongst organizations listed in the NCAA Records Book, even math-based ratings.

Michigan would be the only team in contention. This meant 2 MNCs in a row for Michigan. Pundits across the country did mention Clemson but pooh poohed the great Southern Team's existence in the standings. They suggested that Clemson went 11-0, but their schedule was weak and they performed rather poorly, so they were not a contender at all.

The skinny was that Clemson had played just one team that was ranked by the original AP poll, #20 Wake Forest, and Clemson finished ranked just #11 themselves. They did better in the other poll for 1948 finishing #8, and their Gator Bowl opponent, 8-3 Missouri, was ranked #10.

Clemson won the Gator Bowl 24-23. But that's the only ranked opponent they played according to the pollsters, and they struggled to win 6-0 over 3-6-1 North Carolina State, 13-7 at 3-5 South Carolina, 26-19 at 5-2-2 Boston College, 21-14 over 6-4 Wake Forest, and 7-6 at 1-8-1 Auburn.

Meanwhile, according to the experts, Michigan played 5 ranked teams and only one of their wins was close (touchdown or less), 13-7 at 6-2-2 Michigan State (#17) in their opener. They beat 8-2 Northwestern (#3) 28-0. All commentaries are biased but in this book at least, we show you why the big shots chose not to give Clemson its proper roll of the dice for the Natonal Championship.

Regardless, the Tigers were undefeated and that is pretty darn good when you play eleven games and win them all against tough teams. So, in this book, perhaps one of the only books ever that discusses only Clemson's championship seasons, we give our vote to Clemson as 1948 National Champions. There is more than just our opinion.

California went 10-0 in the regular season, but they lost 20-14 to 8-2 Northwestern in the Rose Bowl to blow a shot at a share of the MNC. This became a habit for Cal: they would go unbeaten during the regular season in 1949 and 1950, and then lose the Rose Bowl following each of those seasons as well.

An always powerful Army team, especially during the WWII years, started this season 8-0, but they were tied by 0-8-1 Navy in their finale to finish 8-0-1, probably the biggest upset in college football history.

10-1 Oklahoma took their upset early, losing 20-17 at 7-2-1 Santa Clara in their opener. 9-1 Tulane lost 13-7 at 7-3 Georgia Tech in their 2nd game, and 8-1 Mississippi lost 20-7 at Tulane. 8-1 Cornell lost 27-6 to 8-0-1 Army at home. Again, 11-0 is not too shabby in anybody's league. Folks, there are no excuses for Clamson's snub.

In the season opener against Presbyterian, Clemson chose to makc it a memorable night game. It was the first time Memorial Stadium hosted a night game -- ever. It was in this season opening shutout W (53-0) victory over Presbyterian. As we have learned Memorial Stadium is where Clemson plays its home games. It is convenient as it sits right on the Clemson Campus in Clemson, SC.

On Oct 2, Clemson beat NC State at home in the Textile Bowl W 6–0. On Oct 9, the Tigers traveled to Scott Field in Starkville MS to play Mississippi State with a nice win W (21-7) Next on Oct 21, South Carolina had designs on an upset over the Tigers but the Gamecocks were brushed back at Carolina Stadium in Columbia, SC on Big Thursday for a Clemson win W (13–7).

Traveling again to the site where the Boston Barves played for years, on Oct 29, the Tigers beat the Eagles of Boston College at Braves Field in Boston, MA W (26–19). On Nov 6, the Tigers beat Furman at home in a big shutout W (41–0).

Finally, Clemson was able to beat Wake Forest at home W (21-14)) on Nov 13. The next week, it was Duquesne at home in a big win W (42-0). Next was Auburn at Ladd Stadium in Mobile AL for a nice win W (7–6). In the final game of the season, on December 4 at The Citadel's Johnson Hagood Stadium in Charleston, SC the Clemson Tigers won as expected W (20–0)

The Tigers had such a great season, they were warded a national bowl bid – the Gator Bowl v Missouri at Gator Bowl Stadium in Jacksonville FL. The Tigers put it all together on January 1, 1949 and beat Missouri W (24-23) for a great Gator Bowl victory W (24-23) in a nail-biter. So, why no national championship?

Highlight Game Clemson 24, Missouri 23

Jan. 1, 1949 at Jacksonville, FL (Gator Bowl)

Clemson's 1948 team was undefeated, but the team was wearing a lucky horseshoe all year long. Clemson had many close games that year, but the Tigers won them all. College Football Coach Darrell Royal's comment might apply here "Luck is what happens when preparation meets opportunity." Of course, Clemson's own John Heisman would take the luck but he preached discipline: "Gentlemen, it is better to have died as a small boy than to fumble this football." Coach Howard took the luck this season and ran with it.

This season had some wins that only fate can explain. For example, Clemson beat NC State 7-0 on a 90-yard punt return by Bobby Gage. Phil Prince blocked a punt at South Carolina that Rabbit Thompson returned for a touchdown, giving the Tigers the 13-7 win over South Carolina. And in the last game of the season, Clemson simply humiliated Auburn 7-6 in a driving rainstorm. Check the scoreboard, folls. Clamson X, Opponents 0.

The Tigers kept the lucky horseshoe for their Gator Bowl appearance against Missouri. This game was voted the best Gator Bowl game of the first 25 that were ever played. Clemson had them 24-16 when the opponents scored a touchdown to cut the margin to one point with about four minutes left. Clemson held. No win for Missiouri.

Clemson got the ball back in this game and Howard was hoping and trying to run out the clock to come home with a one-point win. It was fourth-and-three near midfield. Coach Frank Howard decided to go for it because he felt the team had not effectively stopped Missouri's offense all day. He called a play that gave the ball to Fred Cone on a running play. Cone hit a stone wall, but he kept his legs churning, and he bounced outside a little so that overall, he gained six yards for the first down. Clemson ran the clock out for the victory. As you may be able to determine, Fred Cone was as strong as an ox.

Coach Howard had a problem giving up even little secrets. For example, there is nobody who can relate to anybody else what the coach saw as his most memorable game. However, Frank Howard had no problem telling the world that the run by Fred Cone was his most memorable play.

During the previous season a group of students had come over to see Coach Howard to try to get him to resign. The team was not doing well at 1-5 at the time. Coach Howard stood his ground and he told those boys we were going to win the final three games of the 1947 season, then have a very good season the next year. Some have concluded that Howard did not know what he was talking about, but nonetheless he proved to be correct. Clemson won 14 straight games after he met with those students, including this undefeated season. Aren't true football stories the best?

1949 Clemson Tigers Football Coach Frank Howard

The 1949 Clemson Tigers football team represented Clemson College during the 1949 college football season as a member of the Southern Conference (SoCon). Frank Howard was the head football coach for his tenth of thirty seasons. The Tigers completed their fifty-fourth season overall and their twenty-eighth in the Southern Conference with a record of 4-4-2; 2-2-0. in the SoCon. The Tigers came in eighth in the SoCon out of 16 active SoCon teams. Gene Moore was the team captain for the 1949 Clemson team.

From writing these season summaries, I have learned that one thing you can count on until 1949 is that Presbyterian will show up for the season home opener at whichever stadium Clemson assigns, and they will do their best to defeat the Tigers. You can count on that like a gold standard.

In 1949, Presbyterian came in as usual to play at Clemson Memorial Stadium on the campus of Clemson Univesity in Clemson, SC, even before Clesmosn was a university, and as usual they were overwhelmed by the top-flight play of the Tigers. This year the toll was CU 69, PU 7. It was a big win W (69-7) over Presbyterian and it helped the Clemson squad get accustomed to playing in their new really big stadium.

1950 Clemson Tigers Football Coach Frank Howard <u>Championship</u>

The 1950 Clemson Tigers football team represented Clemson College during the 1950 college football season as a member of the Southern Conference (SoCon). Frank Howard was the head football coach for his eleventh of thirty seasons. The Tigers completed their fifty-fifth season overall and their twenty-ninth in the Southern Conference with a record of 9-0-1; 3-0-1. in the SoCon. The Tigers came in second in the SoCon out of 17 active SoCon teams. Fred Cone was the team captain for the 1950 Clemson team.

Jackie Calvert, Great Player S, QB 1948-1950

Calvert was an NEA first-team All-America safety. He was a great one for sure. He still holds the career record for rushing yards per attempt (5.92). He was designated the honor of team co-captain for the 1951 Orange Bowl team. He was always a top all-purpose yardage gainer that season with 1,220 yards,

<< Jackie Calvert

He could easily be described as a fine all-around back but he was more than that.

When this record was retrieved, Calvert was still second in Tiger history in career yards per pass attempt (8.76)...also seventh in career passing efficiency.

Calvert was a 25th-round draft pick of the Los Angeles Rams after the 1950 season...one of the stalwarts on two undefeated Clemson teams...nicknamed "The Kid".

For years, he resided in Murrells Inlet, SC.

Continuing with the season's games on Sept 23, Presbyterian came to Memorial Stadium on the college campus at Clemson, SC to be shut out W (54–0). On Sept 30, #17 ranked Missouri came to play the Tigers at home and lost W (34-0). Next home game was on Oct 7 as NC State in the Textile Bowl in which the Tigers prevailed W (27-0). Then, on Oct 19 at Carolina Stadium in Columbia SC on Big Thursday, the Gamecocks tied the Tigers T (14-14)) With a little extra rest after the Thursday game, the Tigers beat Wake Forest in a close match at Groves Stadium in Wake Forest NC W (13-12).

On Nov 4, the Tigers beat Duquesne Dukes at home W (53020). Following this, it was a game at Braves Field in Boston v Boston College in which the Tigers prevailed upon the Eagles for the win, W (35-14). Following this it was Furman on Nov 18 at home W (57-2). Auburn was next in a great shutout game for the Tigers at Auburn W (40-0)

Clemson was invited to Miami Burdine Stadium on Jan 1, 1951 for the Orange Bowl and the Tigers beat the Hurricanes in a great victory W (15-14)

1951 Clemson Tigers Football Coach Frank Howard

The 1951 Clemson Tigers football team represented Clemson College during the 1951 college football season as a member of the Southern Conference (SoCon). Frank Howard was the head football coach for his twelfth of thirty seasons. The Tigers completed their fifty-sixth season overall and their thirtieth in the Southern Conference with a record of 7-3-0-; 3-1-0. in the SoCon. The Tigers came in sixth in the SoCon out of 17 active SoCon teams. Bob Patton was the team captain for the 1951 Clemson team.

The Tigers were invited to play the Gator Bowl at Gator Bowl Stadium in Jacksonville on January 1, 1952 and they lost to the Miami Hurricanes L (0-14)

1952 Clemson Tigers Football Coach Frank Howard

The 1952 Clemson Tigers football team represented Clemson College during the 1952 college football season as a member of the Southern Conference (SoCon). Frank Howard was the head football coach for his thirteenth of thirty seasons. The Tigers completed their fifty-seventh season overall and their thirty-first in the Southern Conference with a record of 2-6-1; 0-1-0 in the SoCon. The Tigers came in fifteenth in the SoCon out of 17 active SoCon teams. George Rodgers was the team captain for the 1952 Clemson team.

After playing in the 1950 Orange Bowl and the 1952 Gator Bowl, in spite of the Southern Conference's ban on postseason play, Clemson was declared ineligible for the conference championship. In part, this was due to the ban. Unfortunately, Clemson and six other schools left the Southern Conference where it was tough to compete with the deck stacked. These teams formed the Atlantic Coast Conference (ACC) in 1953. It was a great move for them and a great move for Clemson. Too bad the somewhat corrupt NCAA still exists to punish teams that do not favor their college heritage.

1953 Clemson Tigers Football Coach Frank Howard

The 1953 Clemson Tigers football team represented Clemson College during the 1953 college football season as a member of the newly formed Atlantic Coast Conference (ACC). Frank Howard was the head football coach for his fourteenth of thirty seasons. The Tigers completed their fifty-eighth season overall and their first in the Atlantic Coast Conference with a record of 3-5-1; 1-2 in the ACC. The Tigers came in sixth in the ACC out of 7 active ACC teams. Dreher Gaskin and Nathan Gressette were the team captains for the 1953 Clemson team.

1954 Clemson Tigers Football Coach Frank Howard

The 1954 Clemson Tigers football team represented Clemson College during the 1954 college football season as a member of the newly formed Atlantic Coast Conference (ACC). Frank Howard was the head football coach for his fifteenth of thirty seasons. The Tigers completed their fifty-ninth season overall and their second in the Atlantic Coast Conference with a record of 5-5-0; 1-2-0 in the ACC. The Tigers came in fifth in the ACC out of 8 active ACC teams. Buck George, Scott Jackson, Mark Kane, Clyde White were the team captains for the 1954 Clemson team.

Chapter 15 Frank Howard Era 1955-1969

Coach # 17 Frank Howard

Year	Coach	Record	Conference	Record
1955	Frank Howard	7-3-0	ACC	3-1-0
1956*	Frank Howard	7-2-2	ACC	4-0-1
1957	Frank Howard	7-3-0	ACC	4-3-0
1958	Frank Howard	8-3-0	ACC	5-1-0
1959*	Frank Howard	9-2-0	ACC	6-1-0
1960	Frank Howard	6-4-0	ACC	4-2-0
1961	Frank Howard	5-5-0	ACC	3-3-0
1962	Frank Howard	6-4-0	ACC	5-1-0
1963	Frank Howard	5-4-1	ACC	5-2-0
1964	Frank Howard	3-7-0	ACC	2=4-0
1965*	Frank Howard	5-5-0	ACC	5-2-0
1966"	Frank Howard	6-4-0	ACC	6-1-0
1967*	Frank Howard	6-4-0	ACC	6-0-0
1968	Frank Howard	4-5-1	ACC	4-1-1
1969	Frank Howard	4-6-0	ACC	3-3-0

* Five conference championships from 1955 to 1969

There were a ton of great records as can be seen above from 1955 to 1969 in the Frank Howard years but none in this time period reflected championship seasons or undefeated seasons but clearly there were some great records which brought forth a number of conference championships.

1955 Clemson Tigers Football Coach Frank Howard

The 1955 Clemson Tigers football team represented Clemson College during the 1955 college football season as a member of the newly formed Atlantic Coast Conference (ACC). Frank Howard was the head football coach for his sixteenth of thirty seasons.

The Tigers completed their sixtieth season overall and their third in the Atlantic Coast Conference with a record of 7-3-0;

3-1-0 in the ACC. The Tigers came in third in the ACC out of 8 active ACC teams. Don King was the team captain for the 1955 Clemson team.

1956 Clemson Tigers Football Coach Frank Howard <u>Championship ACC</u>

The 1956 Clemson Tigers football team represented Clemson College during the 1956 college football season as a member of the newly formed Atlantic Coast Conference (ACC). Frank Howard was the head football coach for his seventeenth of thirty seasons. The Tigers completed their sixty-first season overall and their fourth in the Atlantic Coast Conference with a record of 7-2-2; 4-0-1 in the ACC.

The Tigers came in first in the ACC out of 8 active ACC teams. Charley Bussey was the team captain for the 1956 Clemson team. For such a great season, and winning the ACC, Clemson was invited to the Orange Bowl to play Colorado.

In the Orange Bowl played at Burdine Stadium in Miami FL, #20 Colorado defeated #19 Clemson in a tight match L (21-17)

Great Player Joel Wells, RB 1954-1956)

Joel Wells was a running back who wore number-70. In the defense minded 1950s, Wells broke the ACC rushing record his junior season with 782 yards, then bettered that total with 803 as a senior. That junior year he reached 782 yards in just 135 carries, a 5.8 average that still ranks among the top 10 single season averages in Clemson history.

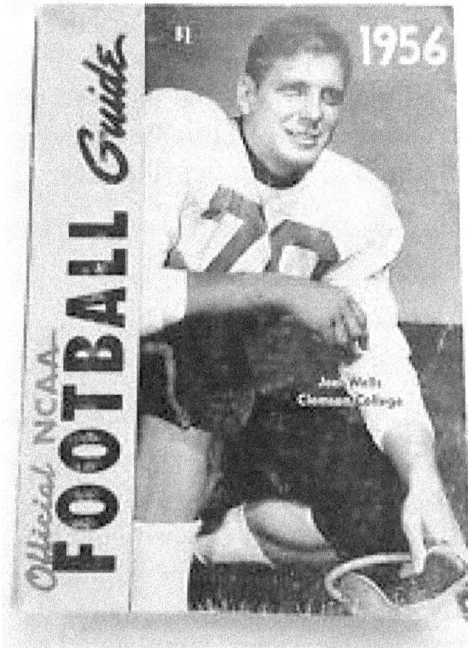

<< Joel Wells

How respected was Wells nationally? In 1956 his picture adorned the cover of the NCAA media guide. He was the first running back in Clemson history to rank among the top 20 in the nation in rushing in consecutive seasons. His number-seven ranking in yards per game in 1955 is still the highest ranking by a Clemson running back.

This two-time All-ACC running back is still in the top 15 in Clemson history in rushing and he led the Tigers in rushing three straight seasons. He might have saved his best game for last when he ran for 125 yards in 18 carries against Colorado in the 1957 Orange Bowl. He scored two touchdowns in that game, including a 58-yard jaunt that is still the Clemson record for a touchdown run in a bowl game by a running back.

He was the first Clemson running back to rank in the top 20 in the nation in rushing in consecutive seasons. He ranked seventh in rushing in 1955 and 18th in 1956.

1957 Clemson Tigers Football Coach Frank Howard

The 1957 Clemson Tigers football team represented Clemson College during the 1957 college football season as a member of the newly formed Atlantic Coast Conference (ACC). Frank Howard was the head football coach for his eighteenth of thirty seasons. The Tigers completed their sixty-second season overall and their fifth in the Atlantic Coast Conference with a record of 7-3-0; 4-3-0 in the ACC. The Tigers came in third in the ACC out of 8 active ACC teams. John Grdijan and Leon Kaltenback were the team captains for the 1957 Clemson team. No bowl games this year.

Kenan Memorial Stadium in Chapel Hill, NC was the venue for the second game of Clemson's 1957 season. North Carolina's Tar Heels pummeled the Clemson Tigers this time on Sept 28 in a shutout L (0-26). NC State got the word that NC teams could win and they did just that in a Clemson home game celebrating the Textile Bowl L (7-13). On Oct 12, at Virginia's Scott Stadium in Charlottesville, VA, the Tigers picked up their second win W 20–6 v the Hokies.

Clemson was ranked #14 nationally when they played the #11 ranked Duke Blue Devils on Nov 16 at Duke Stadium in Durham NC and the Tigers needed just a little more oomph as they lost the game L (6-7).

1958 Clemson Tigers Football Coach Frank Howard Championship ACC

The 1958 Clemson Tigers football team represented Clemson College during the 1958 college football season as a member of the Atlantic Coast Conference (ACC). Frank Howard was the head football coach for his nineteenth of thirty seasons. The Tigers completed their sixty-third season overall and their sixth in the Atlantic Coast Conference with a record of 8-3-0; 5-1 in the ACC.

The Tigers came in first in the ACC out of 8 active ACC teams. Bill Thomas was the team captain for the 1958 Clemson team. Coach Frank Howard's 100th win came September 27 against North Carolina. Clemson also played its first game against #1 ranked team when they played LSU in the January 1959 Sugar Bowl.

Clemson 26, North Carolina 21

Sept. 27, 1958 at Clemson, SC

This was just the second game of the 1958 season. Clemson had begun the season just a week earlier with a come from behind twice effort the week before to beat Virginia. The Tigers had to come from behind three times to win this game against North Carolina. There is a lot of history with this game as it was Coach Howard's 100th win as Clemson head coach. It was also the only time that Howard beat Jim Tatum, who was also a Hall of Fame Coach. Coach Tatum died prior to the next season.

This victory was important for Coach Howard and for Clemson football. Up until this game North Carolina always seemed to beat the Fighting Tigers. In the series, NC held a solid lead. But, this win started a string of six straight wins for Clemson over North Carolina. The lead persists as Clemson is proud to still lead in the series today.

Sugar Bowl

On January 1, 1959, in a great effort, the Clemson Tigers lost to LSU at Tulane Stadium, New Orleans in the Sugar Bowl, L (0-7. Overall, the Bowl game was a bit disappointing but the Howard squad almost beat #1 LSU in the Sugar Bowl that year, but Billy Cannon threw a game-deciding touchdown pass to beat the Clemson Tigers. Cannon's pass was no fluke. As a junior, Cannon was the driving force behind the Fighting Tigers as they carved out a perfect season and captured the 1958 national championship ... He passed for a touchdown and he even kicked the extra point in LSU's 7-0 win over Clemson in the Sugar Bowl, and earned MVP honors.

1959 Clemson Tigers Football Coach Frank Howard Championship ACC

The 1959 Clemson Tigers football team represented Clemson College during the 1959 college football season as a member of the Atlantic Coast Conference (ACC). Frank Howard was the head football coach for his twentieth of thirty seasons. The Tigers completed their sixty-fourth season overall and their seventh in the Atlantic Coast Conference with a record of 9-2-0; 6-1 in the ACC. The Tigers came in first in the ACC out of 8 active ACC teams. Paul Snyder and Harvey White were team captains in 1959. The annual game against South Carolina was played on Thursday at the State Fair for the final time. Clemson's 300th win came in the Bluebonnet Bowl against TCU.

Big Thursday Notes

Coach Frank Howard is shown on the next page blowing a good-by kiss to Big Thursday. Coach Howard felt the yearly matchup at

South Carolina was not in Clemson's best interests. He did not like Big Thursday.

Picture Clemson University Big Thursday Game by Will Vandervort

1960 Clemson Tigers Football Coach Frank Howard

The 1960 Clemson Tigers football team represented Clemson College during the 1960 college football season as a member of the Atlantic Coast Conference (ACC). Frank Howard was the head football coach for his twenty-first of thirty seasons. The Tigers completed their sixty-fifth season overall and their eighth in the Atlantic Coast Conference with a record of 6-4; 4-2 in the ACC. The Tigers came in fourth in the ACC out of 8 active ACC teams. Dave Lynn and Lowndes Shingler were team captains in 1960.

1961 Clemson Tigers Football Coach Frank Howard

The 1961 Clemson Tigers football team represented Clemson College during the 1961 college football season as a member of the Atlantic Coast Conference (ACC). Frank Howard was the head football coach for his twenty-second of thirty seasons. The Tigers completed their sixty-sixth season overall and their ninth in the Atlantic Coast Conference with a record of 5-5; 3-3 in the ACC. The Tigers came in fourth in the ACC out of 8 active ACC teams. Duke was again #1 in the ACC. Ron Andreo, Calvin West were team captains in 1961.

1962 Clemson Tigers Football Coach Frank Howard "Almost" Championship

The 1962 Clemson Tigers football team represented Clemson College during the 1962 college football season as a member of the Atlantic Coast Conference (ACC). Frank Howard was the head football coach for his twenty-third of thirty seasons. The Tigers completed their sixty-seventh season overall and their tenth in the Atlantic Coast Conference with a record of 6-4; 5-1 in the ACC. The Tigers came in second in the ACC out of 8 active ACC teams. Duke was again #1 in the ACC after being the only loss in Clemson's ACC season for 1962. Dave Hynes was the team captain.

Since Clemson stopped playing Presbyterian in every season opener, it was not assured of a victory and a nice warm-up game. This season began with a loss to Georgia Tech on Sept 22 in Grant Field, Atlanta GA L (9-26).

1963 Clemson Tigers Football Coach Frank Howard

The 1963 Clemson Tigers football team represented Clemson College during the 1963 college football season as a member of the Atlantic Coast Conference (ACC). Frank Howard was the head football coach for his twenty-fourth of thirty seasons. The Tigers completed their sixty-eighth season overall and their eleventh in the Atlantic Coast Conference with a record of 5-4-1; 5-2 in the ACC. The Tigers came in third in the ACC out of 8 active ACC teams. The once beaten NC & NC State teams shared the top spot in the ACC. Tracy Childers was the team captain.

1964 Clemson Tigers Football Coach Frank Howard

The 1964 Clemson Tigers football team represented Clemson University during the 1964 college football season as a member of the Atlantic Coast Conference (ACC). Frank Howard was the head football coach for his twenty-fifth of thirty seasons. The Tigers completed their sixty-ninth season overall and their twelfth in the Atlantic Coast Conference with a record of 3-7-0; 2-4-0 in the ACC. The Tigers came in seventh in the ACC out of 8 active ACC teams. The twice-beaten NC State team garnered the top spot in the ACC. John Boyett, Ted Bunton were the team captains.

1965 Clemson Tigers Football Coach Frank Howard   Championship ACC

The 1965 Clemson Tigers football team represented Clemson University during the 1965 college football season as a member of the Atlantic Coast Conference (ACC). Frank Howard was the head football coach for his twenty-sixth of thirty seasons. The Tigers completed their seventieth season overall and their thirteenth in the Atlantic Coast Conference with a record of 5-5-0; 5-2-0 in the ACC. The Tigers came in first tied with co-champion NC State in the ACC out of 8 active ACC teams. Bill Hecht and Floyd Rogers were the team captains.

Clemson was the co-ACC Champion in 1965, compiling a 5-5 record. Jimmy Addison was the QB for the Tigers in 1965 and he often handed the ball to Buddy Gore. Above is a picture of the game program from the game, depicting Little Red Riding Hood, aka the Tiger.

1966 Clemson Tigers Football Coach Frank Howard Championship ACC

The 1966 Clemson Tigers football team represented Clemson University during the 1966 college football season as a member of the Atlantic Coast Conference (ACC). Frank Howard was the head football coach for his twenty-seventh of thirty seasons. The Tigers completed their seventy-first season overall and their fourteenth in the Atlantic Coast Conference with a record of 6-4-0; 6-1-0 in the ACC. The Tigers came in first place in the ACC out of 8 active ACC teams. Mike Facciolo was the team captains.

Looking at the list of scores at the beginning of the Frank Howard chapters and knowing that many teams fire coaches with just six wins, it took a few more Frank Howard wins to convince me of where his priorities were. Every time I looked, despite a so-so season, the Frank Howard led Clemson Fighting Tigers were in the hunt in the ACC, and many times like this year, they were the League Champions against some pretty good teams. Now I know and you know. It is a great honor to win the league championship in any league. As the ACC would become even more respected, the next step would be the national bowl games,

Games of the 1966 Season

Clemson was back to winning opening games. This one was at home in Memorial Stadium located on the campus of Clemson University in Clemson, SC. It was played on Sept 24 featuring Clemson's Tigers and Virginia's Wahoos. The Tigers were dominant on offense and won the flip-flop game by a close margin W (40-35). Clemson had gained its University status in 1964.

Clemson 40, Virginia 35

Sept. 24, 1966 at Clemson, SC

The Clemson Tigers were down 18 points with 17 minutes to play in this game. With a lot of guts and resolve, we came back on the passing of Jimmy Addison. Jimmy passed 65 yards to Jacky Jackson for a touchdown that put Clemson in front. Jackson took off down the sidelines and "Needle" hit him in stride.

That game was memorable because it was the first time that Howard's Rock was in Death Valley. Coach Howard went on his television show the next day and said he told his players prior to the game that if they rubbed that rock they would receive magical powers. But, if they weren't going to give 110 percent, to "keep your filthy hands off that rock." A legend was born on that day. Forever it is known as Howards' Rock!

Virginia had a quarterback named Bob Davis. He and Needle put on quite a passing show, even by the high standards of today. Both teams threw for over 300 yards, the only game that happened in Clemson history over the first 90 years of play. In fact, both QB's were named National Players of the Week by some services.

Clemson's Tigers went on to win the ACC Championship. The team could not have done it if they didn't pull off that comeback against Virginia.

1967 Clemson Tigers Football Coach Frank Howard   Championship ACC

The 1967 Clemson Tigers football team represented Clemson University during the 1967 college football season as a member of the Atlantic Coast Conference (ACC). Frank Howard was the head football coach for his twenty-eighth of thirty seasons. The Tigers completed their seventy-second season overall and their fifteenth in the Atlantic Coast Conference with a record of 6-4-0; 6-0 in the ACC. The Tigers came in first place again in the ACC out of 8 active ACC teams. Jimmy Addison and Frank Liberatore were the team captains.

1968 Clemson Tigers Football Coach Frank Howard

The 1968 Clemson Tigers football team represented Clemson University during the 1968 college football season as a member of the Atlantic Coast Conference (ACC). Frank Howard was the head football coach for his twenty-ninth of thirty seasons. The Tigers completed their seventy-third season overall and their sixteenth in the Atlantic Coast Conference with a record of 4-5-1; 4-1-1 in the ACC. The Tigers came in second place in the ACC out of 8 active ACC teams. Billy Ammons, Ronnie Duckworth were the team captains.

1969 Clemson Tigers Football Coach Frank Howard

The 1969 Clemson Tigers football team represented Clemson University during the 1969 college football season as a member of the Atlantic Coast Conference (ACC). Frank Howard was the head football coach for his thirtieth and last season of thirty seasons. The Tigers completed their seventy-fourth season overall and their seventeenth in the Atlantic Coast Conference with a record of 4-6-0; 3-3-0 in the ACC. The Tigers came in fourth place in the ACC out of 8 active ACC teams. Ivan Southerland & Charlie Tolley were the team captains.

Frank Howard loved Clemson and he chose to remain as Athletic Director for several more years. until 1971. In 1974, the playing field at Memorial Stadium, which he helped to build, was named in his honor. He was a great coach for a ton of teams that could play with the best of them. He was the first Clemson Coach to last for many years.

I would suspect that if Clemson were more interested in National Championships than Conference Championships among the great southern teams, Frank Howard would have been the guy to help tweak the recruiting and the game to assure that the institution got what it needed. No opponent ever pushed around a Frank Howard team, even without a zillion dollars in scholarships and endowments. Bravo Frank Howard! Bravo Clemson University!

Picture from Frank Howard's Last Home Game Nov 1 1969 v Maryland

Frank Howard was on his way out the door and it would have been great if he got a better sendoff but his thirty years at Clemson were absolutely great

If you die, somebody writes a nice Obit

Frank Howard was ready to go when he went but he did lament that the line to keep in at the head coaching job was not a lot longer... I think! He was a piece of work. He coached great teams and great players and nobody ever seemed to complain about his coaching work or the great players he produced. Howard did not even seem to care what they thought.

Clemson had been floundering between success and failure. It was not that they did not have great years and great coaches. It was that nobody until Jess Neely stayed long enough to give the Clemson program a fighting chance. Frank Howard liked to win but he was aware that a lot of coach's bur out by trying too hard to please a constituency that may already be OK with their performance. Frank Howard got thirty years out of simply being a great coach.

Like most observers of his era, it would be easy to suggest tome that Howard did not drive his team to ultimate excellence. Yeah! I get that but if you look at the scores of the games, Howard and company were always there but for very few runaways. Without having the opportunity to interview Frank Howard, I like him immensely and would love to have had or to have a few beers with him some time.

Bear Bryant died a quick death after a phenomenal career with Alabama. He did not get a lot of un after coaching. Frank Howard had it all but he did not have Bear Bryant's record. Howard, IMHO did what he needed to do to get his teams ready and ready to win and somehow when they played v ACC teams, his teams were ready to kill. Some might suggest that he did not do v SEC teams as well but I beg to differ. I say Howard's mission was to win the ACC Championship in which he was always a contender. In this he was extremely successful.

From my observations, Clemson did not fund a national championship caliber team during Thomas's tenure. Oh' don't get me wrong Clemson loved winning but the difference in funding from Conference Champion to National Champion is substantial. Frank Thomas brought a lot of fun to his team and to Clemson University by being the guy that could beat all the teams around him in the south. It meant more to everybody than coming in 32nd in the national championship race meant – or even a close #8. Meanwhile Frank Howard had about twenty great years after retirement. What old fart would not like that?

Here is the Obit which is a great recap of Mr. Frank Howard:

On January 27, 1996 Frank Howard went to his eternal rest at the age of 86 years old. He had quite a life after he retired as Clemson's head football coach in 1969 from Clemson's head coaching duties.

The NY Times Frank Lisky wrote this tribute upon his death on January 27, 1996. His tribute was titled:

Frank Howard, 86, the Coach of Top Clemson Football Teams

Frank Howard, the colorful coach who in 30 years took Clemson University from football obscurity to the ranks of the national elite, died yesterday at his home in Clemson, S.C. He was 86.

The sports information office at the university said the cause of death was congestive heart failure. Howard was hospitalized in November because of circulatory problems, last month after a fainting spell and this month after a minor heart attack.

After retiring from coaching in 1969, he was athletic director at Clemson until mandatory retirement in 1971. He then kept an office in the athletic department and, until three weeks ago, went there five days a week.

"I'm not sure what he did there," the sports information director, Tim Bourret, said. "Whatever a retired legend does."

Howard liked to say he retired for health reasons.

"The alumni got sick of me," he would say.

He had a quick sense of humor. In the late 1950's, after a loss to Duke, he was asked to define the turning point. "It was three years ago," he said, "when I didn't recruit any half backs."

Frank James Howard was born on March 25, 1909, on a cotton farm in Barlow Bend, Ala., a town that he said was "three wagon greasin's from Mobile." He called himself the Bashful Baron of Barlow Bend.

In high school he played football, baseball and basketball and was president of the junior and senior classes. At the University of Alabama, where he was an honor student on an academic scholarship, he was a 185-pound guard on the football team from 1928 to 1930

FOOTBALL AS AN AFTERHOUGHT?

When he could not find work as an accountant, he became an assistant football coach at Clemson under Jess Neely. "I also coached track, was ticket manager, recruited players and had charge of football equipment," Howard said. "In my spare time I cut grass, lined tennis courts and operated the canteen while the regular man was out to lunch."

In 1940, when Neely became coach at Rice, the Clemson athletic council interviewed Howard as a potential successor. As the council discussed what to do, Howard listened from the back of the room. Finally, a council member said, "I nominate Frank Howard."

Long pause.

"I second the nomination," Howard said.

He got the job, lost his copy of the one-year contract and never signed another. From 1940 to 1969 his teams compiled a 165-118-12 record. They won two championships in the Southern Conference and later six in the Atlantic Coast Conference. Between 1949 and 1959 Clemson played in six bowl games.

Shortly after he retired as coach, Clemson named its stadium Frank Howard Field. In 1989, he was inducted into the College Football Hall of Fame.

With all his success, his highest salary was $25,000 a year. The president of the university, Dr. R. F. Poole, feared that professors who earned less would be upset.

"He called me up and said that he didn't want me to tell anybody what I made," Howard once said. "I said: 'Doc, you don't have to worry. I'm as ashamed as you are of what you pay me.' "

Surviving are his wife of 62 years, the former Anna Tribble; a son, Jimmy, of Clemson; a daughter, Alice McClure of Gastonia, N.C., and three grandchildren.

Hootie Ingram Replaces Frank Howard as Clemson Head Football Coach

Hootie Ingram became the next Clemson Football Coach. We highlight his Clemson tenure and his Clemson teams in this book. There are great moments in every season for every football team though in some seasons there are more great moments than others. In the next chapter, we examine the coaching work of Hootie Ingram who took over for the immortal Frank Howard at Clemson in 1970 and left the University after the 1972 season. His record with the Tigers is not very good – 12-21 over the three years in which he was the head coach.

You know from having read this book about every season from the first Clemson Football Season that there have not been many unsuccessful coaches at Clemson, University. Perhaps if he had been given more time, he would have been ready and would have done well.

Ingram had never been a head coach before. He had been a high school football coach and he had worked as an assistant football coach at several colleges, including the University of Georgia and the University of Arkansas, both noteworthy programs, before receiving the head coaching assignment at Clemson University from 1970 to 1972

In 2007, the University of Alabama National Alumni Association presented Ingram with the Paul W. Bryant Alumni-Athlete Award. The award recognizes athletes whose accomplishments since leaving the University are "outstanding based on character, contributions to society, professional achievement and service."

Chapter 16 Hootie Ingram Era 1970-1972

Coach #18 Hootie Ingram I

Year	Coach	Record	Conference	Record
1970	Hootie Ingram	3-8-0	ACC	2-4-0
1971	Hootie Ingram	5-6-0	ACC	4-2-0
1972	Hootie Ingram	4-7-0	ACC	2-5-0

Hootie Ingram 1970-1972 Clemson Coach

1970 Clemson Tigers Football Coach Hootie Ingram

The 1970 Clemson Tigers football team represented Clemson University during the 1970 college football season as a member of the Atlantic Coast Conference (ACC). Hootie Ingram was the head football coach for his first of three seasons. The Tigers completed their seventy-fifth season overall and their eighteenth in the Atlantic Coast Conference with a record of 3-8-0; 2-4-0 in the ACC. The Tigers came in sixth place in the ACC out of 8 active ACC teams. B. B. Elvington, Jim Sursavage, and Ray Yauger were the team captains.

1971 Clemson Tigers Football Coach Hootie Ingram

The 1971 Clemson Tigers football team represented Clemson University during the 1971 college football season as a member of the Atlantic Coast Conference (ACC). Hootie Ingram was the head football coach for his second of three seasons. The Tigers completed their seventy-sixth season overall and their nineteenth in the Atlantic Coast Conference with a record of 5-6-0; 4-2-0 in the ACC. The Tigers came in second in the ACC out of 7 active ACC teams. Larry Hefner and John McMakin were the team captains.

1972 Clemson Tigers Football Coach Hootie Ingram

The 1972 Clemson Tigers football team represented Clemson University during the 1972 college football season as a member of the Atlantic Coast Conference (ACC). Hootie Ingram was the head football coach for his third and last of three seasons. The Tigers completed their seventy-seventh season overall and their twentieth in the Atlantic Coast Conference with a record of 4-7-0; 2-5-0 in the ACC. The Tigers came in fifth place in the ACC out of 7 active ACC teams. Wade Hughes, Buddy King, & Frank Wirth were the team captains.

Just after competing this 4-7 season, the school put pressure on Hootie Ingram to resign as head coach of the football team. Ingram indeed did resign, which paved the way for Red Parker. In his three years as head coach, Ingram's overall record was 12-21.

In the photo above, you can see Hootie Ingram (left), Clemson President R.C. Edwards (center) and Hootie's replacement, Red Parker (right) in a press conference announcing the coaching change.

Chapter 17 Red Parker Era 1973-1976

Coach # 19 Red Parker

Year	Coach	Record	Conference	Record
1973	Red Parker	5-6-0	ACC	4-2-0
1974	Red Parker	7-4-0	ACC	4-2-0
1975	Red Parker	2-9-0	ACC	2-3-0
1976	Red Parker	3-6-2	ACC	0-4-1

Red Parker Coaches the Tigers from the Sidelines

1973 Clemson Tigers Football Coach Red Parker

The 1973 Clemson Tigers football team represented Clemson University during the 1973 college football season as a member of the Atlantic Coast Conference (ACC). Red Parker was the head football coach for his first of four seasons. The Tigers completed their seventy-eighth season overall and their twenty-first in the Atlantic Coast Conference with a record of 5-6-0; 4-2-0 in the ACC. The

Tigers came in third place in the ACC out of 7 active ACC teams. Mike Buckner and Ken Pengitore were the team captains.

1974 Clemson Tigers Football Coach Red Parker

The 1974 Clemson Tigers football team represented Clemson University during the 1974 college football season as a member of the Atlantic Coast Conference (ACC). Red Parker was the head football coach for his second of three seasons. The Tigers completed their seventy-ninth season overall and their twenty-second in the Atlantic Coast Conference with a record of 7-4-0; 4-2-0 in the ACC. The Tigers came in third place in the ACC out of 7 active ACC teams. Willie Anderson, Mark Fellers, Jim Ness, and Ken Peeples were the team captains. This was the first season with more than six victories since 1959.

1975 Clemson Tigers Football Coach Red Parker

<<< Coach Parker.

The 1975 Clemson Tigers football team represented Clemson University during the 1975 college football season as a member of the Atlantic Coast Conference (ACC). Red Parker was the head football coach for his third of four seasons. The Tigers completed their eightieth season overall and their twenty-third in the Atlantic Coast Conference with a record of 2-9; 2-3 in the ACC. The Tigers came in fifth place in the ACC out of 7 active ACC teams. Bennie Cunningham, Neal Jetton, Dennis Smith, Jimmy Williamson were the team captains. This was the first season with more than six victories since 1959.

Bennie Cunningham (1972-75)

Bennie Cunningham continues to today as the most decorated tight end in Clemson history. He is A native of nearby Seneca, SC and gets to see Clemson play regularly. Cunningham was a two-time first-team All-American at Clemson in 1974 and 1975, one of just 12 multi-year All-Americans in school history.

Cunningham was a pro scouts dream. At 6-5 and 250 pounds, he could run like a deer, yet run over the opposition in heavy traffic. In addition to his great hands and quickness, he was a devastating blocker. Cunningham first came on the scene in 1973 when he started all 11 games and caught 22 passes for 341 yards. He also averaged 6.6 yards a rush on 11 carries as a runner. That is a bit more than coming on the scene!

BENNIE CUNNINGHAM

In 1974 Clemson's season long slogan was "Excitement Galore in '74". Cunningham did his part in the 7-4 season that included a perfect 6-0 home record, with seven touchdown receptions among his 24 catches, the most touchdown receptions ever by a Clemson tight end and one of the top five totals nationally that season for tight ends. Cunningham was named a first-team AP All-American that season.

The Tigers stumbled a bit in 1975 with an underclassman offense, but Cunningham still averaged 17-yards a catch, an incredible average for a tight end. After the season, he was named a first-team All-American by Sporting News for the second straight year.

1976 Clemson Tigers Football Coach Red Parker

The 1976 Clemson Tigers football team represented Clemson University during the 1976 college football season as a member of the Atlantic Coast Conference (ACC). Red Parker was the head football coach for his fourth of four seasons. The Tigers completed their eighty-first season overall and their twenty-fourth in the Atlantic Coast Conference with a record of 3-6-2; 0-4-1 in the ACC. For the first time, the Tigers came in seventh (last) place in the ACC out of 7 active ACC teams. Malcolm Marler, Mike O'Cain, Randy Scott, and Joey Walters were the team captains. This was the first season that Clemson played so poorly in the ACC.

Chapter 18 Charley Pell Era 1977 to 1978

Coach # 20 Charley Pell

Year	Coach	Record	Conference	Record
1977	Charley pell	8-3-1	ACC	4-1-1
1978	Charley Pell	11-1-0	ACC	6–0–0

Charley Pell and the Clemson Team

Charley Pell brought a lot of zip back to the Clemson game as his Fighting Tigers almost got a national championshipe

1977 Clemson Tigers Football Coach Charley Pell "almost" championship

The 1977 Clemson Tigers football team represented Clemson University during the 1977 college football season as a member of the Atlantic Coast Conference (ACC). Charley Pell was the head football coach for his first of two seasons. The Tigers completed their eighty-second season overall and their twenty-fifth in the Atlantic Coast Conference with a record of 8-3-1; 4-1-1 in the ACC. The Tigers came in second place in the ACC out of 7 active ACC teams. Steve Fuller, Steve Godfrey, and Randy Scott were the team captains.

On Sept 10, Maryland played Clemson in the home opener at Memorial Stadium on the campus of Clemson University in Clemson, SC. The Terrapins defeated the Tigers in a close match L (14-21). Clemson no longer was playing its opening days against weaker teams. Maryland had been tough during the 1970's and Charley Pell's Tigers, which did very well in this year, had a tough game. On Sept 17 at #17 Georgia's Sanford Stadium in Athens, GA, Clemson prevailed W (7-6) in a nail-biter. On Sept 24 at Georgia Tech's Grant Field in Atlanta, GA, Clemson won handily W (31-14) What a difference a good coach makes. Charlie Pell was a great coach. On Oct 1, at Virginia Tech's Lane Stadium in Blacksburg, VA, the Tigers defeated the Hokies W (31–13).

Virginia came to play Clemson at home on Oct 8 and the Wahoos were shut out by Charley Pell's Tigers W (31-0) before 49,830. On October 15 at Duke's Wallace Wade Stadium in Durham, NC, Clemson was victorious W 17–11. On Oct 22, NC State's Wolfpack played the Tigers at home in the Textile Bowl W (7-3).

On Oct 29, Wake Forest was beaten by #16 ranked Clemson at home W (26–0). On Nov 5, at North Carolina's Kenan Memorial Stadium in Chapel Hill, NC, the #13 Tigers tied the Tar Heels T 13–13 before 50,400 fans. On Nov12, #5 ranked Notre Dame, coached by Dan Devine, came to #15 ranked Clemson at Memorial Stadium on the campus.

The Fighting Irish barely squeaked out a win against a tough Clemson squad L (17-21). Notre Dame won the National Championship in 1977. Charley Pell's Clemson's almost pulled off the big one.

On November 19 at South Carolina, the still ranked #15 Tigers beat South Carolina at Williams-Brice Stadium in Columbia, SC in what was known as the Battle of the Palmetto State W (31–27).

Clemson 31, South Carolina 27 was good enough for Clemson fans. On Nov. 19, 1977 at Columbia, SC, Clemson jumped out ahead 24-0, but South Carolina came back and scored, and scored and scored. How could Clemson stop them? They were like determined rats trying to get off the ship. They had a 27-24 lead with less than three minutes left.

The Tigers took over for one last drive and Steve Fuller came into the Clemson huddle after we got possession and he told the team, "boys we are going down the field and scoring a touchdown to win this game," His first two passes weren't very good and it looked like CU was not going anywhere.

But Fuller finally completed a pass to Rick Weddington to keep the drive alive. He got hit after that. He then clicked with Dwight Clark with a pass on a key play. Then the culmination of the drive was a 20-yard touchdown pass to Jerry Butler, something Clemson has begun to refer to as "The Catch". Butler made a diving backwards catch with just 49 seconds left in the game, giving the Tigers a 31-27 victory.

There might have been an extra motivation for Clemson on that last drive. That year, Coach Charley Pell would give cigars to the team after every Clemson victory. He started it after the team beat Georgia in Athens by stopping the bus at a convenience store on the way back.

Clemson hadn't won in Athens since 1914, so it was a special occasion. That year, someone at South Carolina printed up t-shirts that said, "No Cigars Tonight". A lot of the South Carolina players wore them under their uniform. When they scored to go up 27-24, a lot of them raised up their jerseys and showed the Clemson players and the television audience those t-shirts. I am sure Coach (Jim) Carlen wanted to wring their necks...especially after Butler made that catch.

The Clemson Tigers had a great year. It was the first 8-or better win season since 1959. The Pell Squad was invited to the Gator Bowl played in Gator Bowl Stadium in Jacksonville FL before a crowd of 72,289, against the #10 ranked Pittsburgh Panthers. The Tigers had a few misfires in the Gator Bowl game and lost L (3-34) by a much larger margin than the pundits and scribes expected.

Charley Pell was sure a great coach and the Tigers were an equally great team.

1978 Clemson Tigers Football Coach Charley Pell

The 1978 Clemson Tigers football team represented Clemson University during the 1978 college football season as a member of the Atlantic Coast Conference (ACC). Charley Pell was the head football coach for his second of two seasons. The Tigers completed their eighty-third season overall and their twenty-sixth in the Atlantic Coast Conference with a record of 11-1-0; 6-0-0 in the ACC. The Tigers came in first in the ACC out of 7 active ACC teams. They were also ranked # 6 nationally. Steve Fuller, and Randy Scott were the 1978 team captains.

Player Highlights Steve Fuller QB (1975-78)

Steve Fuller was third-team All-American in 1978 coupled with being on the Academic All-American team for two years. He was smart and he was a great athlete.

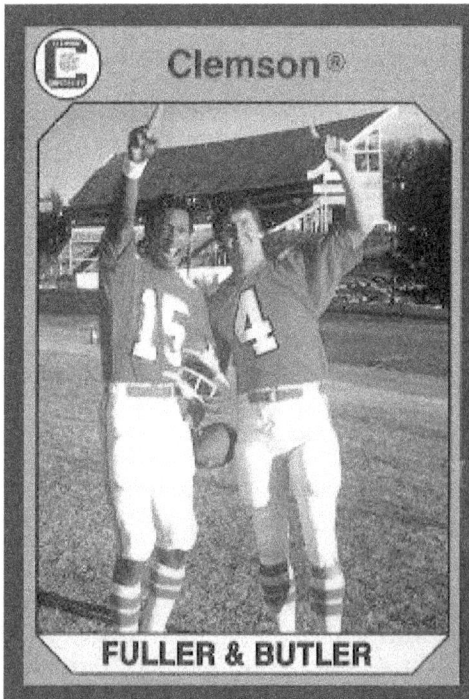

FULLER & BUTLER

He was ACC Player-of-the-Year in 1977,78 in 1978, Fuller led Clemson to the ACC title and then to a Gator Bowl win. The team was 11-1 and ranked sixth in the final poll. Fuller chimed in with 4,359 yards passing and third in total offense with 6,096 yards in his career.

He was second in Tiger history in career touchdown responsibility (44). He was second-best pass interception avoidance percentage (3.33) in NCAA history at the time of his graduation. This tribute he shared with Frank Howard's Award along with with Jerry Butler for the 1978-79 academic year,

Fuller won it outright in 1977-78. He is the only two-time recipient of that award. The pros could not stay away from biffing on grabbing him for their team. He was a first-round draft pick (23rd overall) of the Chiefs in 1979. He played for the Super Bowl Champion Bears in 1985.

Charley Pell coached Steve Fuller for two of his four years. In those years, under Coach Charlie Pell he started 27 consecutive games for him. He was an All-ACC selection in Pell's years -- '77 and '78 and was honored as the ACC Player of the Year both years. He is the only Clemson Tiger to do it twice.

Pell stepped down before the 1978 Bowl game. Nonetheless, that year, Steve Fuller quarterbacked the Tigers to their '78 Gator Bowl victory over Ohio State (the Woody Hayes game) and delivered Danny Ford his first win as a "interim" head coach.

Game Highlights Clemson 28, Maryland 24

Nov. 18, 1978 at College Park, MD

This was a big game -- for the ACC Championship and both teams were ranked in the top 12 in the nation.

It was a truly incredible game of big plays with many long plays. Maryland had a star runner named Steve Atkins who had a 98-yard run in this game. It is still an ACC record. Dwight Clark caught a 62-yard touchdown pass from Steve Fuller and Jerry Butler caught an 87-yard touchdown pass, the longest of his career.

Maryland kicked a field goal to make it 28-24 in the fourth quarter and then got the ball back. They drove into Clemson territory, but couldn't get any closer and the Tigers survived the assault. And won.

When we the team got back to the Greenville Airport there were 7,000 people waiting and cheering. Cars were lined up all the way to I-85. People were out of the cars and all over the place ready to welcome the team. It was a great happy scene. This victory over Maryland gave the Tigers a noteworthy 9-1 record and moved Clemson into the top 10 in the polls for the first time since the 1950s, so it was quite a big win. Of course, it was big enough for the Clemson Fighting Tigers to clinch the ACC Championship. Nobody forgot that.

In the last game of the season. On Nov 25, at home. Clemson beat South Carolina in the Battle of the Palmetto State W (41–23)) It was the best season ever.

The 1978 Gator Bowl

The #7 nationally ranked Tigers were invited to play #20 Ohio State in the Gator Bowl on Dec 29 at Gator Bowl Stadium in Jacksonville, FL. The Clemson Tigers played tough and won the game square W (17–15) before 72,011 fans.

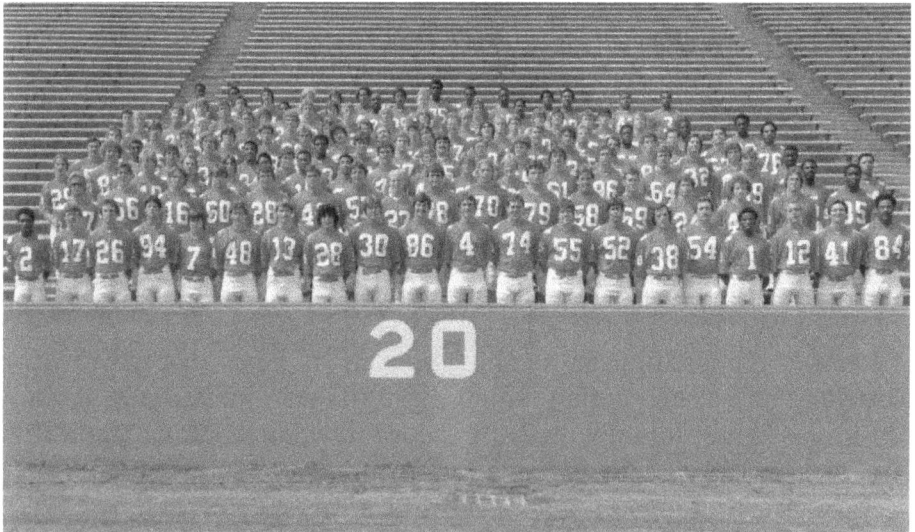

Clemson's 1978 Gator Bowl Champions

Game Highlight Clemson 17, Ohio State 15

Dec. 30, 1978 at Jacksonville, FL (Gator Bowl)

Ohio State always had tough teams and they still do. In 1978, they had a freshman quarterback named Art Schlichter who was a terrific player as both a runner and passer. He completed 16-20 passes in the Gator Bowl.

Of course, the thing everyone remembers is Woody Hayes hitting Charlie Bauman after Bauman made an interception in the final minute.

Charlie Bauman was not even supposed to be in that passing lane on that play. He got knocked backwards, enabling him to make the interception. That was the only interception of his career. He was run out of bounds in the middle of the Ohio State bench, right in front of Woody Hayes and Hayes struck him in a moment of frustration to beat all such moments. Many at the game could not see it for one reason or another.

By the time, the team had exited the field after the game and got in the locker room, everyone was talking about it. Coach Ford felt bad for Coach Hayes and told the players not to comment, just talk about the game.

Bob Bradley, the Clemson Sports Information Director recounts telling Coach Ford before the game that Clemson needed to have a press conference the morning following the game, because the game was scheduled for 9:00 PM. Coach Ford's press conference was scheduled for 10:00 AM. At 9:40 AM the Associated Press reporter came into our press conference to tell us that Hayes had already been fired.

Charlie felt badly about the whole situation because he had grown up an Ohio State fan and thought a lot of Coach Hayes. For years he refused to do interviews about the incident because he didn't want to rekindle the incident and hurt Coach Hayes' legacy. Coach Hayes called him to apologize after it happened. Charlie, who was a sophomore when the play happened, invited him to come down to spring practice, but he never came.

Charley Pell

Coach Pell moved on from Clemson after the 1978 regular season to become head coach at Florida. As you already know, Danny Ford took over the duties of head coach for the Gator Bowl.

Pell is most notably remembered as the head coach of the Clemson University and the University of Florida football teams. Pell created systems at both schools that were enduring. In his second season at Clemson, he had already made the name Clemson stand for success on the field. The systems he created laid the foundation for the later success of the Clemson program and then later the Florida program. Unfortunately, his coaching career was tainted by National Collegiate Athletic Association (NCAA) rules violations.

Pell arrived at Clemson as assistant head coach and defensive coordinator under Red Parker in early 1976. After the poor 3-6-2 1976 outcome, Coach Parker was ordered to fire several assistants. When he refused, Athletic Director Bill McClellan terminated him and asked Pell to take over the reins. He turned the program around,

Charley Pell never intended to be absent for the Gator Bowl. He had made a life decision and made the mistake as some might say of telling some people about it. This stirred up controversy. Clemson officials were outraged. He had accepted the head coaching position at the University of Florida, in Gainesville, on December 4, 1978. It was before the bowl game was played. His assistant, Danny Ford, a great student of Pell's, was named as his replacement almost immediately. Charley Pell's offer to stay with the team 'til the end of the season and coach the bowl game was declined.

Of course, only Charley Pell in a league now with the Lord, where there is no NCAA knows the truth. The alternate thought is that Pell originally said he would coach the Tigers in the Gator Bowl even while building his new program in Gainesville, but had a change of heart -- perhaps prompted by the yelps of outraged alumni and fans -- and announced on Dec. 10 that he was relinquishing the reins. I suspect somebody on earth may also know the truth. My own opinion is that if Clemson wanted Charley to stay, he would have been coaching the Gator Bowl. No aspersions cast on anybody.

Danny Ford, a kid at the time got the full-time job and coached for eleven years. He got Clemson its first National Championship as a kid. His teams are the focus of the next chapter.

Chapter 19 Danny Ford Era 1978-1989

Coach # 21 Danny Ford

Year	Coach	Record	Conference	Record
1978	Danny Ford	1-0	Gator Bowl	WIn
1979	Danny Ford	8-4-0	ACC	4-2-0
1980	Danny Ford	6-5-0	ACC	2-4-0
1981*	Danny Ford	12-0-0	ACC	6-0-0
1982*	Danny Ford	9-1-1	ACC	6-0-0
1983*	Danny Ford	9-1-1	ACC	7-0-0
1984	Danny Ford	7-4-0	ACC	5-2-0
1985	Danny Ford	6-6-0	ACC	4-3-0
1986*	Danny Ford	8-2-2	ACC	5-1-1
1987*	Danny Ford	10-2-0	ACC	6-1-0
1988*	Danny Ford	10-2-0	ACC	6-1-0
1989	Danny Ford	10-2-0	ACC	5-2-0

* ACC Champions

Danny Ford, a kid when he took over the program brought the Clemson Tigers the renown they always deserved including a national championship and many ACC championships. He was a fine coach.

1979 Clemson Tigers Football Coach Danny Ford

The 1979 Clemson Tigers football team represented Clemson University during the 1979 college football season

Danny Ford Leads Clemson Team to National Championship

Clemson is a member of the Atlantic Coast Conference (ACC). Danny Ford was the head football coach for his second of twelve seasons. Ford's first season lasted one game as he was a replacement coach for Charley Pell in the 1978 Gator Bowl. The Tigers completed their eighty-fourth season overall and their twenty-seventh in the Atlantic Coast Conference with a record of 8-4-0; 4-2-0 in the ACC. The Tigers came in second in the ACC out of 7 active ACC teams. They were also ranked # 6 nationally. Steve Fuller, and Randy Scott were the 1978 team captains.

Clemson shut out Furman W (21) in the home opener on Sept 8 at Memorial Stadium, on the campus of Clemson University, Clemson SC before a crowd of 55,000. A tough Maryland Terrapin squad played Clemson at home on Sept 15 and beat the Tigers L (0-19). On Sept 22, Georgia was the next home game. The Tigers beat the Bulldogs W (12-7) in a tight match. Clemson's 300th win came on this day, September 22 against Georgia. On Oct 6, at home, Clemson beat Virginia W 17-17. Then, on Oct 13, at Virginia Tech's Lane Stadium in Blacksburg, VA, Clemson won W 21–0. On October 20, at Duke in Wallace Wade Stadium • Durham, NC, the Tigers defeated the Blue Devils W 28–10.

On Oct 27 at home in the Textile Bowl, Clemson was defeated by NC State L (13-16). On Nov 3 at home, #14 Wake Forest was beaten by Clemson W (31–0). Then on Nov 10 at North Carolina's Kenan Memorial Stadium in Chapel Hill, NC, the then nationally ranked # 18 Tigers beat the Tar Heels W (19–10)   On Nov 17 at Notre Dame Stadium in Notre Dame, the Tigers defeated the Fighting Irish in a close match W 16–10.

Game Highlight Clemson 16, Notre Dame 10

Nov. 17, 1979 at South Bend, IN

Anytime that any team goes to Notre Dame and beats them it is an accomplishment. Notre Dame had beaten Clemson two years before and then went on to win the National Championship.

They weren't quite as good in 1979, but they still had a good ball club. Notre Dame held a 10-0 lead in the first half and looked like they had taken control of the game. Then, there was a big break for

Clemson. An ND player, Tyree Dickerson fumbled a punt that the Tigers recovered. It changed the momentum for the rest of the game.

Tim Bourret who became the Sports Communications Department Director told me later that after Dickerson fumbled the punt, he left the sideline, went to the locker room, got dressed and went back to his dorm. He had quit the team in the middle of the game. He watched the rest of the game on TV in his dorm room and never played football again.

It was Billy Lott who led the Clemson comeback in the second half. He had a 26-yard run that put the Tigers up and then Obed Ariri kicked three field goals and Clemson walked away from Notre Dame Stadium with a nice win W (16-10).

That was quite a first 11 games as head coach for Danny Ford. He was a fine coach. He beat Woody Hayes, Vince Dooley and Dan Devine all within that time. As many know, all three are in the College Football Hall of Fame.

On Nov 24 at #19 South Carolina in Williams-Brice Stadium, Columbia, SC, in the Battle of the Palmetto State, #13 Clemson lost the battle L (9–13)

In the Peach Bowl on Dec 31 v #19 Baylor at Fulton County Stadium in Atlanta, GA, the Clemson Fighting Tigers, the #18 Clemson Fighting Tigers lost the match L (18–24)

Bubba Brown, LB 1976-79

Marlon "Bubba" Brown is the all-time leading tackler in Clemson history. When you review the legendary list of linebackers who have played for Clemson, that is quite a statement. Bubba was finally inducted into the Clemson Hall of Fame.
It has taken a while for Brown to get his due simply because of the great teammates Brown had in his era (1976-79). Of the four players now in the Clemson Ring of Honor, three played on Clemson's 1978 team. But, a look at the statistics tells us that Brown was the team's top tackler, a ferocious hitter and enthusiastic player.

Two games stand out in his career. In 1978 Clemson traveled to Raleigh for an ACC showdown with NC State. NC State was promoting their Brown, running back Ted, for the Heisman Trophy. He had riddled Clemson for four touchdowns and 227 yards rushing three seasons earlier.

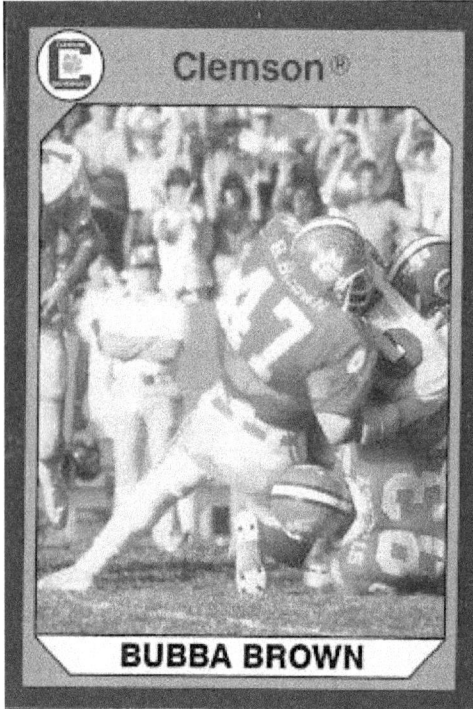

BUBBA BROWN

Although the national media did not portray the game as a "Battle of the Browns" (Clemson also had running back Lester Brown), Bubba took the confrontation as a personal challenge. By the end of the game, Bubba had 17 tackles and had held Ted Brown under 100 yards rushing, and out of the endzone. When Sports Illustrated was released the next week, it was Bubba who caught the national headlines with his selection as National Defensive Player of the Week.

Clemson finished the 1978 season with a 10-1 record and was chosen to play Ohio State in the Gator Bowl on national television. Clemson won the historic game ,17-15. Again, the pregame headlines were all about Danny Ford's first game as head coach and his meeting with future Hall of Fame mentor Woody Hayes. Brown personally stymied the Ohio State rushing game with 22 tackles, still the second highest single game total in Clemson history.

1980 Clemson Tigers Football Coach Danny Ford

The 1980 Clemson Tigers football team represented Clemson University during the 1980 college football season as a member of the Atlantic Coast Conference (ACC). Danny Ford was the head football coach for his third of twelve seasons. The Tigers completed their eighty-fifth season overall and their twenty-eighth in the Atlantic Coast Conference with a record of 6-5-0; 2-4-0 in the ACC. The Tigers came in 4th in the ACC out of 7 active ACC teams. Lee Nanney, and Willie Underwood were the 1978 team captains.

1981 Clemson Tigers Football Coach Danny Ford   <u>National Championship</u>

The 1981 Clemson Tigers football team represented Clemson University during the 1981 college football season as a member of the Atlantic Coast Conference (ACC). Danny Ford was the head football coach for his fourth of twelve seasons. The Tigers completed their eighty-sixth season overall and their twenty-ninth in the Atlantic Coast Conference with a record of 12-0-0; 6-0-0 in the ACC. The Tigers came in 1st in the ACC out of 7 active ACC teams. Nelson Stokely was the offensive coordinator. Jeff Davis was the team captain. This year a dream came true. The Clemson Tigers won the National Championship. It was a consensus of the coaches and AP polls.

On Sept 5 in the home opener, Clemson defeated Wofford W (45-10) at Memorial Stadium on Sept 12, at Tulane in the Louisiana Superdome, New Orleans, LA, Clemson won W (13–5). Then on Sept 19 at home, #4 Georgia lost to Clemson W (13-3.

Game Highlight Clemson 13, Georgia 3

Sept. 19, 1981 at Clemson, SC

Georgia came to Clemson as the defending national champion. It was a season highlight for sure for Clemson to compete well in this game. To win the game was simply remarkable. There is no question that this was Clemson's key regular season win on the way to winning the coveted national championship.

No one had Clemson on their scopes in their preseason top 20. As you all know, the Tigers were just coming off a frustrating 6-5 season. On top of that, Clemson vs. Georgia is a special rivalry and this is one of the games that made it that way. Herschel Walker, a name everybody knows had led Georgia to the National Championship the year before and he was ready to destroy Clemson if given the opportunity. He was a marked man by the Clemson defensive unit this day and it was quite effective.

The Clemson defense was ready as it forced nine turnovers against the Bulldogs. It was the most turnovers forced in a game in history. Clemson took a 10-0 early lead in the first half on an eight-yard touchdown pass from Homer Jordan to Perry Tuttle and a 39-yard field goal by Donald Igwebuike. Thigs were looking good.

Clemson and Georgia traded field goals in the second half and Coach Danny Ford let the defense take control to shut down the Bulldogs offensive threat. Jeff Davis was outstanding and followed Walker everywhere he went. Herschel Walker ended the day with 111 yards rushing on 28 carries, but the Tiger defense made sure that he never got into the Clemson endzone.

Georgia entered this game ranked fourth in the nation. It is still the highest ranked win in Clemson history in Death Valley. Go Tigers!

On Oct 3 at Kentucky's Commonwealth Stadium in Lexington, KY, the #14 Clemson Tigers beat the Wildcats W (21–3). On Oct 10 at home, #9 Clemson shut out Virginia W (27–0) before 63,064. Then, on Oct 17 at Duke's Wallace Wade Stadium in Durham, NC, #6 Clemson beat the Blue Devils W (38–10)

In the Textile Bowl at home on Oct 24, the #4 Tigers beat the Wolfpack of NC State W (17-7). On Oct 31 in another home game, the #3 ranked Tigers routed the Demon Deacons of Wake Forest before 60,383. Then, on Nov 7 at # 9 North Carolina's Kenan Stadium in Chapel Hill, NC, the #2 Tigers got by the Tar Heels by a thread W 10–8, keeping their unbeaten season streak intact.

Clemson's Jeff Davis celebrates after a victory in the magical 1981 season
Photo courtesy of Clemson Tigers

Game Highlights Clemson 10, North Carolina 8

Nov. 7, 1981 at Chapel Hill, NC

The thing I remember about this game was the play that Jeff Bryant made in the closing moments. We had a 10-8 lead in the closing minutes and Dale Hatcher punted the ball out of bounds at the North Carolina two.

They hadn't driven for a touchdown against us all day, so it looked good for the Tigers.

But, Scott Stankavage started to lead North Carolina up field. With 57 seconds left they had the ball on their 40 and Stankavage threw a swing pass to the right flat. It was incomplete and every player relaxed...except for Bryant. He chased after the ball and pounced on it.

Sure enough, the referees said it was a lateral and it was Clemson ball. We ran out the clock and kept our perfect record.
That one play might have helped him become a first-round draft choice because it showed his alert play. That play was shown on the Saturday night news all over the country because it was the big game of the day in college football. We were ranked second in the nation and North Carolina was eighth, the first time in history two top 10 ACC teams faced each other.

The headline in the Greenville News the next day was Tigers read "10-8cious". Since I did not get it at first either, think how *tenacious* the Tigers play had to be.

This is such a memorable game against such a major foe and it was so critical to the 1981 national Championship, that I have "borrowed a great piece of Tiger News from ClemsonTigers.com witten on September 23, 2014 by Sam Blackman. It is a great account of the game. http://www.clemsontigers.com/ViewArticle.dbml?ATCLID=209671838

Clemson is "10-8cious"

By: ClemsonTigers.com
Release: Tuesday 09/23/2014

by Sam Blackman

Clemson's road to the National Championship in 1981 included a classic game with North Carolina in Chapel Hill, N.C. on November 7th. It's considered to be one of the greatest games ever played in Atlantic Coast Conference history.

It was eighth-ranked North Carolina against second-ranked Clemson, the first meeting of top-10 ACC teams in league history.

"The North Carolina game did more for us winning the national championship than any other game," said senior linebacker and captain Jeff Davis. "It was the ultimate test for us. We expected to win in Death Valley and we expected teams to already be behind when the whistle blew to start the game. But, to go into the backyard of a top-10 football team with everything at stake, and win, that did it for us.

"Remember, North Carolina had everything to play for. It's right there for them. You can think there were people wondering 'Can Clemson stay focused?' And we beat them in a fight. It was an all-out brawl. May the best man win! It was man-on-man."

With an ACC Championship and a major bowl bid at stake, it was dubbed the biggest game to ever be played in the state of North Carolina.

"North Carolina came to play," defensive tackle and All-American Jeff Bryant said. "They were at home and they were a top-10 team. We both were striving for that goal which was to win the ACC and take it further from there.

"It was a very physical game. I can remember being sore for a couple of days after that."

It was also Homecoming Weekend in Chapel Hill, NC and it was the last game at Kenan Stadium for UNC's seniors – a class that had helped the Tar Heels win an ACC Championship the year before and beat traditional powers such as Texas and Oklahoma along the way.

To top things off, there were bowl representatives from eight bowl games in attendance, more than at any other game that afternoon across the country. Sports Illustrated had been at Clemson all week to chronicle the Tigers' magical run and was in Chapel Hill on that afternoon. ABC was broadcasting it as part of their regional coverage and carried the game throughout most of the country.

All of America's eyes seem to be placed on this small school from the foothills of South Carolina, and then Clemson Head Coch Danny

Ford knew he had to do something to turn his team's focus to what was really important – beating the Tar Heels.

"Were we excited about the hype? Yes! We wanted the stakes high," said Davis. "It didn't get any better than this. This was another opportunity for us to do something in Clemson football history that had never been done.

"We took all of that into consideration. We would not have approached that game any other way because there was the crown jewel of college football standing right in front of us. We could almost touch it.

"The world was watching. We had a great opportunity. It was everything that a young man and a young student-athlete could want."

"North Carolina, for me, was a big game," Davis said. "I'm from Greensboro, North Carolina, and I wanted to beat them more than anyone else we played. This was my last opportunity to make a statement in North Carolina that I made the right decision in coming to Clemson."

"Both teams knew it was going to be a hard-fought, physical game. They had some very good athletes and they were a very good football team. We were going into their backyard. It was going to be tough."

Ford knew it was going to be tough too.

"I was concerned about how we can play physically with this team," he said. "We were out-muscled in 1980, which did not happen too often with our football teams. Their game plan in 1980 was to out-muscle Clemson, and I think they did it.

"We knew that's what they were going to try and do again."

The game started as a defensive struggle and lived up to its billing. The score was 0-0 at the end of the first quarter.

McCall had a game-high 84 yards before he left the game injured and scored the game's lone touchdown – a seven-yard run with 6:54 to play in the second quarter.   Clemson led 7-5 at the half.

North Carolina ranked second in the country running the football coming in, but Clemson held the Tar Heels to 84 yards on 42 carries. Stopping the run had been the Tigers ammo all season. With new defensive coordinator Tom Harper at the helm, Clemson led the ACC in rushing defense and ranked second in the country.

"We would put a goose egg on our (defensive) board before every game," Davis said. "We didn't do it as a mark or just to put something up there. No, we actually believed it. It was symbolic to us. You were not going to score on us. Even if you get in our territory, you might have a chance to get a field goal, but you can forget about scoring a touchdown on us.

"We took pride in that. You were not supposed to score on us. We even took pride in goal line situations in practice. I don't care how close you put the ball you were not going to score on our defense. We believed that. That was not some tough guy talk or something to motivate people. We believed it."

North Carolina running back and three-time All-ACC selection, Kelvin Bryant believed it. In his first game back after arthroscopic knee surgery earlier, he gained just 31 yards on 13 carries as did fellow running back Tyrone Anthony on eight carries.

"When I see Kelvin, he likes to joke that he gets a headache right when he sees me because we were hitting him so hard that day," Davis smiled.

Clemson's defense was stifling.

No team that season learned that any better than the Tar Heels. Twice, North Carolina had first-and-goal inside the Clemson 10, and both times it was held to short field goals by Brooks Barwick.

Early in the second quarter, North Carolina appeared to have a possible touchdown on a third-down swing pass in the flats to Tyrone

Anthony, but Clemson All-American safety Terry Kinard came out of nowhere to drag him down at the five. The Tar Heels settled for a 22-yard Barwick field goal and led 3-0.

Now Trailing 10-5, following a Donald Igwebuike 39-yard field goal, North Carolina took its second drive of the third quarter and marched down to the Clemson four thanks to a 21-yard halfback pass from Anthony to Griffin. But, Davis and Kinard stuffed Kelvin Bryant for a five-yard loss on the next play and then Stankavage threw incomplete on second and third down, forcing the Tar Heels to settle for a 26-yard Barwick field goal.

The Tigers led 10-8 heading into the fourth period.

In the fourth quarter, North Carolina again had an opportunity to take the lead following a muffed punt by Billy Davis at the Clemson 37. After gaining just four yards on first and second down, the Tar Heels hopes for taking the lead were dashed when freshman nose guard William Perry broke through and sacked quarterback Scott Stankavage for a 10-yard loss.

"With the kind of defense we had, we never panicked," defensive tackle, Jeff Bryant said. "We are going to make the big play. It was always role call to the ball."

Following a Clemson punt, UNC again moved into Tiger territory to the 39, but again the defensive stiffened, with a tackle for a loss and two incomplete passes.

Unable to move the ball, Clemson punter Dale Hatcher then pinned the Heels deep in their own territory at the two-yard line following a 47-yard punt with 2:19 to play, setting up the final dramatics in one of the biggest victories in Clemson history.

After moving the ball out from the shadow of their own goal post , the Tar Heels found themselves with a first down at their own 40 thanks to a 12-yard scramble by Stankavage on third-and-10 from the two, then a nine-yard pass to wide receiver Ron Richardson and a 14-yard pass to Anthony.

With just over a minute to play and one timeout left, the Tar Heels called a screen pass to fullback Alex Burrus. Stankavage threw the ball behind the line of scrimmage and when Burrus went to make the catch, defensive end Bill Smith met him, knocking the ball to the ground.

The ball rolled 15 yards backwards towards the Clemson sideline, and that is where defensive tackle Jeff Bryant jumped on the football at the UNC 25-yard line.

Smith is sort of the unsung hero. The play everyone remembers is Bryant having the presence of mind to jump on what appeared to be an incomplete pass with 57 seconds to play.

The pass was ruled a lateral, and by jumping on the loose football Bryant secured Clemson's 10-8 victory in front of a then record crowd at Kenan Stadium of 53,611. But, what people don't recall is who actually caused the fumble.

That would be Bill Smith, a current member of the Clemson University Board of Trustees.

"They were moving the ball down the field, and all they needed was a field goal to win," Smith said. "That was just a timely play that happened."

Timely indeed, it was perhaps the calling-card of the 1981 defense. In 1981, Clemson ranked seventh in the nation in turnover margin and led the ACC in forced turnovers with what is still a school-record 41.

Jeff Bryant, who played 12 seasons in the NFL, had a stellar career at Clemson, but it wasn't until Tom Harper became the defensive coordinator in the spring of 1981 when he finally realized what kind of player he could be.

Harper did wonders for Bryant's play. He not only helped him become sound fundamentally, he helped him with his technique. He helped him become a better football player, and a better person.

"Tom Harper was very instrumental in my development," Bryant said. "He was a great guy. I wish I had Tom Harper all four years. I'm thankful I had him when I did, though, because he really made a difference with me."

Bryant credited Harper's instruction as one of the reasons he stayed alert and recognized the lateral on North Carolina's final drive.

"I was coming up field pretty hard because I figured they were going to pass the ball. I had a good rush on and I was about as deep as the quarterback," he said. "I noticed him throwing the ball, and I saw the hit, but I noticed he threw the ball behind him.

"Bill made a great hit, and I saw the ball coming out, so my thinking was to rush over there and get on it because no one else thought it was a lateral. I thought it was one because of the angle I was at because I was right there behind the quarterback as he threw the ball."

Smith, who admits he did not know it was a lateral at the time, sometimes wonders about the "what ifs" had Bryant not jumped on the loose ball.

"Who knows what would have happened had we lost that game, but thank goodness we can say 'what if' all we want because we didn't lose it," he said. "We won it and we did all we could do to win it. That was the mentality of that team all year."

After Jordan fell to the ground three times to run out the final 57 seconds, a mass celebration broke out on the Clemson sideline. As Tar Heel fans made their way to the exit, the Clemson players and the 10,000 or so Tiger fans that traveled up to Chapel Hill, stayed and enjoyed what they had accomplished, a 10-8 victory over North Carolina.

The next day, "The Greenville News" had in its headlines, in bold print, a very clever headline, "Clemson is 10-8cious."

"We knew that anything was possible at that point," Bryant said.

With a victory over the eighth-ranked Tar Heels behind them, Clemson for the first time, admitted the possibility of going undefeated and playing for a national championship was on its mind.

"It was important because we started thinking a little bit now about being undefeated," Davis said. "Until that point, we were not trying to touch it. There might have been a few rumblings here and there, but we were all about one game at a time.

"At that point, and where we were at, you were going to have to do something phenomenal to beat us."

The Tigers were simply 10-8cious that day and that season.

-- End of article reprint--

On Nov 14, at home the #2 Clemson Fighting Tigers beat Maryland W (21–. On Nov 21, at South Carolina's Williams-Brice Stadium in Columbia, SC, in the Battle of the Palmetto State, the #1 Tigers beat the Gamecocks W (29–13), finishing the season undefeated and in first place.

The #1 Clemson Tigers played in the Orange Bowl Game on January 1, 1982 at 8:00 p.m. against # 4 Nebraska in the Miami Orange Bowl, Miami, FL, and the Tigers came away with the victory and the National Championship

Game Highlights Clemson 22, Nebraska 15

Jan. 1, 1982 at Miami, FL (Orange Bowl)

This game was definitely for the national championship. Nebraska had future Heisman Trophy Mike Rozier, Dave Rimington, the Outland Trophy Winner and many other talented players. But Clemson had some pretty good players in our own right with Jeff Davis, Perry Tuttle, William "Refrigerator" Perry, and many others.

Nebraska scored and cut the lead to seven points, 22-15 when they converted a two-point play from the eight-yard line in the fourth quarter.

But, Clemson held the ball about the last five minutes. Homer Jordan was the key to running out the clock and not giving Nebraska another chance. He made a great run with about two minutes left that gave the Tigers a first down. What a run that was, he made so many cut backs. We held the ball to the final seconds. Nebraska had one last play with six seconds left, but Andy Headen knocked down a long pass attempt.

Homer made it to the dressing room, but he passed out once he got there from dehydration. It was a tough game. All the press wanted to talk to Homer after the ballgame, but he was in there for a long time getting IVs. By the time he got out of the training room it was past deadline for the writers. That is why all the accounts of that game don't have any quotes from Homer. He didn't do any interviews until the next day. That was certainly a magic night in Miami. Clemson was happy with the win and so what about the interviews.

Clemson's Fighting Tigers finished the 1981 season undefeated and untied (12-0) and were voted #1 in the AP and UPI polls. When they won the Orange Bowl over Nebraska, the Tigers were selected as Consensus National Champions by the AP, UPI, Football Writers Association of America (FWAA), and National Football Foundation (NFF). In the 1980-s with Danny Ford as the head coach for most of the run, Clemson was the fifth winningest Division I college football team of the decade, with a record of 86-25-4 (.765).

Danny Ford was awarded the 1981 Coach of the Year Award by the American Football Coaches Association (AFCA) and the FWAA. At the time, Coach Ford was the youngest ever to receive the award, and the youngest (33 yrs. old) to have won a National Championship.

In the 1982 Orange Bowl, Clemson QB Homer Jordan received Offensive Most Valuable Player honors. Homer earned first-team All-ACC honors in 1981, his junior season, and finished first in the ACC in passing efficiency and 12th in the nation. Jordan was an honorable mention All-American selection in 1981. He was runner-up for ACC MVP behind teammate Jeff Davis, but the team voted him MVP in 1981.

Even though Jordan was injured for much of his senior season, he helped lead the 1982 team to a 9-1-1 record and number-eight national ranking. He also earned honorable mention All-American honors as a senior. He ranked as Clemson's 18th greatest player of the century. Jordan was inducted into the Clemson Hall of Fame in 1993.

1982 Clemson Tigers Football Coach Danny Ford   Championship ACC

The 1982 Clemson Tigers football team represented Clemson University during the 1982 college football season as a member of the Atlantic Coast Conference (ACC). Danny Ford was the head football coach for his fifth of twelve seasons. The Tigers completed their eighty-seventh season overall and their thirtieth in the Atlantic Coast Conference with a record of 9-1-1; 6-0-0 in the ACC. The Tigers came in 1st in the ACC out of 7 active ACC teams. Nelson Stokely was the offensive coordinator. Homer Jordan and Terry Kinard were the team captains. This year, with a great coach after a National Championship Season, the Clemson Tigers played great football

If I am out of line, on the NCAA, please skip this part. Somehow whenever smaller, less important teams do something well like win a National Championship the NCAA seems to like to step in a ruin the party. Clemson was placed on probation near the end of this season for recruiting violations, and was ineligible for a bowl bid. Some think it was because Clemson won the National Championship and not a team the corrupt NCAA was supporting. Who knows? In this book about Clemson, I give my support to the Tigers and not to the faux Tigers in the NCAA.

"I was a senior on the 1982 team, and we voted as seniors to accept the unprecedented extra year of probation which the ACC handed down on top of two year NCAA sanctions. We were offered the invitation to play SMU in the Cotton Bowl, and turned it down so that the future teams at Clemson could accept a bowl invitation in 1985." (Carl Martin). Why is it that when adults mete out punishment, it is student athletes who get hurt? I really would like to feel differently but please note this is the fifth Great Moments book I have written. Nobody escapes the scourge of the corrupt NCAA with all of their rich and famous officials. Unless…

The home opener was not the first game this year. Instead, on Sept 6 at #7 ranked Georgia's Sanford Stadium in Athens, GA, this famous rival Bulldogs beat the former champion Clemson Tigers by no more than a hair. L (7–13). More and more fans were able to squeeze into larger and larger stadiums as in the 1980's there was a lot of building going on. On Sept 18, for the first time in a while, the always-tough Boston College Eagles played the #16 Clemson Fighting Tigers at home to a tie in the home opener at Memorial Stadium on the campus of Clemson University in Clemson, SC T (17-17).

On Sept 25 at home, Clemson beat Western Carolina W (21–10) before 61,369. On Oct 2 at home the Tigers beat the Kentucky Wildcats W (24–6). On Oct 9 at Virginia in Scott Stadium, Charlottesville, VA, Clemson pummeled the Wahoos W (48–0). Then, on Oct 16 at home, the #20 Tigers beat the Duke Blue Devils W (49–14). On Oct 23 in the Textile Bowl at NC State's Carter–Finley Stadium in Raleigh, NC, the #18 Tigers beat the Wolfpack W (38–29).

On Nov 6 at home playing #18 North Carolina, the #13 Clemson Tigers managed to beat the Tar Heels W (16–13). On Nov 13, the eternally tough #18 ranked Maryland Terrapins took on the #11 Tigers at Byrd Stadium in College Park, MD and lost W (24–22). On Nov 20, at home in the regular season finale, the big in-state rival South Carolina in the Battle of the Palmetto State lost in a nice match W (24-6 before a great crowd of 66,210.

#10 Clemson had a good year and got to go to Japan's National Olympic Stadium in Tokyo, Japan to play an always-tough Wake Forest team in the Mirage Bowl. As tough a game as it was, it was a treat for the players and the Clemson Tigers emerged victorious W (21–17) before 80,000 spectators.

1983 Clemson Tigers Football Coach Danny Ford   Championship ACC

The 1983 Clemson Tigers football team represented Clemson University during the 1983 college football season as a member of the Atlantic Coast Conference (ACC). Danny Ford was the head football coach for his sixth of twelve seasons. The Tigers completed their eighty-eighth season overall and their thirty-first in the Atlantic Coast Conference with a record of 9-1-1; 7-0-0 in the ACC. The Tigers came in 1st in the ACC out of 8 active ACC teams. Nelson Stokely was the offensive coordinator. James Farr and James Robinson were the team captains. This year, with a great coach again, the Clemson Tigers played great football. Clemson was on probation for recruiting violations, and was ineligible for the ACC championship or a bowl bid.

On Sept 3, to begin the home season at Memorial Stadium on the campus of Clemson University, Clemson, SC, the Tigers overwhelmed the Catamounts of Western Carolina W (44–10) before an opening day crowd of 69,962. On Sept 10, Clemson picked up its only loss of the year at Boston College's Alumni Stadium, Chestnut Hill, MA L (16–31). On Sept 17, at home the Tigers settled for their only other mar on their record with a tie (16-16) against the Georgia Bulldogs. On Sept 24, the other Georgia team came to Clemson and the Tigers defeated the Georgia Tech Yellow Jackets W (41-14). On Oct 8 for the third home game in a row, the Tigers defeated the Virginia Wahoos W (42-21.

Duke was next on Oct 15 at Wallace Wade Stadium • Durham, NC, W (38–31). On Oct 22, at home, the Tigers beat NC State's Wolfpack in the Textile Bowl W (27-17). At home again on Oct 29, Wake Forest played tough football and came close to upsetting Clemson W (24-17). On Nov 5, Clemson defeated #10 North Carolina at Kenan Memorial Stadium in Chapel Hill, NC W (16–3). The following week on Nov 12 at home, the Tigers defeated the Maryland Terrapins W (52-27). In the season finale, with no ACC championship though no losses in the ACC, and no Bowl games to be played, the Battle of the Palmetto State was the next and final item on the season's agenda. The Tigers won this game W (22-13) for a great season record of 9-1-1 and an ACC record of 7-0-0. That's great Clemson football.

1984 Clemson Tigers Football Coach Danny Ford

The 1984 Clemson Tigers football team represented Clemson University during the 1984 college football season as a member of the Atlantic Coast Conference (ACC). Danny Ford was the head football coach for his seventh of twelve seasons. The Tigers completed their eighty-eighth season overall and their thirty-first in the Atlantic Coast Conference with a record of 7-4-0; 5-2-0 in the ACC. The Tigers came in 2nd in the ACC out of 8 active ACC teams. Nelson Stokely was the offensive coordinator. Mike Eppley, and William Perry were the team captains. This year, with a great coach again, the Clemson Tigers played great football. Clemson was on probation for recruiting violations, and was ineligible for the ACC championship or post season play.

William Perry (1981-84)

As a freshman at Clemson, Perry helped the Tigers to the 1981 national title. That season, Perry came off the bench to 48 tackles and four sacks, including two in a key win over North Carolina.

That was only the start for the 300-pound lineman, who earned his nickname as a senior at Clemson after earning consensus All-America honors as a junior. In his final season in 1984, Perry led the nation with 27 tackles for a loss and had 100 tackles – as a nose guard – to earn ACC Player of the Year honors.

Only three ACC defensive players and two players from Clemson since then have earned such honors.

"The Refrigerator" made a great debut at Clemson. They say he had a knack for the "big" debut, even before he helped the Chicago Bears' dominant defense to the Super Bowl as a rookie in 1985.

Fridge Starring on the Bob Hope Show

1985 Clemson Tigers Football Coach Danny Ford

The 1985 Clemson Tigers football team represented Clemson
University during the 1985 college football season as a member of the
Atlantic Coast Conference (ACC). Danny Ford was the head football
coach for his eighth of twelve seasons. The Tigers completed their
eighty-ninth season overall and their thirty-second in the Atlantic
Coast Conference with a record of 6-6-0; 4-3-0 in the ACC. The
Tigers came in 4th in the ACC out of 8 active ACC teams. Nelson
Stokely was the offensive coordinator. Steve Berlin and Steve Reese
were the team captains.

1986 Clemson Tigers Football Coach Danny Ford   Championship ACC

The 1986 Clemson Tigers football team represented Clemson
University during the 1986 college football season as a member of the
Atlantic Coast Conference (ACC). Danny Ford was the head football
coach for his ninth of twelve seasons. The Tigers completed their
ninetieth season overall and their thirty-third in the Atlantic Coast
Conference with a record of 8-2-2; 5-1-1 in the ACC. The Tigers
came in 1st in the ACC out of 8 active ACC teams. Terrence Flagler
and Terence Mack were the team captains.

Clemson began the season on Sept 13 losing one of just two games that it would lose in the entire season. This game was the home opener in Memorial Stadium on the campus of Clemson University, Clemson, SC. The Hokies of Virginia Tech defeated the Clemson Fighting Tigers L (14-20) before 75,930. On Sept 20, at #14 Georgia's in Sanford Stadium, Athens, GA, Clemson prevailed W (31–28). Then on Sept 27 at Georgia Tech's Grant Field in Atlanta, GA, Clemson won W (27–3). On Oct 4, at home, the Tigers shut out The Citadel W (24–0). On Oct11 at Virginia's Scott Stadium in Charlottesville, VA, Clemson won another W (31–17).

On Oct 18 at home against Duke, the #17 ranked Tigers walloped the Blue Devils W (35–3). On Oct 25 at #20 NC State's Carter–Finley Stadium in Raleigh, NC, playing in the annual Textile Bowl, Clemson bowed to the Wolfpack L (3–27). On Nov 1 at Wake Forest's Groves Stadium in Winston-Salem, NC, the Tigers squeaked by the Demon Deacons W (28–20). On Nov 8 at home the Clemson Fighting Tigers defeated the North Carolina Tar Heels W (38-10). On Nov 15, at Maryland at Memorial Stadium, Baltimore, MD, the teams played to a tie T (17–17). On Nov 22, at home, South Carolina tied the Tigers in the Battle of the Palmetto State T (21–21).

The #21 Tigers were invited to the Gator Bowl on Dec 27, 1986 to play #20 Stanford in Gator Bowl Stadium in Jacksonville Florida before 80,104. The Tigers defeated the Cardinal in a well-played close game W (27-21).

1987 Clemson Tigers Football Coach Danny Ford   Championship ACC

The 1987 Clemson Tigers football team represented Clemson University during the 1987 college football season as a member of the Atlantic Coast Conference (ACC). Danny Ford was the head football coach for his tenth of twelve seasons. The Tigers completed their ninety-first season overall and their thirty-fourth in the Atlantic Coast Conference with a record of 10-2-0; 6-1-0 in the ACC. The Tigers came in 1st in the ACC out of 8 active ACC teams. Michael Dean Perry and John Phillips were the team captains.

On Sept 5 in the home opener played on the campus of Clemson University at Memorial Field in Clemson, SC, Coach Danny Ford's Clemson Fighting Tigers shut out Western Carolina to get the season rolling W (43-0). On Sept 12, at Virginia Tech's Lane Stadium in Blacksburg, VA, the #10 Tigers won again W (22–10). Back home, on Sept 19, the #18 Georgia Bulldogs were defeated by Clemson's Tigers W (21-20).

Game Highlights Clemson 21, Georgia 20

Sept. 19, 1987 at Clemson, SC

Clemson was down 20-16 with about five minutes left in this game when Rusty Seyle hit a punt that was downed by Chinedu Ohan on the half-yard line. A couple of plays later, the Clemson Tigers defense swarmed on Georgia quarterback John Jackson and tackled him for a safety and the two points that come with it.

The Tigers took the "safety kickoff," which was a punt with about five minutes left and drove the ball down the field, one successful play after another behind the running of Terry Allen and Wesley McFadden.

Clemson was behind by two at this point and successfully drove the ball to the three yard-line. Clemson brought out kicker David Treadwell to make the winning kick. It was just like an extra point. Thigs got confused near the end of the game and it was a little hairy because the Clemson team was all out of timeouts. Nonetheless Coach Ford got the Clemson squad / the field goal team on the field and Treadwell got the kick through the uprights with just two seconds left.

Treadwell a great kicker and this was not the first time he had amazed the crowd. He had a number of game winning kicks. He had done the same thing the year before at Georgia, kicking a 46-yard field goal to win 31-28 in Athens. I wonder if Treadwell had his own horseshoe.

In addition to the success so far in the season, Clemson also won four more home games in the following five home encounters. The first was when #9 ranked Clemson went against Georgia Tech on Oct 3 W (22-12). The second was when the #8 Tigers went against the Virginia Wahoos on Oct 10 W (33–12). And then the third was when

#7 Clemson played Duke's Blue Devils on Oct 17 for the win W (17-10). At this point, at 6-0 for the season, The Tigers suffered a tough home loss to NC State in the Textile Bowl on Oct 24 L (28-30). The fourth win of the last five home games came on Oct 31, when the #14 Tigers defeated the Wake Forest Demon Deacons W (31-17).

On Nov 7, at North Carolina's Kenan Memorial Stadium, Chapel Hill, NC, the Tigers beat the Tar Heels in a close game W (13–10) Next on Nov 14 at home, the Tigers back to #9 nationally, handily beat Maryland W 45–16. Now, looking for a nice top ten finish and a great Bowl Game, the #8 Clemson Tigers were disappointed in the Battle of the Palmetto State as #12 South Carolina pulled out all the stops and defeated CU at South Carolina's Williams-Brice Stadium • in Columbia, SC L (7-20 Clemson was ranked #14 after the game and were invited to the Citrus Bowl.

Citrus Bowl

On Jan 1, 1988, the #14 Clemson Tigers squared off in the Florida Citrus Bowl Game against the #20 Penn State Nittany Lions in the Citrus Bowl Stadium, Orlando, FL (Florida Citrus Bowl). Clemson beat up Penn State in the game W (35–10) and finished #11 in the AP poll and #12 in the Coach's Poll for the year. The Tigers had previously won the ACC Championship.

John Phillips OG 1984-1987

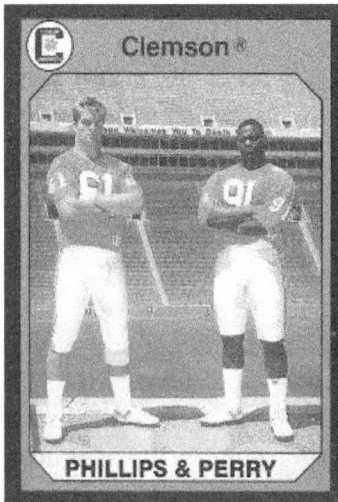
PHILLIPS & PERRY

John Phillips was named first-team All-American as a junior and became a second-team All-American as a senior. He made the All-ACC team two consecutive years and captured the Jacobs Blocking Trophy for South Carolina two years in a row.

Phillips had the single-season record of 103 knockdown blocks as a junior, he concluded his career with 245 knockdown blocks, which at the time was third in Clemson history. He is still the only Tiger with a pair of 100-knockdown block seasons, he had 100 in 1986 and 103 in 1987.

Phillips started 32 games and played in 47 for his career. He was co-captain of Clemson's 1987 team with Michael Dean Perry. He was a graduate assistant coach at Clemson for 1990 and 1991. Phillips was inducted into Clemson's Hall of Fame in Fall in 1999.

Michael Dean Perry, 1984-87

Some knew him as the Refrigerator's brother. But, he was more than just a familiar name along the Clemson defensive line. Michael Dean Perry picked up right where his brother left off and he exceeded him in some areas. Like his brother, he was one of a handful of defensive players to win ACC Defensive Player of the Year (1987). Michael also broke William's ACC records for career tackles for a loss (61) and career sacks (28).

He remains Clemson's sole record holder for career tackles for a loss and was tied for career sacks by Gaines Adams in 2006. Perry's best season came in 1987 when he recorded 24 tackles for a loss and 10 sacks as Clemson went 10-2 with an ACC title.

1988 Clemson Tigers Football Coach Danny Ford Championship ACC

The 1988 Clemson Tigers football team represented Clemson University during the 1988 college football season as a member of the Atlantic Coast Conference (ACC). Danny Ford was the head football coach for his eleventh of twelve seasons. The Tigers completed their ninety-second season overall and their thirty-fifth in the Atlantic Coast Conference with a record of 10-2-0; 6-1-0 in the ACC. The Tigers came in 1st in the ACC out of 8 active ACC teams. Rodney Williams, and Donnell Woolford were the team captains.

The Tigers began the season with three home games in a row. On Sept 3 in the home opener played on the campus of Clemson University at Memorial Field in Clemson, SC, Coach Danny Ford's Clemson Fighting Tigers defeated Virginia Tech W (40-7) to get the season rolling. On Sept 10, #3 ranked Clemson beat Furman W 23–

3 before   80,620. Then, on Sept 17, the Tigers suffered their first loss at home against #10 Florida State in a nail biter L (21-24).

On Sept 24, at Georgia Tech's Bobby Dodd Stadium in Atlanta, GA, the #12 Tigers defeated the unranked Bulldogs W (30-13). Then, at Virginia's Scott Stadium in Charlottesville, VA, Clemson got the best of the Wahoos W 10–7. On Oct 15 at home, the #11 Tigers beat the #22 Duke Blue Devils W (49–17) before a packed house of 83,356. Then, on Oct 22 at #24 ranked NC State's Carter–Finley Stadium in Raleigh, NC in the Textile Bowl, the Wolfpack got the best of the Tigers L (3–10).

On Oct 29 at Wake Forest's Groves Stadium in Winston-Salem, NC, the Tigers defeated the Demon Deacons W 37–14. On Nov 5, at home North Carolina was defeated by Clemson W (37–14). On Nov 12, at Maryland's Byrd Stadium in College Park, MD, the Tigers defeated the Terrapins W (49–25). Then, in the season finale v South Carolina—the Battle of the Palmetto State, the Tigers beat the Gamecocks W 29–10. Of the second year in a row, Clemson accepted an invitation to play in the Citrus Bowl.

Citrus Bowl

On Jan 1, 1989, in the Florida Citrus Bowl post-season game, Coach Danny Ford's #9 Clemson Fighting Tigers defeated Coach Barry Switzer's #10 ranked Oklahoma Sooners in the game played at the Citrus Bowl Stadium in Orlando, FL. The Tigers won W (13-6) The game was seen on ABC TV and by the 53,571 in the stadium.

1989 Clemson Tigers Football Coach Danny Ford

The 1989 Clemson Tigers football team represented Clemson University during the 1989 college football season as a member of the Atlantic Coast Conference (ACC). Danny Ford was the head football coach for his twelfth and last of twelve seasons. The Tigers completed their ninety-third season overall and their thirty-sixth in the Atlantic Coast Conference with a record of 10-2-0; 5-2 in the ACC. The Tigers came in 3rd in the ACC out of 8 active ACC teams.

On Sept 9 at No. 16 Florida State in Doak Campbell Stadium, Tallahassee, FL, the Tigers beat the Seminoles W (34–23).

Game Highlight Clemson 34, Florida State 23

Sept. 9, 1989 at Tallahassee, FL

This might have been the best performance ever for Clemson. The Tigers were ahead 21-0 in the first quarter after two 73-yard plays. Wayne Simmons had a 73-yard interception return and Terry Allen had a 73-yard run for a touchdown. Allen's run was simply amazing because it took place right before half-time. Clemson was simply trying to run out the clock on a sweep and it went all the way.

The Tigers controlled this game the entire night. Clemson held a nice 34-17 lead with six seconds left before Florida State scored a very late touchdown. This was not a fluke against a poor FSU team. No! This Florida State team ended the season at #2 in the nation in the final Coach's poll. When you talk to Clemson fans who attend lots of Tiger games, this might have been the most fun they have ever had at a road game. This was the year after the "puntrooskie Game" so Clemson Fans were pretty fired up.

To help with that memory, in the prior year's Florida State against Clemson-- in the famous 1988 "Puntrooskie Game;" Dayne took the snap from center on the play, put the ball between the legs of the upback, Leroy Butler, who then raced down the sideline for 78-yards to the three-yard line. Bobby Bowden's squad orchestrated the play to perfection and it had its intended result—a Clemson loss after the field goal L (21-24).

Gator Bowl

On Jan 1, 1989, in the Gator Bowl post-season game, Coach Danny Ford's #14 Clemson Fighting Tigers defeated Coach Don Nehlen's #17 ranked West Virginia Mountaineers in the game played at the Gator Bowl Stadium in Jacksonville, FL. The Tigers won W (27-7) The game was seen on ESPN and by the 82,911 in the stadium.

Chapter 20 Ken Hatfield Era 1990 - 1993

Coach # 22 Ken Hatfield

Year	Coach Record	Record		Conference	
1990	Ken Hatfield	10-2-0	ACC	5–2-0	
1991	Ken Hatfield	9-2-1	ACC	6-0-1	
1992	Ken Hatfield	5-6-0	ACC	3-5-0	
1993	Ken Hatfield	9-3-0	ACC	5-3-01	
1993	Tommy West	Bowl Game WIn		Score	20-0

Ken Hatfield was the perfect guy to come in after Danny Ford as he kept up the Clemson winning tradition.

1990 Clemson Tigers Football Coach Ken Hatfield

<<< Coach Ken Hatfield
The 1990 Clemson Tigers football team represented Clemson University during the 1990 college football season as a member of the Atlantic Coast Conference (ACC). Ken Hatfield was the head football coach for his first of four seasons. The Tigers completed their ninety-fourth season overall and their thirty-seventh in the Atlantic Coast Conference with a record of 10-2-0; 5-2-0. They were tied for second in the ACC. out of 8 active ACC teams. Stacy Fields and Vance Hammond were team captains.

Hall of Fame Bowl

On January 1, 1991, the #14 ranked Clemson Fighting Tigers took on the # 16 ranked Illinois Fighting Illini in Tampa Stadium • Tampa, FL in the Hall of Fame Bowl. It was viewed on NBC. The Fighting Tigers shut out the Fighting Illini W (20-0) before 82,911 spectators.

1991 Clemson Tigers Football Coach Ken Hatfield   Championship ACC

The 1991 Clemson Tigers football team represented Clemson University during the 1991 college football season as a member of the Atlantic Coast Conference (ACC). Ken Hatfield was the head football coach for his second of four seasons. The Tigers completed their ninety-fifth season overall and their thirty-eighth in the Atlantic Coast Conference with a record of 9-2-1; 6-0-1. They took first place in the ACC. out of 8 active ACC teams. Rob Bodine, DeChane Cameron, and Levon Kirkland were team captains.

The Clemson Fighting Tigers began the season with a home game. On Sept 7 in the home opener played on the campus of Clemson University at Memorial Field in Clemson, SC, Coach Ken Hatfield's #8 Clemson Fighting Tigers shut-out Appalachian State W (34-0) to get the season rolling quickly in a positive direction. On Sept 21, Temple played # 8 Clemson at home in Memorial Stadium.

The Tigers beat the Owls W (37-7) before 74,575. On Sept 28, at home Clemson barely got by a tough Georgia Tech Team W (9-7) On Oct 5, at Sanford Stadium in Athens, #6 Clemson lost to the Yellow Jackets L (12–27) before 85,434 fans. Then on Oct 12 at home against Virginia, Clemson tied the Wahoos T (20-20).

On Oct 26 at home against # 12 NC State, the Tigers beat the Wolfpack W (29-19) before 79,832. On Nov 2 at home, the Tigers beat the Demon Deacons W 28–10. Then a week later on Nov 9 at North Carolina at Kenan Memorial Stadium in Chapel Hill, the Tigers won W (21–6). On Nov 16, at home, the Fighting Tigers defeated the Terrapins W (40-7) before 71, 881.

On Nov 23, in the Battle of the Palmetto State at South Carolina's Williams-Brice Stadium, Columbia, SC, #12 Clemson beat the

Gamecocks W (41–24). On Dec 1, in the season finale, the Tigers defeated the Blue Devils of Duke in the Tokyo Dome Japan in the Coca Cola Classic W (33-21) before 50,000. For a great season, Clemson accepted a bid to the Citrus Bowl.

Citrus Bowl

On Jan 1, 1992, the #13 ranked Tigers of Clemson lost to #14 California in the Florida Citrus Bowl played at Citrus Bowl Stadium in Orlando, Florida before 64,192. The score was L 13-27).

1992 Clemson Tigers Football Coach Ken Hatfield

The 1992 Clemson Tigers football team represented Clemson University during the 1992 college football season as a member of the Atlantic Coast Conference (ACC). Ken Hatfield was the head football coach for his third of four seasons. The Tigers completed their ninety-seventh season overall and their fortieth in the Atlantic Coast Conference with a record of 5-6-0; 3-5-0 in ACC. They finished in seventh place in the ACC. out of 9 active ACC teams. It was a poor year for Clemson by recent standards. Robert O'Neal, Daniel Telley, and Wayne Simmons were team captains.

On Oct 10, the barely ranked #25 Tigers squeezed out a one-point win against #10 Virginia at Scott Stadium, Charlottesville, VA W (29–28).

Game Highlights Clemson 29, Virginia 28

Oct. 10, 1992 at Charlottesville, VA

This game is known as "The greatest comeback in Clemson Football History." Some may take issue with that but none can argue how great a comeback this game actually was. Virginia was up on Clemson 28-0 with 32 minutes left in the game.

Right before the half Louis Solomon made a 64-yard touchdown run to give the Tigers some momentum going into halftime. Coach Hatfield made some second half defensive adjustments which were more than enough to shut Virginia out.

Clemson made this comeback simply by running the ball effectively. The squad clocked off over 400 yards rushing for the day, a highly unusual way to make a major comeback. Rudy Harris had a big day and Rodney Blunt scored a key late touchdown. In the second half, Virginia just couldn't stop Clemson.

The Tigers got the ball back in the final minutes, down by two-points, 28-26. Using the running game, Clemson drove the ball up the field, very effectively on the ground. The crowd was still as the snap came for the field goal. Nelson Welch made the 32-yard field goal look easy to win the game. It was phenomenal comeback because Clemson did it on the road against a top 10 team. It is still the greatest comeback by an ACC team against another ACC team. I bet you cannot prove me wrong on that one.

1993 Clemson Tigers Football Coach Ken Hatfield

The 1993 Clemson Tigers football team represented Clemson University during the 1993 college football season as a member of the Atlantic Coast Conference (ACC). Ken Hatfield was the head football coach for his fourth and last of four fine seasons. Because Ken Hatfield moved on from Clemson after the regular season, Tommy West took over for the bowl game in his first year as head coach for 1994. The Tigers completed their ninety-eighth season overall and their forty-first in the Atlantic Coast Conference with a record of 9-3-0; 5-3-0 in the ACC. They finished in third place in the ACC out of 9 active ACC teams. It was another fine year for Clemson. Richard Monreef was the team captain.

Peach Bowl

Tommy West took over for coach Hatfield in the Peach Bowl as this Bowl game was his first game as head coach for the Clemson Tigers and for 1994. On Dec 31 @ 6:00 p.m. New Year's Eve, Kentucky squared off against # 23 ranked Clemson at the Georgia Dome in Atlanta, GA for the (Peach Bowl. It was a thrilling game and the Tigers got it all together to win in the end, W (14–13) before 63,416 fans.

Emery Smith Starred in Coach Tommy West's 1993 Peach Bowl Win!

Chapter 21 Tommy West Era 1993 to 1998

Coach # 23 Tommy West

Year	Coach	Record	Conference	Record
1993	Tommy West	Bowl Game WIn	Score 20-0	
1994	Tommy West	5–6	ACC	4-4-0
1995	Tommy West	8-4	ACC	6-2
1996	Tommy West	7-5	ACC	6-2
1997	Tommy West	7–5	ACC	4–4
1998	Tommy West	3-8	ACC	1-7

The team slowed down a bit in Tommy West's six season tenure.

1994 Clemson Tigers Football Coach Tommy West

Clemson Coach Tommy West

The 1994 Clemson Tigers football team represented Clemson University during the 1994 college football season as a member of the Atlantic Coast Conference (ACC). Tommy West was the head football coach for his second of six seasons.

Because Ken Hatfield moved on from Clemson after the 1993 regular season, Tommy West was asked to take over for the bowl game in his first year as head coach (one Bowl game) in the 1993 post-season.

The Tigers completed their ninety-ninth season overall and their forty-second in the Atlantic Coast Conference with a record of 5-6-0; 4-4-0 in the ACC. They finished in sixth place in the ACC, out of 9 active ACC teams. It was at best a mediocre year for Clemson. Tim Jones and Louis Solomon were the team captains.

1995 Clemson Tigers Football Coach Tommy West

The 1995 Clemson Tigers football team represented Clemson University during the 1995 college football season as a member of the Atlantic Coast Conference (ACC). Tommy West was the head football coach for his third of six seasons. The Tigers completed their one hundredth season overall and their forty-third in the Atlantic Coast Conference with a record of 8-4-0; 6-2-0 in the ACC. They finished in third place in the ACC, out of 9 active ACC teams. It was a fine year for Clemson. Louis Solomon was the team captain.

Gator Bowl

Typically, great performers in Bowl Games, the # 23 Clemson Tigers were unexpectedly shut out in the Gator Bowl on January 1, 1996 by the Syracuse Orangemen at Jacksonville Memorial Stadium in Jacksonville FL L (0-41) before 45,202 and an NBC TV national audience.

1996 Clemson Tigers Football Coach Tommy West

The 1996 Clemson Tigers football team represented Clemson University during the 1996 college football season as a member of the Atlantic Coast Conference (ACC). Tommy West was the head football coach for his fourth of six seasons. The Tigers completed their one hundred-first season overall and their forty-fourth in the Atlantic Coast Conference with a record of 7-5-0; 6-2-0 in the ACC. They finished in third place in the ACC, out of 9 active ACC teams. It was a fine year for Clemson. Louis Solomon was the team captain.

Due to a "rules change" during the postseason of 1995, college football games played from 1996 on cannot end in a tie. At the beginning of this season, the NCAA Football Rules Committee added an overtime procedure to end the chance of a tied game. Though Clemson had no ties in 1996, it would have had a tie in 1997 if it were not for this new rule. Every now and then, the NCAA does something because it is the right thing. Don't count on many more NCAA decisions that take fans or entities other than the NCAA insiders into consideration.

After this season's games, the Tigers found they were eligible for a Bowl Game and they chose to play in the Peach Bowl.

The Peach Bowl

On Dec 28, 1996, at 8:00 PM, the Fighting Tigers of Clemson University engaged the #17 Louisiana State Tigers at the Georgia Dome in Atlanta, GA for the Peach Bowl, seen by 63,622 at the stadium and millions of others on ESPN. The Tigers played a tough game but were beaten L (7–10) by the other Tigers from Louisiana.

1997 Clemson Tigers Football Coach Tommy West

The 1997 Clemson Tigers football team represented Clemson University during the 1997 college football season as a member of the Atlantic Coast Conference (ACC). Tommy West was the head football coach for his fifth of six seasons. The Tigers completed their one hundred-second season overall and their forty-fifth in the Atlantic Coast Conference with a record of 7-5-0; 4-4-0 in the ACC. They finished in fifth in the ACC, out of 9 active ACC teams. It was an OK year for Clemson. Raymond Priester and Raymond White were the team captains. For a great year, the unranked Clemson Tigers, were invited to the Peach Bowl

January 2, 1998 Peach Bowl

On January 2, 1998 at 3:00 p.m., the Clemson Tigers squared off against the Auburn Tigers in the first game between the two in many

years. This was a post-season game called *The Peach Bowl* played at
the Georgia Dome in Atlanta, GA (Peach Bowl) L (17–21) before
71,212 fans.

1998 Clemson Tigers Football Coach Tommy West

The 1998 Clemson Tigers football team represented Clemson
University during the 1998 college football season as a member of the
Atlantic Coast Conference (ACC). Tommy West was the head
football coach for his sixth and last of six seasons. The Tigers
completed their one hundred-third season overall and their forty-sixth
in the Atlantic Coast Conference with a record of 3-8; 1-7 in the
ACC. They finished in eighth in the ACC, out of 9 active ACC
teams. It was a terrible year for Clemson. Donald Broomfield and
Holland Postell were the team captains.

Chapter 22 Tommy Bowden Era 1999-2008

Coach # 24 Tommy Bowden

Year	Coach	Record	Conference	Record
1999	Tommy Bowden	6-6	ACC	5-3
2000	Tommy Bowden	9–3	ACC	6-2
2001	Tommy Bowden	7-5	ACC	4-4
2002	Tommy Bowden	7-6	ACC	4-4
2003	Tommy Bowden	9–4	ACC	5-3
2004	Tommy Bowden	7-5	ACC	4-4
2005	Tommy Bowden	8-4	ACC	4-4
2006	Tommy Bowden	8-5	ACC	5-3
2007	Tommy Bowden	9-4	ACC	5-3
2008	Tommy Bowden	7-6	ACC	4-4
2008	Dabo Swinney	4-3	interim coach last 7 games	

Tommy Bowden, sone of great coach Bobby Bowden took the reins for ten years and brought some nice victories and a lot of ACC firsts but no national championships

Coach Tommy Bowden Prepares to lead his Clemson Tigers onto the Field

1999 Clemson Tigers Football Coach Tommy Bowden

The 1999 Clemson Tigers football team represented Clemson University during the 1999 college football season as a member of the

Atlantic Coast Conference (ACC). Tommy Bowden was the head football coach for his first of ten seasons.

The Tigers completed their one hundred-fourth season overall and their forty-seventh in the Atlantic Coast Conference with a record of 6-6; 5-3 in the ACC. They finished in fourth in the ACC, out of 9 active ACC teams. It was a terrible year for Clemson. Donald Broomfield and Holland Postell were the team captains.

On Dec 30 at 7:30 PM vs. Mississippi State in the Peach Bowl postseason battle, the Tigers played at the Georgia Dome in Atlanta, GA, and lost to the Bulldogs L (7-17) in a tough played match before 73,315

2000 Clemson Tigers Football Coach Tommy Bowden

The 2000 Clemson Tigers football team represented Clemson University during the 2000 college football season as a member of the Atlantic Coast Conference (ACC). Tommy Bowden was the head football coach for his first of ten seasons. The Tigers completed their one hundred-fifth season overall and their forty-eighth in the Atlantic Coast Conference with a record of 9-3; 6-2 in the ACC. They finished in third in the ACC, out of 9 active ACC teams. Chad Carson, Rod Gardner, and Chad Speck were the team captains.

2000 Gator Bowl.

On January 1, 2001 at 12:30 PM, the #16 Tigers took on #6 Virginia Tech at Alltel Stadium in Jacksonville, FL in the Gator Bowl. The Tigers could not get a full head of steam rolling and lost to the Hokies L (20–41). 68,741 were in attendance

2001 Clemson Tigers Football Coach Tommy Bowden

The 2001 Clemson Tigers football team represented Clemson University during the 2001 college football season as a member of the Atlantic Coast Conference (ACC). Tommy Bowden was the head football coach for his third of ten seasons. The Tigers completed their one hundred-sixth season overall and their forty-ninth in the Atlantic Coast Conference with a record of 7-5; 4-4 in the ACC. They finished in fourth in the ACC, out of 9 active ACC teams. Brad Scott served as the offensive coordinator, and Reggie Herring served as the defensive coordinator.

On Sept 29, The Tigers put it in gear and had enough left to finish off the Georgia tech Yellow Jackets W (47-44).

Game highlights Clemson 47 v GA Tech 44 (OT)
Sept 29, 2001 in Atlanta Georgia.

This game was another overtime thriller. It was also another victory on the road for Clemson against a top-10 team.

In 2001, Clemson had high hopes to capture the ACC title. Standing in its way was rival Georgia Tech, a team going into this game ranked #9 in the nation.

It was quarterback Woody Dantzler who made play after play, guiding the Tigers to a thrilling overtime victory by being personally responsible for 418 of the team's 502 total yards.

In overtime, on a 3rd-and-6 play from the Tech 11-yard line, Dantzler ran a draw untouched into the end zone to win the game.

2001 Humanitarian Bowl

Thirty days after the close of the regular season, the Clemson Fighting Tigers were ready to face another opponent in the Humaniatarian Bowl The opponent was Louisiana Tech and the venue was Bronco Stadium in Boise, Idaho. The Tigers prevailed against Tech W (49-24) before 23,472 and a national TV audience provided by ESPN.

2002 Clemson Tigers Football Coach Tommy Bowden

The 2002 Clemson Tigers football team represented Clemson University during the 2002 college football season as a member of the Atlantic Coast Conference (ACC). Tommy Bowden was the head football coach for his fourth of ten seasons. The Tigers completed their one hundred-seventh season overall and their fiftieth in the Atlantic Coast Conference with a record of 7-6; 4-4 in the ACC. They finished in fifth, out of 9 active ACC teams. Nick Eason, Bryant McNeal, and Jackie Robinson were the captains for 2002.

Tangerine Bowl

The Tigers won enough to be scheduled in a non-January Bowl game. On December 23at 5:30 p.m. vs. Texas Tech in the Citrus Bowl Stadium in Orlando, FL, playing in the Tangerine Bowl. Texas Tech whooped the Tigers Texas-style in the fashion of Florida State's whoopings. The Tigers were making a great reappearance on the national stage but every great showing needs a little time.

2003 Clemson Tigers Football Coach Tommy Bowden

The 2003 Clemson Tigers football team represented Clemson University during the 2003 college football season as a member of the Atlantic Coast Conference (ACC). Tommy Bowden, son of Florida State's famous Coach Bobby Bowden was the head football coach for his fifth of ten seasons. The Tigers completed their one hundred-eighth season overall and their fifty-first in the Atlantic Coast Conference with a record of 9-4; 5-3 in the ACC. They finished in third, out of 9 active ACC teams. Tony Elliott, DeJuan Polk, and Gregory Walker were the team captains for 2003.

On Nov 8, history was made in the Bowden Bowl at 7:45 p.m. as #3 Florida State went in to Clemson Memorial Stadium expecting another blowout but instead faced strong opposition. The younger Tommy Bowden's team defeated his dad Bobby Bowden's team for the first time. History was made with the Clemson win W 26–10

Game highlights Clemson 26, Florida State 10
Nov 8, 2003 in Death Valley

No single win from the past decade tasted sweeter than on a clear November night. The son finally bested the father.

After 11-consecutive losses against Florida State, Clemson finally got the monkey off its back and got Tommy Bowden his first ever win against his dad.

The Tigers thoroughly dominated the game, especially considering FSU didn't get its first (and only) touchdown until 2:14 left in the fourth quarter.

The Seminoles came into the game ranked third in the nation, making them the highest ranked opponent Clemson knocked off the entire decade.

Clemson out-rushed the Noles 152 to 11, and had a 13-minute advantage in time of possession.

This win was monumental in that it really helped turn things around for Tommy Bowden. Just a week before, Clemson had been humiliated by Wake Forest 45-17, a loss that had many fans calling for Bowden's job.

He would finish the season on a four-game winning streak, including this win, a win over Duke, the 63-17 thrashing of South Carolina, and knocking off Tennessee in the Peach Bowl.

Bowden's job may not have been cast in cement but it was on firm footing after this great win.

The 2003/2004 Peach Bowl

On the day after New Year's Day on Sunday January 2, 2004 at 4:30 in the afternoon, # 6 Tennessee and unranked Clemson paired off to play a tough Peach Bowl Game in the Georgia Dome, Atlanta, GA, shown on TV by ESPN and watched by 75, 125 at the Dome. The Clemson Fighting Tigers played the best that day and beat Tennessee W (27–14).

Game highlights Clemson 27, Tennessee 14
Jan 2, 2004 in Peach Bowl Game Atlanta GA.

For at least one evening, Clemson laid claim to this truth: The ACC can outplay the SEC.

The Vols, ranked No. 6 in the nation, were run all over by the Tigers, namely Chad Jasmin who rushed for a career high 106 yards and a touchdown in the Peach Bowl win.

The win capped off what could be defined as the best season Clemson had under Tommy Bowden. But even this postseason bowl win wasn't the best Tiger W of the decade.

2004 Clemson Tigers Football Coach Tommy Bowden

The 2004 Clemson Tigers football team represented Clemson University during the 2004 college football season as a member of the Atlantic Coast Conference (ACC). Tommy Bowden, son of Florida State's famous Coach Bobby Bowden was the head football coach for his sixth of ten seasons. The Tigers completed their one hundred-ninth season overall and their fifty-second in the Atlantic Coast Conference with a record of 6-5; 4-4 in the ACC. They finished in seventh, out of 11 active ACC teams. Eric Coleman, Airese Currie, and Leroy Hill were the team captains for 2004.

On Sept 25 at 3:30 p.m.   against #8 Florida State in their home park of Doak Campbell Stadium, Tallahassee, FL in the now infamous Bowden Bowl, the Seminoles did not forgive anything about being beaten the prior year and proved their dominance again against the younger Bowden L 22–41 before 83,538.

On Nov 6 at #11 Miami (FL) in a game played in the Miami Orange Bowl in Miami, FL, the Clemson Tigers were on-key and ready to play. They came up with the victory over the Hurricanes in OT W 24–17 before 55,225.

Game Highlights Clemson 24, Miami 17
Nov 6, 2004 in Miami Orange Bowl.

Miami and Clemson have a record together that shows they just can't finish games in four quarters.

In fact, every game between the two teams in this particular decade has been decided in overtime. This one was completely unexpected. Clemson wasn't having its best of seasons—having been crushed by

Florida State, Texas A&M, and Virginia earlier in the season. Miami was ranked first in the ACC and #10 nationally.

Reggie Merriweather had 114 yards rushing and three touchdowns to spark the Tigers. It was the Clemson defense, however, that got the job done in overtime, forcing three straight Miami incompletions to seal the deal.

To commemorate the win Clemson celebrated over a tombstone – a ceremony they put on for every road win against a top-25 team.

2005 Clemson Tigers Football Coach Tommy Bowden

The 2005 Clemson Tigers football team represented Clemson University during the 2005 college football season as a member of the Atlantic Coast Conference (ACC). Tommy Bowden, son of Florida State's famous Coach Bobby Bowden was the head football coach for his seventh of ten seasons. The Tigers completed their one hundred-tenth season overall and their fifty-third in the Atlantic Coast Conference with a record of 8-4; 4-4 in the ACC. They finished in third out of 6 ACC Atlantic Division teams. The Offensive Coordinator was Rob Spence and the Defensive Coordinator was Vic Koenning.

The Clemson Fighting Tigers season opener resulted in a tough win on Sept 3 at home against #17 Texas A &M W (25-24) This home opener was played as always at Memorial Stadium on the campus of Clemson University in Clemson, SC before 79,917.

Game highlights Clemson 25 v Texas A&M 24
Sept. 3, 2005 at Death Valley.

Many recall the ugly loss to the Aggies in 2004. This year, Clemson kicked off the 2005 season with a rematch against A&M, this time it was in Death Valley with the Aggies ranked No. 17 in the nation.

It took WR Chansi Stuckey returning a punt 47 yards for a touchdown and Jad Dean kicking a Tiger-record six field goals, including the game winner with six seconds remaining, to send the Tigers to their victory party.

Champs Sports Bowl

In the post-season, Clemson received an invitation to play in the 2005 Champs Sports Bowl at the Citrus Bowl Stadium in Orlando FL. The game was played on Dec 27 against Colorado. Clemson won the game, W (19–10), to finish the full season at 8–4.

Clemson had a great year by all accounts. It could have been a little better with some better luck. The Tigers finished the season ranked in the top 25 (21st in both the AP and the Coaches' Poll) for the second time in three years. Clemson also recorded wins against three AP top 20 teams in the 2005 season for just the fourth time in school history. Clemson lost its four games by a combined 14 points. The two words *if only* come to mind but nobody was complaining.

2006 Clemson Tigers Football Coach Tommy Bowden

The 2006 Clemson Tigers football team represented Clemson University during the 2006 college football season as a member of the Atlantic Coast Conference (ACC). Tommy Bowden, son of Florida State's famous Coach Bobby Bowden was the head football coach for his eighth of ten seasons. The Tigers completed their one hundred-eleventh season overall and their fifty-fourth in the Atlantic Coast Conference with a record of 8-5; 5-3 in the ACC. They finished in fourth out of 6 ACC Atlantic Division teams. The Offensive Coordinator was Rob Spence and the Defensive Coordinator was Vic Koenning.

Entering the season, the Tigers had high expectations, hoping to compete for a spot in the ACC Championship Game. After a heartbreaking loss at Boston College in the second game of the season, Clemson rolled off six straight victories, during which they averaged nearly 42 points a game. But things soon fell apart, with Clemson losing four out of their last five, including a loss to Kentucky in the Music City Bowl, and a 31–28 loss to arch rival South Carolina. The team finished the season with a disappointing 8–5 record.

On Oct 21, at home the Tigers defeated the Yellow Jackets of # 13 Georgia Tech W (31-7).

Game highlights Clemson 31 v GA Tech 7
Oct 21, 2006 at Death Valley.

ESPN's College Gameday show made its first-ever appearance in Clemson for the game between the Tigers and the Georgia Tech Yellow Jackets on October 21. Kirk Herbstreit mentioned both during and after the show, that he felt that Clemson hosted one of the best Gameday audiences he'd ever seen. The Gameday audience at Clemson also set a new noise record when measured in the latter-half of the show.

The Tigers were ranked 12th nationally, while the Yellow Jackets came in No. 13 in the nation. The game was the most hyped game the ACC had seen in years.

And yes, Clemson rocked with all purple uniforms.

James Davis ran for 216 yards and two touchdowns while CJ Spiller had some mind-numbing touchdown plays of his own to lead Clemson to the easy victory. GT star wide receiver Calvin Johnson was held without a catch.

This was perhaps the most dominating performance Clemson had all decade against a top 25 team.

Music City Bowl

On Dec 29 at 1:00 p.m. vs a tough Kentucky squad, at LP Field in Nashville, TN, the Wildcats defeated the Tigers in the Music City Bowl, shown on ESPN and 68,024 fans at the stadium L (28–20)

2007 Clemson Tigers Football Coach Tommy Bowden   Almost ACC CHamps

The 2007 Clemson Tigers football team represented Clemson University during the 2007 college football season as a member of the Atlantic Coast Conference (ACC). Tommy Bowden, son of Florida State's famous Coach Bobby Bowden was the head football coach for his ninth of ten seasons. The Tigers completed their one hundred-twelfth season overall and their fifty-fifth in the Atlantic Coast Conference with a record of 9-4; 5-3 in the ACC. They finished in second of 6 ACC Atlantic Division teams. The Offensive Coordinator was Rob Spence and the Defensive Coordinator was Vic Koenning.

Clemson started 4-0, including a victory in the season and conference opener over the Florida State Seminoles in the ninth "Bowden Bowl", which pits father Bobby Bowden, coaching the Seminoles, against his son, Tommy. Following their 4-0 start, Clemson gave up two losses to Georgia Tech and Virginia Tech respectively. Following the two-game losing streak, the Tigers went on to another four-game winning streak. The team then finished the season with its toughest loss of the season (losing in the final seconds to Boston College, 20-17) and greatest triumph (defeating rival South Carolina 23-21 with a last-second field goal). With a record of 9-3, the Tigers received a bid to play in the 2007 Chick-fil-A Bowl.

Clemson played host to the Florida State Seminoles on Labor Day, Monday, September 3, 2007 in both teams' season opener. The game was played before a primetime national audience on ESPN as the only college football game in that time slot. It was only Clemson's second regular season Monday night game, the last being in 1982 against the University of Georgia.

The unranked Clemson Fighting Tigers season opener resulted in a great win on Sept 2 at home against Florida State W (24-18) in the annual Bowden Bowl. This home opener was played at Memorial Stadium on the campus of Clemson University in Clemson, SC before 81993.

Game highlights Clemson 24 v Florida State 18
Sept. 3, 2005 at Death Valley.

In this Labor Day night classic, Clemson knocked off the No. 19 Seminoles 24-18 behind James Davis' solid performance running the ball (18 carries, 102 yards, one TD) and Will Proctor's efficiency (14-24, 160 yards, 2 TDs).

The Tigers jumped out to a 21-0 lead, but FSU would storm back to be down by only six in the fourth quarter. Clemson's defense held off the Seminoles on three-straight drives to end the game.

He may not have known it, but Tommy Bowden would coach his last game ever against his father that night.

After this win, on Sept 8, the #25 Tigers played at home again against Louisiana Monroe and won W (49-26). During this September 8th game against UL-Monroe, Clemson quarterback Cullen Harper threw five touchdown passes, setting a new school record for most touchdown passes thrown in a single game

Chick-Fil-A Bowl

Ranked at #16, Clemson's Tigers took on the #21 Auburn Tigers in the 2008 Chick-Fil-A Bowl game, played at the Georgia Dome in Atlanta GA on New Year's Eve. The Clemson Tigers entered the post-season ranked 15th nationally, while Auburn came in 22nd. The game was particularly notable as it was Walter Riggs (Clemson's first football coach) who came to coach at Clemson from Auburn and who brought with him many traditions, including the Tiger Mascot

Auburn barely beat the Tigers L (20-23) but got the win nonetheless. 74,413 were in attendance plus the ESPN audience.

2008 Clemson Tigers Football Coach Tommy Bowden

Following a 9–4 season in 2007, in which Clemson finished second in the ACC Atlantic Division and played in the Chick-Fil-A Bowl, and with several players returning in the skill positions, many expected Clemson to be a strong candidate to win the ACC and a dark horse in the national championship picture.

The Tigers' main areas of concern heading into the 2008 season was on the offensive line and linebackers. The offensive line would be very young and inexperienced heading into the season, while the linebacker corps was thinned by graduation and off-field issues. Despite these areas of concern, Clemson was tabbed as preseason favorites to win the ACC and was ranked 9th in both the AP and ESPN/USA Today preseason polls. In addition, QB Cullen Harper was tabbed as the preseason favorite for the ACC's Player of the Year. The best laid plans of mice and men gang oft aglay.

The 2008 Clemson Tigers football team represented Clemson University during the 2008 college football season as a member of the Atlantic Coast Conference (ACC). Tommy Bowden, son of Florida State's famous Coach Bobby Bowden was the head football coach for his tenth (last) of ten seasons. The Tigers completed their one hundred-thirteenth season overall and their fifty-sixth in the Atlantic Coast Conference with a record of 7-6; 4-4 in the ACC. They finished in fifth of 6 ACC Atlantic Division teams. The Offensive Coordinator was Rob Spence and the Defensive Coordinator was Vic Koenning.

Head coach Tommy Bowden stepped down after the first six games of his tenth and last season. He was replaced by coach Dabo Swinney in the interim. Swinney was retained and of course in 2016, his Tigers brought in the School's second National Championship. Rob Spence left after Six games and was replaced by Billy Napier in the interim.

For their efforts this season, Clemson was invited to the Gator Bowl.

2009 Gator Bowl

On January 1, 2009 at 1:00 p.m. Nebraska squared off against
Clemson at Jacksonville Municipal Stadium in Jacksonville, FL for
the Gator Bowl. It was a close loss but a loss nonetheless L (21-26)
for the Tigers before a crowd of 67,282 plus a TV audience.

The Nebraska win was a come-from-behind 26–21 finish to the 2009
Gator Bowl. The game remained in doubt until the very end, as
Clemson marched from their own 23 to the Nebraska 10. With 1st
and goal to go and about two minutes remaining on the clock, Cullen
Harper came up short, resulting in a 16-yard sack and three Clemson
incompletions to seal the outcome of the game. The game was played
only days after Nebraska's Head Coach Bo Pelini and Defensive
Coordinator Carl Pelini returned from their father's funeral in Ohio.

The best way to describe Tommy Bowden's departure from Clemson
after a reasonably good tenure is to turn the writing floor over to
Mark Schlabach an ESPN Senior writer who wrote this piece right
when it happened in mid-season, 2008. He tells it as he saw it right
after it happened.

Schlabach titled his piece:

"Bowden out at Clemson; coach 'deserved' fate, QB says.

It was written on Oct 14, 2008. Here it is:

Mark Schlabach ESPN Senior Writer

"Clemson ousted football coach Tommy Bowden on Monday, four days after the Tigers -- who were the favorites to win the ACC championship -- lost to Wake Forest and fell to 3-3.

Bowden informed his assistant coaches of his ouster Monday morning. Assistant head coach/wide receivers coach Dabo Swinney has been named interim coach for the final six regular-season games and potential bowl game. Clemson offensive coordinator Rob Spence also has been ousted, a source close to the situation said.

Athletic director Terry Don Phillips said his intent Monday morning was to have a candid heart-to-heart with Bowden about the football team. But Phillips said he was surprised when Bowden offered to resign.

"There wasn't a gun to his head," Phillips said.

"He put it on the table for the sake of the program," Phillips said. "I agreed."

...

Bobby Bowden said in a statement Monday that his son "felt like it was fixin' to happen; he felt like it was inevitable."

Clemson's 10th season under Tommy Bowden unraveled quickly. The Tigers were expected to contend for the ACC

"He's thankful for the experience he got there at Clemson," Bobby Bowden said. "He has no hard feelings towards them. This is just the nature of this game right now. He's disappointed but he's got his priorities in order in his life, so he'll move on and won't lose a minute of sleep over it. At least I don't have to worry about him beating me again."

Clemson center Thomas Austin said he was "caught off guard" by Bowden's departure. ...

Chapter 23 Dabo Swinney Era 2008-2019+

Coach # 25 Dabo Swinney

Year	Coach	Record	Conference	Record
2009	Dabo Swinney	9-5	ACC	6-2
2010	Dabo Swinney	6-7	ACC	4-2
2011	Dabo Swinney	10-4	ACC	6-2
2012*	Dabo Swinney	11-2	ACC	7-1
2013	Dabo Swinney	11-2	ACC	7-1
2014	Dabo Swinney	10-3	ACC	6-2
2015*	Dabo Swinney	14-1	ACC	8-0
2016*	Dabo Swinney	14-1	ACC	7-1
2017	Dabo Swinney		ACC	

* ACC Championship; 2016 National Championship

Wow! Look at Swinney's record. It speaks for itself.

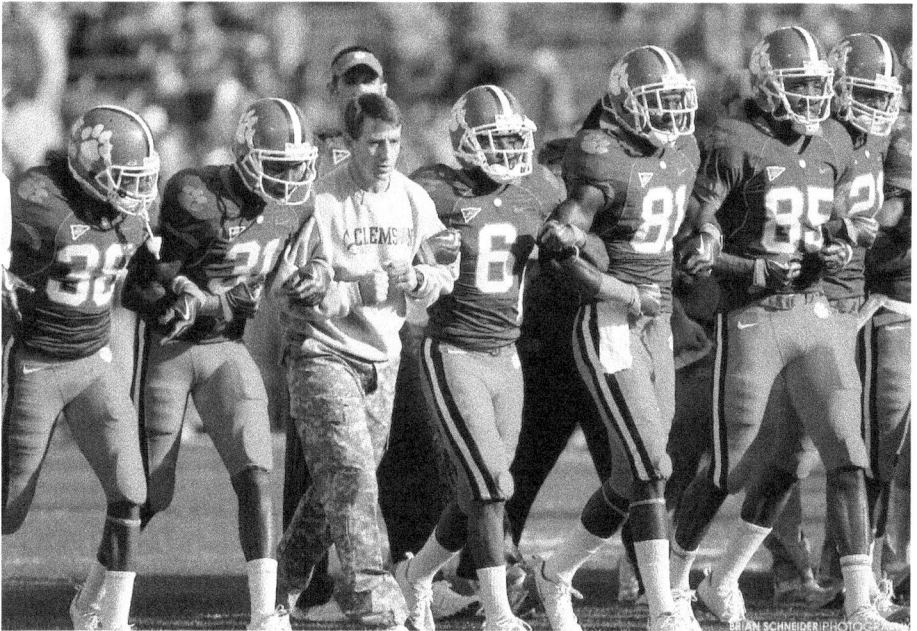

2009 Clemson Tigers Football Coach Dabo Swinney

The 2009 Clemson Tigers football team represented Clemson University during the 2009college football season as a member of the Atlantic Coast Conference (ACC). Dabo Swinney was the head football coach for his second of many seasons.

This was Swinney's first full season after completing seven games of Coach Tommy Bowden's final year in 2008. The Tigers completed their one hundred-fourteenth season overall and their fifty-seventh in the Atlantic Coast Conference with a record of 9-5; 6-2 in the ACC. They finished in first place of 6 ACC Atlantic Division teams. The Offensive Coordinator was Bill Napier and the Defensive Coordinator was Kevin Steele.

The Tigers had an overall good year and won the ACC Atlantic Division, but after securing the title lost to in–state rival South Carolina in the Palmetto Bowl 34–17, before losing for the second time in the season to Georgia Tech in the ACC Championship Game. Clemson closed the season with a win over Kentucky in the Music City Bowl.

The unranked Clemson Fighting Tigers home season opener resulted in a win on Sept 5 at home against Middle Tennessee W (37-14). This home opener was played as always at Memorial Stadium on the campus of Clemson University in Clemson, SC before 78371. After this home win, on Sept 10, the unranked Tigers played at No. 13 Georgia Tech's Bobby Dodd Stadium in Atlanta, GA where they were defeated by the Yellow Jackets L (27–30) before 52,029. On Sept 19, at home, Boston College took it on the chin big time W (25-7).

On Sept 26, at home, Clemson lost to #14 TCU L (10-14). Then, on Oct 3, at Maryland's Byrd Stadium in College Park, MD, Clemson lost again L (21-24) before 46,243. Two weeks later on Oct 17 at home, the Tigers defeated the Wake Forest Demon Deacons W (38-3). On Oct 24, unranked Clemson played the #10 Hurricanes of Miami University at Land Shark Stadium in Miami Gardens, FL., The game was nip and tuck and finally the Tigers beat the Hurricanes W (40-37) in OT before 43, 778.

Game highlights Clemson 40 v Miami 37 (OT)
Oct 24, 2009 in Miami Gardens FL.

This was a huge game for Clemson's 2009 season.

The Tigers were coming off two tough losses to Maryland and TCU. Clemson had hammered Wake Forest the week before. Heading to Miami, Clemson was considered a huge underdog against the #8 Hurricanes.

There were more back-and-forth blows in this game than a heavyweight fight. Nonetheless, Clemson managed to outlast the Canes in overtime 40-37. CJ Spiller had 300-plus all-purpose yards while Kyle Parker threw for 326 yards and three touchdowns, including a 26-yard pass in overtime to cap off an instant classic.

On Oct 31, as Dabo Swinney's team was beginning to know how great they were, Coastal Carolina's Chanticleers came to Clemson's campus for the Clemson Homecoming game. It was a great homecoming as the Tigers got the best of the visitors in a walloping game W (49-3). In the non-Bowden Bowl of 2009, it was Bobby Bowden's last year coaching Florida State. The game was Nov 7 and it was at home in a celebration called Solid Orange Day. The Tigers hit the Seminoles with all they had and the Seminoles fought back but lost the game W (40-24), giving Dabo Swinney a great win and putting a mar in Bobby Bowden's last season (7-6) at FSU with Jimbo Fisher as his offensive coordinator.

On Nov 14 at NC State's Carter-Finley Stadium in Raleigh, NC, the Tigers outplayed the Wolfpack in the Textile Bowl W (43–23) before 57,583. Then, on Nov 21 at home, #19 Clemson beat Virginia's Wahoos W (34-21) before 77,568. Finishing up a better season than was ever delivered by a fine coach Tommy Bowden, on Nov 28, at South Carolina's Williams-Brice Stadium in Columbia, SC, the #16 Tigers lost the game to the unranked Gamecocks L (17–34)). But, there was still one or two games left in the postseason.

At the end of the season, Head Coach Dabo Swinney announced that they would retire the #28 jersey worn by C. J. Spiller at a ceremony when the Tigers play Maryland at home on Oct. 16, 2010.

2009 Post Season – Championships and Music City Bowl

On December 5 at 8:00 p.m. vs. #12 Georgia Tech, at Raymond James Stadium in Tampa, FL, Clemson lost the ACC Championship L (34–39).

The Tigers got a bowl bid anyway. On Dec 27at 7:30 p.m. vs. Kentucky at LP Field in Nashville, TN, the Clemson Tigers with Dabo Swinney found enough muster to defeat Kentucky in the Music City Bowl W (21–13) before 57,280.

Game highlights Clemson 21 v Kentucky 13
Dec 27, 2009 in Nashville TN.

Not only was it Dabo Swinney's first bowl win as Clemson's head coach, it was also CJ Spiller's last game as a Clemson Tiger.

Spiller gained 172 all-purpose yards and scored a touchdown in his 14th consecutive game.

Kentucky came out and scored quickly on its first drive. Clemson's defense then snapped from its slumber and held UK to just a couple of field goals the rest of the game. This was just Clemson's fourth bowl win of the decade despite being bowl eligible every single season.

2010 Clemson Tigers Football Coach Dabo Swinney

The 2010 Clemson Tigers football team represented Clemson University during the 2010college football season as a member of the Atlantic Coast Conference (ACC). Dabo Swinney was the head football coach for his third of many seasons. The Tigers completed their one hundred-fifteenth season overall and their fifty-eighth in the Atlantic Coast Conference with a record of 6-7; 4-4 in the ACC. They finished fifth of 6 ACC Atlantic Division teams. The Offensive Coordinator was Bill Napier and the Defensive Coordinator was Kevin Steele.

Meineke Car Care Bowl Game

On Dec 31 at Noon, against South Florida at Bank of America Stadium in Charlotte, NC, after playing the entire Meineke Car Care Bowl, South Florida had beaten Clemson L (26–31) before 41,122.

2011 Clemson Tigers Football Coach Dabo Swinney   Championship ACC

The 2011 Clemson Tigers football team represented Clemson University during the 2011college football season as a member of the Atlantic Coast Conference (ACC). Dabo Swinney was the head football coach for his fourth of many seasons. The Tigers completed their one hundred-sixteenth season overall and their fifty-ninth as a member of the Atlantic Division of the Atlantic Coast Conference. Their overall record was 10-4; 6-2 in the ACC. They finished first of 6 ACC Atlantic Division teams. The Offensive Coordinator was Chad Morris and the Defensive Coordinator was Kevin Steele.

Clemson finished the previous season 6–7, losing in the Meineke Car Care Bowl to South Florida. They began the 2011 season unranked, but after a three-game winning streak against ranked opponents in late September, rose to #8 in the AP and Coaches Poll. However, the Tigers lost three of their final four regular-season contests (with two of the losses to unranked opponents). And, so, they fell back to #21 in the polls.

However, their early start was enough to clinch a spot in the 2011 ACC Championship Game. They won that game with a dominant performance over Virginia Tech, 38–10. In the process, they won their first ACC title since 1991, and with it, they received an automatic berth in the 2012 Orange Bowl.

It was the Tigers' first-ever Bowl Championship Series berth, as well as their first major-bowl appearance since the 1982 Orange Bowl. They lost the game to West Virginia and made history at the same. The game's score of 70–33, set a bowl record for points conceded in a game.

The Games of the 2011 Season

The unranked Clemson Fighting Tigers home season opener resulted in a win on Sept 3 against Troy W (43–19). The Clemson home opener was played as always at Memorial Stadium (also known as Death Valley) on the campus of Clemson University in Clemson, SC before 73,458. In the game, The Tigers offense had a shaky first half adapting to offensive coordinator Chad Morris's faster new spread set. They had a tough time getting it going and were 0-for-8 on third down conversions and had only four first downs. Sophomore quarterback Tajh Boyd had several bad throws and near interceptions as the team was actually booed off the field at half time.

Clemson was down 16–13 with 6:56 left in the third quarter, but Swinney's squad finally converted their first third down as tight end Dwayne Allen grabbed a 54-yard touchdown pass from Boyd to put the Tigers ahead. On the next drive, Boyd completed all of his passes including a seven-yard touchdown pass to Jaron Brown. The scoring run continued in the fourth quarter, ending in a 43–19 rout.

Boyd finished the game 20-for-30 for 364 yards and three touchdowns in his debut as Clemson's starting quarterback. Sammy Watkins had seven catches for 81 yards while Andre Ellington rushed 18 times for 89 yards. Freshmen accounted for 266 of Clemson's 468 yards. They promised good things to come.

After this home win, on Sept 10, the unranked Tigers played again at home this time against Wofford. The Tigers won the close match W (35-27). In week two, the inexperienced Tigers defense struggled to contain Wofford's triple-option offense throughout the game. The Terriers led 21–13 with 4:03 remaining in the second quarter, but Tajh Boyd led a six-play, 72-yard drive and a two-point conversion to tie the game before half time.

Wofford's last lead in the game came in the opening series of the second half with a field goal. Clemson scored a touchdown each in the third and fourth quarters before stopping Wofford on fourth-and-2 with 3:30 remaining in the game to hold on for a 35–27 victory. Boyd was 18-for-29 for 261 yards and three touchdowns. Andre Ellington had 22 carries for 165 yards. His 74-yard touchdown run was the longest of his career.

On Sept 17, at home again against the #21 Auburn Tigers, the Clemson Tigers prevailed W (38–24) before 81,514. Defending national champions #21 Auburn took a 14–0 lead in the first quarter before Tajh Boyd began finding his passing rhythm. Boyd completed 30 of 42 passes for 386 yards and four touchdowns. The game was tied 21–21 at half time, but Clemson's defense restricted Auburn to a field goal in the second half while Boyd threw two touchdown passes to earn a 38–24 win, ending a 17-game winning streak for Auburn.

Clemson's offense totaled 624 yards, its record against an SEC opponent. Fans swarmed the field at the end of the game. Coach Dabo Swinney remarked, "I couldn't think of a better place to end the streak than Death Valley, South Carolina, baby."

On Sept 24, at home against #11 Florida State, the #21 ranked Tigers beat the Seminoles W (35-30). After Auburn, Clemson entered week four ranked #21. They faced Atlantic Division champions Florida State in their fourth straight home game. FSU was without injured starting quarterback E. J. Manuel. Clemson opened up a 21–10 lead by halftime, and were in control for the rest of the game. Tajh Boyd was 23-for-37 for 344 yards and three touchdowns and had a rushing touchdown. Freshman receiver Sammy Watkins had eight catches for 141 yards and two touchdowns while Andre Ellington rushed for 72 yards.

On Oct 1, at # 11 Virginia Tech's Lane Stadium in Blacksburg, VA, Clemson's Tigers defeated the Hokies W (23–3) before 66,233. For Clemson's first road game, The Tigers' defense turned in its best effort of the season in a 23–3 victory against the #11 Hokies. The Clemson defense led by Andre Branch held the Hokies to 258 yards and no touchdowns. Branch had three sacks and was involved in 11 tackles. Tajh Boyd threw one touchdown to Dwayne Allen and one interception while Andre Ellington and Mike Bellamy both recorded a rushing touchdown apiece. This win marked the first time any ACC team had ever beaten three top 25 AP opponents in a row. It was also the second time Virginia Tech had not scored a touchdown in Lane Stadium under Frank Beamer and was the first time since 1995.

On Oct 8, at home, the #8 Tigers beat the Boston College Eagles on Homecoming W (36-14) and the Tigers picked up the O'Roarke-McFadden Trophy. Clemson controlled the Eagles for the majority of the game. Boyd scored 2 touchdowns (1 passing, 1 rushing) before being replaced by Cole Stoudt after suffering a hip injury. Andre Ellington (rushing) and Jaron Brown (receiving) each scored a touchdown, Sammy Watkins recorded 152 receiving yards, while Chandler Catanzaro hit a career-high 5 field goals (38, 42, 28, 20, and 47 yards). This win marked Clemson's best start since 2000.

On Oct 15 at Maryland's Byrd Stadium in College Park, MD, the #8 Tigers beat the Terrapins in a shootout W (56–45). Tajh Boyd threw four touchdown passes, Andre Ellington rushed for a career-high 212 yards and two touchdowns for the Tigers, and freshman Sammy Watkins scored three TDs (two passing, one kick-off return) as No. 8 Clemson rallied from an 18-point deficit against Maryland to remain unbeaten with a 56–45 victory.

The defense, however, yielded 468 yards and had no answer for sophomore quarterback C.J. Brown, who ran for 162 yards and a touchdown and threw three scoring passes in his first college start. The 18-point deficit was the second largest in Clemson University history. Sammy Watkins also broke the school record for most all-purpose yards in a game (345 yards) held previously by Clemson great C.J. Spiller (312 yards).

On Oct 22 at home, the #8 Tigers beat the North Carolina Tar Heels in another shootout W (59-38) Clemson was scoring big while giving up a large # of points. A 35-point third quarter explosion highlighted Clemson's home win over the Tar Heels, including a 5-touchdown performance by quarterback Tajh Boyd. Defensive end Kourtney Brown scored two defensive touchdowns, once on an interception and another on a fumble return. Boyd threw for 367 yards and rushed for one touchdown. Wide receiver DeAndre Hopkins had 157 yards receiving and a touchdown. Clemson's defense held UNC running back Giovani Bernard to 44 yards rushing, ending his five-game streak of 100 yards or more.

On Oct 29. At, 8-0 things looked very promising. Then came arch rival Georgia Tech. On Oct 29 at Georgia Tech's Bobby Dodd Stadium in Atlanta, GA, the #6 Tigers lost its first game of the season against the Yellow Jackets L (17–31) before 55,646. Georgia Tech's triple option attack was seemingly unstoppable for the Clemson defense as Yellow Jacket quarterback Tevin Washington scampered for 176 yards on 27 carries and a touchdown.

Clemson's high-powered offense never left the gates in the first half, although the Tigers made a play for a comeback in the second half with a 48-yard touchdown catch by Sammy Watkins. Following a Rashard Hall interception to the Georgia Tech 9, the Tigers looked to have a chance to rally back, but Tajh Boyd threw an interception in the end zone to Jemea Thomas on the next play. Clemson's four turnovers in the game would ultimately prove to be costly for the Tigers.

On Nov 12, at home, Wake Forest's Demon deacons came in tough and almost beat the Tigers in a close match W (31-28) but Clemson won the game in the end. Clemson clinched its second ACC Atlantic Division title in a nail-biter game against the Demon Deacons in Death Valley. The Tigers' 14–7 third quarter lead quickly deteriorated following a 50-yard Mike Campanaro punt return for Wake Forest. Demon Deacon running back Brandon Pendergrass added two more scores to put Wake Forest up 28–14.

Clemson also lost Sammy Watkins for the second half following an injury on a third-quarter kick return. The Tigers, however, rallied back with two touchdown tosses from quarterback Tajh Boyd. Following a missed 47-yard field goal try by Demon Deacon kicker Jimmy Newman, the Tigers orchestrated a drive to set up a 43-yard game-winning kick by Chandler Catanzaro as time expired. With the win, Clemson secured its trip to Charlotte for the ACC Championship Game and finished undefeated at home for the first time since 1990.

On Nov 19, the #7 ranked Tigers lost to the NC State Wolfpack at Carter–Finley Stadium in Raleigh, NC in the annual Textile Bowl L (13-37). NC State shocked a heavily favored Clemson team in Raleigh, including a dominant 27-point second quarter performance.

Wolfpack quarterback Mike Glennon threw for 253 yards and three touchdowns while Clemson quarterback Tajh Boyd, despite throwing 238 yards, threw two interceptions, no touchdowns, and was replaced in the 4th quarter by Cole Stoudt. NC State's aggressive pass rush hindered Boyd and Clemson's big play ability throughout the game, and the Tigers' four turnovers to NC State's none proved costly. The Wolfpack stymied Clemson's running game with running back Andre Ellington the team leader at only 28 yards

Then, on Nov 26 at #12 South Carolina's Williams-Brice Stadium in Columbia, SC, the Gamecocks beat #18 Clemson and won the big Battle of the Palmetto State L (13–34) before 83,422. Still reeling from the loss to NC State, the Tigers entered hostile territory in Columbia against the 12th-ranked Gamecocks. Clemson's offense again felt the heat from South Carolina's stingy defense, which held the Tigers to 153 total yards.

Clemson's defense struggled as well against the Gamecocks' balanced attack and quarterback Connor Shaw, who threw for 210 yards and three touchdowns as well as rushing for 107 yards and a touchdown. The Tigers' tone for the game was set early when wide receiver Sammy Watkins dropped a sure touchdown pass early in the game. Although Clemson was able to keep the turnovers down this game, the tough Gamecock defense proved too relentless for the Tigers to open up any options on offense. The loss marked Clemson's third straight to its archrival.

2011 Post Season Games

#21 Clemson won their division championship in the ACC and got to play #5 Virginia Tech for the full ACC Championship on December 3 at 8:00 p.m. at Bank of America Stadium in Charlotte, NC. The Clemson Tigers won the game and grabbed the championship W (38–10) before 73,675 football fans. Clemson was invited to the Orange Bowl game for winning the championship.

Devastating losses to NC State and South Carolina had Clemson's future looking bleak for the rematch against Virginia Tech in the ACC Championship. Nonetheless, the Tigers regained their form from earlier in the season to secure their first ACC Championship game win and their first ACC title in 20 years.

Quarterback Tajh Boyd threw for 240 yards and three touchdowns, including a 53-yard strike to Sammy Watkins during the Tigers' 21-

point third quarter rally. Clemson defense forced three touchdowns and kept the Hokies scoreless in the second half. The defense also held running back David Wilson, the ACC's player of the year, to only 32 yards rushing. Clemson running back Andre Ellington ran for 125 yards and one touchdown on 20 carries. With the win, Clemson solidified its first 10-win season since 1990, a spot in the Orange Bowl and its first BCS bowl bid in school history

On January 4, 2012 at 8::30 p.m., the #14 Clemson Tigers took on the #23 West Virginia Mountaineers at Sun Life Stadium in Miami Gardens, FL. The Tigers were beaten in a shootout L (33–70) before 67,563. Not everything goes as planned. Clemson's best season in 20 years came to a crashing halt with arguably the worst bowl loss in school history. What at first appeared to have the makings of a high-scoring shootout between the Tigers and West Virginia turned into a shellacking on par with a video game score in the second quarter.

Following Andre Ellington's fumble at the goal line and the 99-yard touchdown return by Mountaineer safety Darwin Cook, the floodgates opened for the Tigers. West Virginia quarterback Geno Smith was electrifying, and Clemson's defense did not have an answer for him as he rattled off 407 yards passing and 6 touchdowns. Although Clemson coughed the ball up four times on offense, the real story lay in the defense's inability to stop Smith and the Mountaineer offense. The result was a record in points in a bowl game for West Virginia.

2012 Clemson Tigers Football Coach Dabo Swinney   <u>Co-Champions ACC</u>

The 2012 Clemson Tigers football team represented Clemson University during the 2012college football season as a member of the Atlantic Coast Conference (ACC). Dabo Swinney was the head football coach for his fifth of many seasons. The Tigers completed their one hundred-seventeenth season overall and their sixtieth as a member of the Atlantic Division of the Atlantic Coast Conference. Their overall record was 11-2; 7-1 in the ACC. They finished tied for first with Florida State of 6 ACC Atlantic Division teams. Since FSU beat the Tigers in head to head, they got to compete for the ACC title. The Offensive Coordinator was Chad Morris and the Defensive Coordinator was Brent Venables. They were invited to the Chick-fil-A Bowl where they defeated LSU. The Tigers had their first 11-win season since 1981.

The unranked Clemson Fighting Tigers season opener resulted in a win on Sept 1 in the Chick-fil-A Kickoff Game against Georgia at the Georgia Dome in Atlanta GA. W (26-19). The Clemson home opener was played at Memorial Stadium (also known as Death Valley) on the campus of Clemson University in Clemson, SC before 79,557. In this game on Sept 8, the #12 Tigers defeated Ball State W (52-27).

Chick-Fil-A Bowl

On Dec 31 at 7:30 p.m. the #15 Clemson Tigers faced the #9 LSU Tigers at the Georgia Dome in Atlanta, GA in the Chick-fil-A Bowl game and Clemson won the match by one point W (25–24) before 68,027.

2013 Clemson Tigers Football Coach Dabo Swinney

The 2013 Clemson Tigers football team represented Clemson University during the 2013college football season as a member of the Atlantic Coast Conference (ACC). Dabo Swinney was the head football coach for his sixth of many seasons. The Tigers completed their one hundred-eighteenth season overall and their sixty-first as a member of the Atlantic Division of the Atlantic Coast Conference. Their overall record was 11-2; 7-1 in the ACC. They finished second of 6 ACC Atlantic Division teams. The Offensive Coordinator was Chad Morris and the Defensive Coordinator was Brent Venables. They were invited to the Orange Bowl where they defeated Ohio State.

2014 Orange Bowl

On January 3, 2014 at 7:30 p.m., the #12 Clemson Tigers defeated the #7 Ohio State Buckeyes at Sun Life Stadium in Miami Gardens, FL when playing the Orange Bowl Game. W (40–35) before 72,080

2014 Clemson Tigers Football Coach Dabo Swinney

The 2014 Clemson Tigers football team represented Clemson University during the 2014 college football season as a member of the Atlantic Coast Conference (ACC). Dabo Swinney was the head football coach for his seventh of many seasons. The Tigers completed their one hundred-nineteenth season overall and their sixty-second as a member of the Atlantic Division of the Atlantic Coast Conference. Their overall record was 10-3; 6-2 in the ACC. They finished second of 6 ACC Atlantic Division teams. The Offensive Coordinator was Chad Morris and the Defensive Coordinator was Brent Venables. The Captains were Stephone Anthony, Sam Cooper, Adam Humphries, and Grady Jarrett. Clemson was invited to the Russell Athletic Bowl where they defeated Oklahoma. Clemson was invited to the Russell Athletic Bowl.

Russell Athletic Bowl

On Dec 29 at 5:30 p.m., the Oklahoma Sooners squared off against the #18 Clemson Tigers in the Russell Athletic bowl played at the Orlando Citrus Bowl Stadium in Orlando, FL. The Tigers whooped the Sooners W (40-0) before 40,071.

2015 Clemson Tigers Football Coach Dabo Swinney Championship ACC

Clemson finished the 2015 as the # 2 team in the nation

The 2015 Clemson Tigers football team represented Clemson University during the 2015 college football season as a member of the Atlantic Coast Conference (ACC). Dabo Swinney was the head football coach for his eighth of many seasons. The Tigers completed their one hundred-twentieth season overall and their sixty-third as a member of the Atlantic Division of the Atlantic Coast Conference. Their overall record was 14-1; 8-0 in the ACC. They finished first of 6 ACC Atlantic Division teams and they won the ACC Championship. The Offensive Coordinators were Tony Elliott and Jeff Scott Chad Morris and the Defensive Coordinator was Brent Venables. The Captains were Travis Blanks, B.J. Goodson, Eric MacLain, Charone Peake, D.J. Reader, and Stanton Seckinger.

Clemson had a great year with just one major disappointment. The Tigers won the 2015 ACC Championship Game by defeating the North Carolina Tar Heels, 45–37, capping their first undefeated regular season since winning the national title in 1981. Ranked No. 1 throughout the College Football Playoff (CFP) rankings, Clemson defeated the No. 4 Oklahoma Sooners, 37–17, in the 2015 Orange Bowl to advance to the College Football Playoff National Championship. On January 11, 2016, the No. 2 Alabama Crimson Tide (13–1) defeated the No. 1 Clemson Tigers (14–0) in the 2016 national championship, 45–40. Both Clemson and Alabama finished the season 14–1.

Clemson announced their 2015 football schedule on January 29, 2015. The 2015 schedule consisted of seven home and five away games in the regular season. The Tigers hosted ACC foes Boston College, Florida State, Georgia Tech, and Wake Forest, and travelled to Louisville, Miami, NC State, and Syracuse. Clemson hosted #4 seed Oklahoma in the Orange Bowl in the first round of the 2015-16 College Football Playoff. The Tigers then hosted #2 seed Alabama in the 2016 College Football Playoff National Championship in University of Phoenix Stadium.

The unranked Clemson Fighting Tigers season and home opener resulted in a rout against Wofford W (49-10) before 81,345. The game was played on Sept 5 at Memorial Stadium (also known as Death Valley) on the campus of Clemson University in Clemson, SC. On Sept 12 at home, Clemson beat Appalachia State W (41-10). In the next game on Sept 17, at Louisville's Papa John's Cardinal Stadium in Louisville, KY, the Tigers nipped the Wildcats for the win W (20-17)

On Oct 3 in a pivotal game at home, with the start at 8:00 p.m. in what most would call torrential rain at Memorial Stadium, the undefeated #12 Clemson Tigers got the best of the #6 Notre Dame Fighting Irish W (24-22). All-Everything Deshaun Watson threw for two touchdowns, ran for a third and Clemson's defense stopped DeShone Kizer on a tying two-point conversion as the 12th-ranked Tigers held on to beat No. 6 Notre Dame.

On Oct 10 at home, the #6 Tigers beat Georgia Tech W (43–24) before 80,983. On Oct 17, at home, the Tigers beat the Eagles on homecoming night W (34-17). On Oct 24, at Miami (FL) at Sun Life Stadium, Miami Gardens, FL, the Clemson Tigers shellacked the Miami Hurricanes W 58–0 before 45,211. On Oct 31, at NC State's Carter–Finley Stadium in Raleigh, NC in the annual Textile Bowl, the Clemson Tigers defeated the NC State Wolfpack in a major shootout W (56–41) before 57,600.

In what might have been the season spoiler at home, the #3 Tigers engaged #16 Florida State and prevailed W (23-13) before 83,099. On Nov 14 at the Syracuse carrier Dome in Syracuse NY against Syracuse, the #1 ranked Tigers defeated the Orangemen W (37-27) before 36,736. On Nov 21 at home, the #1 Clemson Tigers defeated the Demon Deacons of Wake Forest W (33-13). Then, on Nov 28 at South Carolina's Williams-Brice Stadium in Columbia, SC in what is now known as the Palmetto Bowl, Clemson squeaked out its second-last win to earn an undefeated regular season W (37–32). The Tigers also won their Division Championship and would next play for the big ACC honors.

2015 Post Season Games

On Dec 5 at 8:00 p.m. v #8 ranked North Carolina, Coastal Division Champ, the #1 Clemson Tigers, Atlantic Division Champs engaged at the Bank of America Stadium in Charlotte, NC in the ACC Championship Game. In a tough game, Clemson prevailed W (45-37 before 74,514.

On Dec 31, New Year's Eve, at 4:00 p.m. vs. No. 4 Oklahoma, #1 Clemson defeated the Sooners at Sun Life Stadium in Miami Gardens, FL in the Orange Bowl Game – CFP Semifinal. Clemson won the encounter W (37-17) setting the stage for a game against Alabama for the National Championship.

On January 10, 2016, at 8:30 p.m., #1 Clemson played #2 Alabama at University of Phoenix Stadium in Glendale, AZ for the CFP National Championship. In a great game, Alabama held on for the win L (40-45) before 75,765

2016 Clemson Tigers Football Coach Dabo Swinney Championship National

The 2016 Clemson Tigers football team represented Clemson
University during the 2016 college football season as a member of the
Atlantic Coast Conference (ACC). Dabo Swinney was the head
football coach for his ninth of many seasons. The Tigers completed
their one hundred-twenty-first overall and their sixty-fourth as a
member of the Atlantic Division of the Atlantic Coast Conference.
Their overall record was 14-1; 7-1 in the ACC. They finished tied for
first of 7 with Louisville but got to play in the championship because
they had beaten Louisville in head to head earlier in the season. They
also won the ACC Championship. The Offensive Coordinators were
Tony Elliott and Jeff Scott Chad Morris and the Defensive
Coordinator was Brent Venables.

The # 2 ranked Clemson Fighting Tigers season opener was played
on Sept 3 at Auburn's Jordan-Hare Stadium, Auburn, in the long-
time rivalry. Clemson won the close game W (19-13) before a packed
house of 87,451. On Sept 10, game # 2 was played at home at
Memorial Stadium (also known as Death Valley) on the campus of
Clemson University in Clemson, SC. The Tigers had another close
game against Troy but prevailed W (30-24). On Sept 17 at home
against South Carolina State, Clemson shut out the Bulldogs W (59-
0). On Thursday, Sept 22 at Georgia Tech's Bobby Dodd Stadium in
Atlanta, GA, the Tigers won again W (26-7) before 53,932.

On Oct 1, now at 4-0 for a great season start after a #2 finish in 2015,
the #5 Clemson Tigers took on #3 Louisville at home and beat the
Cardinals in a close one W (42-36).

Sometimes, Top 5 matchups fail to live up to their billing. They're
blowouts—decided long before the final horn. Or maybe they're
slogs, where points are at a premium, and turnovers are prevalent.
That wasn't the case with Clemson-Louisville. The No. 5 Clemson
Tigers and No. 3 Louisville Cardinals put on a show that the 80,000-
plus in attendance at Memorial Stadium will likely never forget.

At halftime, it appeared that the quarterback showdown between
Clemson's Deshaun Watson and Louisville's Lamar Jackson was
one-sided on Watson's behalf, with the Tigers holding a 28-10 lead.
But Jackson was just getting started, leading a Cardinals rally with

his arm and legs that spanned 22 minutes in the third and fourth quarters for a 26-0 run and a 36-28 Louisville edge with 7:52 left.

The Tigers and Watson struck back, with Watson leading a pair of touchdown drives, the second ending with a 31-yard Jordan Leggett catch-and-run score for a 42-36 lead with 3:14 remaining. Jackson led one final drive inside the Clemson 15, and on 4th-and-12, he found James Quick. But one yard short of the first down, Quick was forced out of bounds, and Clemson hung on for a wild 42-36 win and a huge feather in its College Football Playoff push.

Lamar Jackson and Louisville came up just short against Clemson

Then on Oct 7 at Boston College's Alumni Stadium in Chestnut Hill, MA, the Tigers snagged the O'Rourke–McFadden Trophy again in a blowout W (56–10) before 44,500. On Homecoming Day, Clemson played the Textile Bowl game against NC State and in a nail-biter overtime game, escaped with the win W (24-17). On Oct 29 in another nail-biter game—this one against #12 Florida State at Doak Campbell Stadium, Tallahassee, FL, the #4 Tigers escaped with the win W (37–34).

Bleacher report suggests that Clemson-Florida State is always meaningful in the ACC race. Lately, it has taken on importance in the College Football Playoff picture, too. When the Tigers and Seminoles met in late October, a pair of FSU losses had robbed the game of some of its significance. But that didn't stop the rivalry tilt from turning into an instant classic.

In 2016, Florida State erased an early 14-0 Clemson lead and led 28-20 after three quarters. A Wayne Gallman touchdown and a Greg Huegel field goal gave the Tigers a one-point lead with 5:25 remaining, but FSU had one final push. The Seminoles struck back with an eight-play, 80-yard touchdown drive, capped off by Dalvin Cook's eight-yard touchdown run with 3:23 left

That was too much time for Deshaun Watson and Clemson, however. He led a five-play, 75-yard drive that finished with a 34-yard touchdown to tight end Jordan Leggett, and the Tigers held on for a tense 37-34 victory.

On Nov 5, at home, the #3 Tigers shut-out the Syracuse Orangemen W (54-0) before 80, 609. Sitting at 9-0 at home with recent ACC team Pittsburgh coming to play football, Clemson could not grab the win and lost by one point L (42-43).

Clemson made a habit of edge-of-your-seat victories in 2016. Call Dabo Swinney's Tigers the Cardiac Cats; six games were decided by a touchdown or less. Play with fire that much, however, and you're bound to get burned eventually. Clemson found that out the hard way at home on Nov. 12 against Pitt. The cats had run out of luck.

The No. 2 Tigers hadn't lost to an unranked foe since November 2011, but a combination of mistakes, poor defense and untimely penalties caught up with them against the scrappy Panthers. Even with quarterback Deshaun Watson throwing for an ACC-record 580 yards, Clemson couldn't put Pitt away, with its biggest lead being eight points. Pitt closed to 42-40 on James Conner's 20-yard touchdown run with 5:17 left, and the Tigers just had to run out the clock. But the Panthers stuffed Wayne Gallman on 4th-and-1 from their 35 with 58 seconds left, giving themselves one more chance.

Pitt quickly got into field-goal position, and the aptly named Chris Blewitt nailed a 48-yard field goal on the game's final play, lifting the Panthers to a shocking 43-42 upset. Clemson still made the College Football Playoff, but Pitt and head coach Pat Narduzzi had a win they'll never forget.

Clemson 42 Pittsburgh 43

On Nov 19, the #5 Tigers recovered and beat Wake Forest's Demon Deacons at BB&T Field, Winston-Salem, NC, W (35–13). The next scheduled game was on Nov 26 at home against South Carolina in the Palmetto Bowl. The Tigers defeated the Gamecocks in a big-time shellacking W (56-7)

The 2016 Post Season

After finishing the regular season 12-1 with a win over Coastal Division champion #23 Virginia Tech in the 2016 ACC Championship game, the #2 Tigers advanced to the 2016 College Football Playoff semifinal and went on to defeat the #3 Ohio State

Buckeyes 31-0, in the 2016 Fiesta Bowl on December 31, 2016. Both top ranked Clemson and Alabama met again in college football's first rematch in National Championship game history, the 2017 CFP National Championship game in Tampa, Florida.

On January 9, 2017, the Clemson Tigers would go on to defeat the Alabama Crimson Tide in the rematch by a score of 35 to 31, winning their first consensus National Football Championship since 1981. Clemson subsequently finished with #1 rankings in both the Associated Press Poll and the AFCA Coaches' Poll for the 2016 season. Here are the stories

In the ACC Championship game on Dec 3, against #19 Virginia Tech, played at Camping World Stadium in Orlando, Clemson prevailed in a close match W (42-35) to gain the full ACC Championship before 50,628. Ranked #2, the Tigers would be playing in the Fiesta Bowl in a game known as the CFP Semifinal.

On December 31, New Year's Eve two games were played and the winner would play on January 9 for the National Championship. #2 Clemson shut out #3 Ohio State in the Fiesta Bowl at 7:00 p.m. at University of Phoenix Stadium, Glendale, AZ CFP Semifinal. W (31-0). In a game earlier in the day at 3:00 PM, #1 Alabama beat the #4 Washington Huskies W (24-7) earning them a berth to play Clemson for the championship on January 9, 2017

On Monday, January 9, 2017 at 8:30 p.m., the #1 ranked Alabama Crimson Tide (14-0) were looking for a repeat National Championship against the #2 ranked Clemson Tigers (13-1) at Raymond James Stadium in Tampa, FL in the CFP National Championship game. Clemson pulled out the win in a magical fashion.

The 2017 National Championship Game

Uncommitted football fans across the world enjoyed one of the best football games of all-time on Monday evening January 9, 2007, from 8:00 PM to way past bedtime at 12:25 AM. For the committed Clemson fans, the victory was sweet after waiting a year for a rematch. For the committed Crimson Tide fans, the loss was simply heartbreaking. Clemson knew the feeling for the prior year and the victory was even that much sweeter.

In this game, the song lyrics, *what a difference a day makes* took a back seat to *what a difference a few seconds make*. Clemson did all it could to win, battling to the last second. Alabama came literally one second away from a repeat title. Clemson fans all remember that with Alabama holding a three-point lead after rolling down the field and scoring on a Jalen Hurts' 30-yard touchdown run with just 2:01 remaining, Clemson took the second-last kickoff of the game and simply refused to be stopped. It was exhilarating to watch for sure.

Deshaun Watson was the game's super-hero. However, Watson had to perform "all night long" to get the win and he had the ball in his hands again as the game ended after a Clemson onside kick was recovered by Clemson with one second still on the clock.

It took many fans and the entire Crimson Tide by surprise as Clemson executed an onside kick with one second left in this Monday night national championship game. The Tigers, had kicked it after scoring a game-winning touchdown so as to avoid letting Alabama run the kick back, recovered it, leaving just a kneel down left for the Tigers to seal their big victory.

Just before that, without his two-yard TD pass with 1-second left after the score, the super-hero acclaim would have gone to the Alabama defense. The big guys from the Crimson Tide spent the night chasing Watson, keeping the talented QB from overcoming Alabama's early lead.

But, not this time. Not this game. Clemson would not be denied and the Tigers had both the talent and the luck, on their side. Clemson's heralded QB, and the best QB in the nation per his coach Dabo Swinney calmly led his team to victory and to him goes the credit as game super-hero.

This QB, who is also a two-time Heisman Trophy finalist, (who should have received the Heisman -- third in the Heisman voting in 2015, then second in 2016) performed flawlessly on this all-important drive down the field. Watson was the master on the field and the results have already made the history books. Clemson won by four.

They are the 2017 National Champions for the 2016 season and will be so forever.

DeShaun Watson, interviewed after the game told reporters that his message to his teammates on the drive was to stay calm; don't get nervous; and they would prevail. They did.

Watson guided the Clemson Tigers 68 yards in nine plays, completing a 24-yard pass to Mike Williams to Alabama's 39-yard line and a 17-yard pass to tight end Jordan Leggett that gave Clemson a first-and-goal at the 9. The Tigers got to the 2 when Alabama cornerback Anthony Averett was flagged for pass interference in the end zone.

"Everything was calm, and nobody panicked," Watson said. "I walked up to my offensive line and my receivers, and I said, 'Let's be legendary.' God put us here for a reason."

Coach Swinney offered: "He didn't lose out on the Heisman. The Heisman lost out on him."

From the two-yard line, with about 6 seconds left, Alabama was either going to be playing in OT with a field goal if Clemson's next play did not work; or time would run out by mistake; or of course option 3 was that the play would result in a touchdown.

Much to Alabama's chagrin, option 3 was operative. When Alabama double-teamed 6' 3" Mike Williams on the left side, Clemson decided to go right against man to man coverage. They executed a perfect touchdown play that some Alabama fans still claim was illegal. But, in football, the referees have the final word.

Regardless, along with other referee miscues, the officials said it was legal. On the play, Deshaun Watson's rolled right and threw a perfect 2-yard touchdown pass to Hunter Renfrow with just 1 second remaining. Clemson can take that call to the bank.

This gave Clemson their wild 35-31 win over Alabama in the College Football Playoff national championship game. Clemson fans were ecstatic as they felt they should have won the marbles one year earlier. Alabama fans of course were generally heartsick.

Sure, Alabama could have played better. Their offense was sluggish and they depended on their defense after Bo Scarbrough was no longer on the field. Clemson did not miss an opportunity when the going got tough. There is no denying the Tigers this great win.

There were a lot of ups and downs in the game, especially at the end. Alabama quarterback Jalen Hurts had just given the Crimson Tide a 31-28 lead on his 30-yard scramble with 2:01 remaining. This had countered Wayne Gallman's 1-yard touchdown run with 4:38 remaining that had put the Tigers up 28-24. Two minutes is an awful long time and Watson engineered a drive that used it all up right to the last second before he passed for the score.

Last year Watson threw for almost 500 yards and this year, the Crimson Tide managed him better; but he still stole 420 yards on 36-of-56 passing and three touchdowns. Renfrow caught ten of his passes for 92 yards and two touchdowns and big 6'3" leaping Mike Williams adding eight receptions for 94 yards and one score.

Clemson packed in 511 total yards to 376 by Alabama and the Tigers posted a 31-16 edge in first downs. Alabama's bright side in the game was not its offensive production and because of that, its D had little time to rest.

Clemson ran 99 plays. All season long it was only Arkansas W (49-30) that had anything close to that (84 plays). Though in great shape, the D was not as well backed up as the 2016 team. Some say that this huge number of plays helped wear down the mighty Tide defense with tempo and consistent movement on offense. One thing for sure is that Clemson bested the vaunted Crimson Tide.

Alabama did not get much rest as the offense ran just 66 plays. Its defensive depth was not at the same level as the 2015 team. The wear of those extra plays on the Alabama defense was evident in the second half. Clemson visited the red zone four times and they scored four times. Alabama had typically rejected opponents on two of every three red zone attempts. On the field, fatigue surely was a factor though there are no real excuses. Nick Saban is not looking for excuses. He knows his team was beaten.

Nick Saban's Crimson Tide were clearly denied a fifth national championship in eight seasons under this highly successful coach. The Tide managed just 131 passing yards, as Hurts had a tough night going 14-of-32.

Nick Saban saw it as it was. "They made the plays and we didn't," Saban said. "We could have done some things better, but I'm proud of the way our guys competed." Dabo Swinney has proven that he is one of the best coaches of all time at any university.

Alabama struggled in the second half but did take a 24-14 lead on a 68-yard touchdown pass from Hurts to O.J. Howard with 1:53 remaining in the third quarter. Clemson fans quickly remembered Howard as the MVP of last year's title game with 208 yards on five receptions. Alabama had faked the look of a quick screen before Howard raced behind a confused Clemson secondary for the catch. And the TD.

"Not to have him [Bo Scarborough] was probably a little bit of a disadvantage for us," Saban gave it a positive slant when he said. "I was pleased with our other backs who had an opportunity in this game, Josh Jacobs and Damien Harris, but we always miss a guy who's Bo Scarbrough 's size when we want to run the ball and take some time off the clock."

Alabama had to punt after a three-and-out on the night's opening possession. Clemson on its first drive then moved across midfield before they were stuffed by Tony Brown on a fourth down and 1 try on a pitch to Gallman. Alabama then took over on their own 41.

Bama got going on their second possession on a 20-yard scramble by Hurts down the right sideline to the Clemson 39-yard line and grabbed a 7-0 lead at the 9:23 mark of the first quarter on Bo Scarbrough's 25-yard scamper around left end.

Watson was a bit shaky at first but calmed down as the O-line settled down. He fumbled a low shotgun snap late in the first quarter. Alabama outside linebacker Ryan Anderson recovered the fumble at Clemson's 35-yard line, Mistakes stopped an Alabama advance. There was a false start on Cam Robinson and a 2-yard loss by Scarbrough and the Tide was forced to punt.

When they got the ball back, ArDarius Stewart started Alabama's second touchdown drive with a 25-yard run to Clemson's 49-yard line early in the second quarter. From here, Scarbrough broke loose moments later from 37 yards out to make it 14-0.

The Alabama fans and the Clemson fans had a feeling that Alabama was on the verge of breaking things open until Tigers receiver Deon Cain took a short Watson pass and weaved 43 yards to Alabama's 39. It was the juice Swinney's Clemson squad needed to convince them they "could." It was a major momentum shift.

Watson was energized and calm by then. He completed a third-and-10 pass for Leggett for 26 yards to the Alabama 13 and ran in for an 8-yard score to pull the Tigers within 14-7 with 6:09 before halftime. That would be the end of the first-half scoring, with the Tide held the seven-point lead at the break even though they had been outgained 203-183.

Alabama's Anderson struck again early in the second half, stripping Tigers tailback Gallman of the ball and returning the fumble to the Clemson 16. For whatever reason Alabama, just as it had done after Anderson's first fumble recovery, could not move the ball and had to settle for a 27-yard Adam Griffith field goal for a 17-7 lead.

Clemson was no longer intimidated to say the least. They reduced the lead to 17-14 with 7:10 left in the third quarter on a 24-yard touchdown pass from Watson to Renfrow. After a Tide, TD, The Tigers then pulled within 24-21 in the first minute of the fourth quarter on a 4-yard touchdown pass from Watson to Williams.

Clemson coach Dabo Swinney is one of Alabama's own. Swinney became just the second person to have won an Associated Press national championship as a player and coach. Swinney was a wide receiver on Gene Stallings' 1992 Alabama team that won the AP national championship and now he has coached Clemson to a national title over his alma mater Crimson Tide. Swinney still has a lot of love for Alabama and its supporters. He is a good guy

Coach Dabo Swinney was all emotion as he described the victory for Clemson: "This has been the most incredible team I've ever been around," Swinney said. "You saw their heart, and it's been there all year."

It was a big loss for Nick Saban. It was his first ever in a championship game. in six tries. Afterwards, speaking with ESPN's Tom Rinaldi, he was very gracious in defeat. Saban praised his team for all it accomplished in 2016, while also congratulating Dabo Swinney and Clemson on the victory.

Watch out next year folks! It will be another great Clemson football year. You can take that to the bank.

Deshaun Watson QB (2014-16)

Only if you have never seen him in action would there be any doubt? Following the Tajh Boyd era, a great era, which ended with an Orange Bowl win over Ohio State, the Clemson Tigers began the 2014 season with QB Cole Stoudt at QB due in part to DeShaun Watson having suffered a collar bone injury prior to the season. In the season opener in Athens v and always tough Georgia Tech Yellow Jackets squad, Watson did take a few snaps and he secured his first TD pass as a Tiger.

From that moment, Clemson fans knew they had another one of those magical quarterbacks, and they knew the next few years would be special. Watson unfortunately was plagued with injuries for most of that 2014 season. He famously played with a torn ACL in the Palmetto Bowl and beat South Carolina to snap their five-game winning streak. Not ever to like seeing a loss on the scorecard, Watson would go 3-0 in his career against the Gamecocks.

Deshaun Watson shook the injury prone label the following year in 1915 as he led the Tigers to their first undefeated regular season since 1981. He was a finalist for the Heisman. He was simply a superman but for some reason, though John Heisman coached at Clemson, Clemson is always skipped over for the Heisman Trophy. Watson's stats were remarkable as he posted 5,209 total yards (4,104 passing, 1105 rushing) and 42 TDs (35 passing, 12 rushing). After beating UNC in a high scoring ACC Championship game and Oklahoma in the Orange Bowl, the DeShaun Watson-led Clemson Tigers played for the National Championship v Alabama, Clemson would lose that game due to defensive lapses and special team gaffes, but the contest is largely remembered for the 405 yard, 4 TD performance by a great QB, Deshaun Watson.

In his final season as a Tiger, Deshaun Watson tallied 4,593 passing yards and was once again a Heisman finalist. Again, Clemson was denied a Heisman. Lamar Jackson won the award, but after what Watson did in three postseason games that came after the vote, there was no doubt about him being the best player in the nation. Following an 11-1 regular season, the Tigers used a five TD performance from Deshaun Watson to get past Virginia Tech, earn a second-consecutive ACC title and make another trip to the College Football Playoff.

The Tigers would win their first ever Fiesta Bowl by beating Urban Meyer's tough Ohio State team 31-0. In the title game, as noted, they got to play Alabama again.

The Tigers fell behind 0-14, but then, Coach Swinney's squad with Watson leading the offensive action outplayed the Tide for most of the night and finally took the lead with under five minutes remaining. Despite struggling to move the ball since early in the game, Alabama used a third-and-long completion, a fourth down conversion, a WR-pass, and a QB scramble to score the go-ahead touchdown with 2:07 remaining.

242 Clemson Tigers' Championship Seasons

That's when Deshaun Watson calmly told his teammates to be "legendary," and they were. The greatest QB and greatest player in Clemson history took the field for the final drive of his illustrious career and cemented his legacy with "The Drive." Go Tigers!

2017 Clemson Tigers Football Coach Dabo Swinney <u>Championship ACC</u>

The 2017 Clemson Tigers football team represented Clemson University during the 2017 college football season as a member of the Atlantic Coast Conference (ACC). Dabo Swinney was the head football coach for his tenth of many seasons. The Tigers completed their one hundred-twenty third overall and their sixty-sixth as a member of the Atlantic Division of the Atlantic Coast Conference. Their overall record should be very good overall and in the ACC as they have a fine returning team

Tigers entered the 2017 season as defending national champions, having finished the 2016 season 14–1 with a win over Alabama in the CFP National Championship game.

Clemson won the ACC for the third consecutive season by beating Miami (FL) in the ACC Championship game, 38–3. They received their third straight bid to the College Football Playoff, earning the number one seed. The Tigers unfortunately fell to eventual national champion Alabama in the semifinal game played at the Sugar Bowl, 6–24. Wait til next year.

2018 Clemson Tigers Football Coach Dabo Swinney Championship ACC

The 2018 Tigers also won the National Championship v Alabama.

The 2018 Clemson Tigers football team represented Clemson University during the 2018 college football season as a member of the Atlantic Coast Conference (ACC). Dabo Swinney was the head football coach for his tenth full year and eleventh after taking over the team midway through the 2008 season. The Tigers completed their one hundred-twenty second overall and their sixty-fifth as a member of the Atlantic Division of the Atlantic Coast Conference. Their overall record was 15-0 and in the ACC they turned in an 8-0 performance coming in #1 again.

The Tigers entered the 2018 season from being the #2 team from 2017 having lost the national championship to Alabama and having finished the 2017 season 12-2 with a loss to Alabama in the CFP National Championship game. This year was another championship for Clemson plus other honors

To refresh our collective memories, Clemson was coming off a big College Football Playoff semi-final loss to Alabama in 2017, began the year ranked second in the preseason AP Poll and Coaches Poll. The Fighting Tigers won all 12 of their regular season games, securing their first undefeated regular season since 2015. They also grabbed their fourth consecutive ACC title by defeating Pittsburgh in the 2018 ACC Championship Game. I

n the final College Football Playoff rankings of the 2018 season, Clemson was ranked second, earning them their fourth consecutive playoff bid and a spot in the 2018 Cotton Bowl Classic against third-ranked Notre Dame. The Tigers won that game by a whopping 30-3, advancing them to the 2019 College Football Playoff National Championship against Alabama. This was their fourth consecutive year meeting the Crimson Tide in the playoff and third time doing so in the national title game.

Clemson won that game in a dominant fashion, 44-16, to win the Tigers' third national championship in school history and second in three years. They were the first undefeated College Football Playoff champion and the first major college football program to finish with a record of 15-0 since Penn in 1897. What a performance!

The Tigers were led offensively by true freshman quarterback Trevor Lawrence, who won a highly publicized battle for the starting role over 2017 starter Kelly Bryant.[2] Sophomore running back Travis Etienne contributed significantly, rushing for over 1,600 yards and an FBS-leading 24 rushing touchdowns. He was named ACC Player of the Year following the regular season. On defense, the team was anchored by a highly touted, veteran defensive line consisting of Clelin Ferrell, Christian Wilkins, Dexter Lawrence, and Austin Bryant all of whom were subsequently drafted in the 2019 NFL Draft.

They played these games in 2018

On Sep 1, CU played #23 (FCS) Furman at home and whopped them big time W (48–7) before   80,048. Then, on Sep 8 at Texas A&M the #2 ranked Tigers had a tough bout at Kyle Field in College Station, TX in a College Game Day celebration W (28–26) before 104,794. On Sep 15, Georgia Southern came to #2 Clemson to play at home W (38–7) before 79,844   . On Sep 22-at Georgia Tech #3 CU pounded the Yellow Jackets in Bobby Dodd Stadium W (49–21) before 50,595. Wrapping up September, #3 Clemson hosted Syracuse on Sep 29 Syracuse and captured the game W (27–23) before 80,122.

On Oct 6 at Wake Forest in BB&T Field Winston-Salem NC, the #4 Tigers whopped them W (63–3) before a big crowd for them 31,608. At home v NC State on Oct 20, then ranked #16 NC State tried to knock off $3 Clemson at home at home but failed big time W (41–7) before 81,295. Then, on Oct 27 at Florida State, #2 CU prevailed at Doak Campbell Stadium in Tallahassee, FL W (59–10) before 68,403.

Still no losses, On Nov 3, #2 Clemson hosted Louisvillev and overpowered them W (77–16) before 78,741. CU was a powerful team for sure. Then, on Nov 10 at #17 Boston College, the #2 Tigers defeated the strong #17 Eagle at Alumni Stadium W (27–7) before 44,500 in Chestnut Hill, MA. For this accomplishment Clemson won the (O'Rourke–McFadden Trophy) for a game that was televised by College GameDay.

On Nov 17 Duke was ready to beat the Tigers who were #2 at the time, playing the Tigers at home but they lost as all comers did this year W (35–6) before 81,313 in Clemson, SC. Then on Nov 24, South Carolina took its shot against # 2 Clemson at home, and were soundly defeated W (56–35) before 81,436 at   Clemson, SC in the Palmetto Bowl. This ended the regular season. The post season is listed below:

On Dec 1 at Pittsburgh in Bank of America Stadium, #2 CU beat the Panthers W (42–10_ before 67,784 in Charlotte, NC for the ACC Championship.

With a four week rest, Clemson played #3 Notre Dame on Dec 29 at AT&T Stadium. The Irish were tepid and weak compared to CU's always ready Tigers and Clemson picked them apart for the win W (30–3) before 72,183 in a game with multiple names in Arlington, TX (Cotton Bowl–CFP Semifinal).

After winning & then losing to Alabama in the past two years, nobody knew who would win on Jan 7 2019 when Clemson faced #1 ranked Alabama at Levi's Stadium. Clemson let no grass grow under their feet as from the whistle at kickoff, the Tigers did their best to pound Alabama into submission—which is exactly the game which Alabama plays against the unsuspecting. Clemson was given a chance at winning but not by much if it won. Instead, the Tigers upset all the oddsmakers by giving an old-fashioned licking o the Crimson Tide W (44–16) before 74,814. Alabama did not understand what had hit them in this Santa Clara, CA (CFP National Championship.) Clemson fans, however, we knew.

Looking back at the big game at the beginning of 2019 we all find that SANTA CLARA, California had nothing to do with the result. Nobody gets blowouts against Nick Saban's Alabama like Clemson did—at least very often—or ever, in fact. And yet, that's exactly what Clemson did by pounding the Crimson Tide 44-16 to win the 2019 College Football Playoff National Championship and capture its second national title in three years. Each championship game victory came against Nick Saban's Crimson Tide—who were no pushovers.

Nonetheless, the Clemson Fighting Tigers became the first team in modern college football history to finish a season 15-0. Clemson was the first to accomplish this major feat since Penn in 1897. Meanwhile many #1 seeds fell to 3-5 in CFP games and a resounding 0-X in the national championship.

Alabama-Clemson IV was exhilarating and even polarizing in a number of ways. There was no doubt that these were the two best teams in college football, as they had been the top two wire-to-wire from preseason until now. However, with "fatigue" apparently setting in among casual fans, this game didn't quite have the build-up as previous editions did. That view looked to be silly early on, though, with a 27-point first quarter that had plenty of momentum swings –

from pick-sixes to long touchdowns, only one of the teams looked completely tuned-in – Clemson.

In the end, Clemson pulled away in an amazingly stunning fashion as it accounted for 482 yards of offense on just 63 plays. Quarterback Trevor Lawrence threw for 347 yards for his second straight postseason game and nearly became the 10th college quarterback to throw for 350 yards against a Saban-led defense. Lawrence became the first true freshman starting quarterback to win a national championship since Oklahoma's Jamelle Holieway in 1985. But, hey, Perhaps Lawrence forgot who he was playing. Then, again, maybe, just maybe he did not forget and the world has a great three CFP games left before he checks out for the pros. Just maybe. Wow, what a team! Clemson's Fighting Tigers know how to fight for championships. That's for sure. See you next time around.

In addition to being consensus national champion, Clemson was also the ACC champion, the ACC Atnaltic Division Champion; and the Cotton Bowl Classic Champions. In the ACC Championship Game Clemson was victorious over Pitts burgh (W (42-10). In the Cotton Bowl Classic (CFP SemiFinal) the team whooped Notre Dame W (30-3) and then they clobbered Alabama in the CFP National Championship W (44-16). It took just one year for Dabo Swinney to replace the powerhouse QB DeSesean Watson but he did. What a coach.

The Tigers won all 12 of their regular season games, securing their first undefeated regular season since 2015. Clemson won their fourth consecutive ACC title by defeating Pittsburgh in the 2018 ACC Championship Game. In the final College Football Playoff rankings of the 2018 season, Clemson was ranked second, earning them their fourth consecutive playoff bid and a spot in the 2018 Cotton Bowl Classic against third-ranked Notre Dame.

The Tigers won that game 30–3, advancing them to the 2019 College Football Playoff National Championship against Alabama, their fourth consecutive year meeting the Crimson Tide in the playoff and third time doing so in the national title game. Clemson won that game in dominant fashion, 44–16, to win the Tigers' third national championship in school history and second in three years. They were the first undefeated College Football Playoff champion and the first major college football program to finish with a record of 15–0 since Penn in 1897.[1]

The Tigers were led offensively by true freshman quarterback Trevor Lawrence, who won a highly publicized battle for the starting role over 2017 starter Kelly Bryant. Sophomore running back Travis Etienne contributed significantly, rushing for over 1,600 yards and an FBS-leading 24 rushing touchdowns. He was named ACC Player of the Year following the regular season. On defense, the team was anchored by a highly touted, veteran defensive line consisting of Clelin Ferrell, Christian Wilkins, Dexter Lawrence, and Austin Bryant—all of whom were subsequently drafted in the 2019 NFL Draft.

That's All Folks!

We hope you enjoy this book of many championships. Our intention is to refresh versions of our four Clemson titles on a periodic basis to add data as time goes by. This will permit a better focus on Tiger football and permit us to offers a commentary on what's new Thank you for choosing this book among the many that are in your options list. We sincerely appreciate it!

The best to you all – Go Tigers!

Other Books by Brian W. Kelly: (amazon.com, and Kindle)

Hope for Wilkes-Barre-John Q. Doe Next Mayor Wilkes-Barre PA: John Doe Plan, help create better city!
Democrat Secret for Power & Winning Elections: Open borders & amnesty & millions of new Dem Voters
The Cowardly Congress Whatever happened to Congress doing the work of the people?
Help for Mayor George and Next Mayor of Wilkes-Barre How to vote for the next Mayor &Council
Ghost of Wilkes-Barre Future: Spirit's advice for residents about how to pick the next Mayor and Council
Great Players in Air Force Football: Air Force's best players of all time
Great Coaches in Air Force Football: From Coach 1 to Coach Troy Calhoun
Great Moments in Air Force Football: From day 1 to today
Great Players in Navy Football: Navy's best including Bellino & Staubach
Great Coaches in Navy Football: From Coach 1 to Coach #39 Ken Niumatalolo
Great Moments in Navy Football: From day 1 to coach Ken Niumatalolo l
No Tree! No Toys! No Toot Toot! Heartwarming story. Christmas gone while 19 month old napped
How to End DACA, Sanctuary Cities, & Resident Illegal Aliens . best solution to wipe shadows in America.
Government Must Stop Ripping Off Seniors' Social Security!: Hey buddy, seniors can no longer spare a dime?
Special Report: Solving America's Student Debt Crisis!: The only real solution to the $1.52 Trillion debt
How to End DACA, Sanctuary Cities, & Resident Illegal Aliens . best solution to wipe shadows in America.
The Winning Political Platform for America Unique winning approach to solve big problems in America.
Lou Barletta v Bob Casey for US Senate Barletta's unique approach to solving big problems in America.
John Chrin v Matt Cartwright for Congress Chrin has a unique approach to solve big problems in America.
The Cure for Hate !!! Can the cure be any worse than this disease that is crippling America?
Andrew Cuomo's Time to Go? "He Was Never that Great!": Cuomo says America never that great
White People Are Bad! Bad! Bad! Whoever thought a popular slogan in 2018 would be It's OK to be White!
The Fake News Media Is Also Corrupt !!!: Fake press / media today is not worthy to be 4th Estate.
God Gave US Donald Trump? Trump was sent from God as the people's answer
Millennials Say America Was "Never That Great": Too many pleased days of political chumps not over!
White People Are Bad! Bad! Bad! In 2018, too many people find race as a non-equalizer.
It's Time for The John Doe Party… Don't you think? By By Elephants.
Great Players in Florida Gators Football… Tim Tebow and a ton of other great players
Great Coaches in Florida Gators Football… The best coaches in Gator history.
The Constitution by Hamilton, Jefferson, Madison, et al. The Real Constitution
The Constitution Companion. Will help you learn and understand the Constitution
Great Coaches in Clemson Football The best Clemson Coaches right to Dabo Swinney
Great Players in Clemson Football The best Clemson players in history
Winning Back America. America's been stolen and can be won back completely
The Founding of America… Great book to pick up a lot of great facts
Defeating America's Career Politicians. The scoundrels need to go.
Midnight Mass by Jack Lammers… You remember what it was like Great story
The Bike by Jack Lammers… Great heartwarming Story by Jack
Wipe Out All Student Loan Debt--Now! Watch the economy go boom!
No Free Lunch Pay Back Welfare! Why not pay it back?
Deport All Millennials Now!!! Why they deserve to be deported and/or saved
DELETE the EPA, Please! The worst decisions to hurt America
Taxation Without Representation 4th Edition Should we throw the TEA overboard again?
Four Great Political Essays by Thomas Dawson
Top Ten Political Books for 2018… Cliffnotes Version of 10 Political Books
Top Six Patriotic Books for 2018… Cliffnotes version of 6 Patriotic Boosk
Why Trump Got Elected!.. It's your chance to hear about a great milestone in America!
The Day the Free Press Died. Corrupt Press Lives on!
Solved (Immigration) The best solutions for 2018
Solved II (Obamacare, Social Security, Student Debt) Check it out; They're solved.
Great Moments in Pittsburgh Steelers Football... Six Super Bowls and more.
Great Players in Pittsburgh Steelers Football ,,,Chuck Noll, Bill Cowher, Mike Tomin, etc.
Great Coaches in New England Patriots Football,,, Bill Belichick the one and only plus others
Great Players in New England Patriots Football… Tom Brady, Drew Bledsoe et al.
Great Coaches in Philadelphia Eagles Football..Andy Reid, Doug Pederson & Lots more
Great Players in Philadelphia Eagles Football Great players such as Sonny Jurgenson
Great Coaches in Syracuse Football All the greats including Ben Schwartzwalder
Great Players in Syracuse Football. Highlights best players such as Jim Brown & Donovan McNabb
Millennials are People Too !!! Give US millennials help to live American Dream
Brian Kelly for the United States Senate from PA: Fresh Face for US Senate
The Candidate's Bible. Don't pray for your campaign without this bible
Rush Limbaugh's Platform for Americans… Rush will love it
Sean Hannity's Platform for Americans… Sean will love it
Donald Trump's New Platform for Americans. Make Trump unbeatable in 2020
Tariffs Are Good for America! One of the best tools a president can have

Great Coaches in Pittsburgh Steelers Football Sixteen of the best coaches ever to coach in pro football.
Great Moments in New England Patriots Football Great football moments from Boston to New England
Great Moments in Philadelphia Eagles Football. The best from the Eagles from the beginning of football.
Great Moments in Syracuse Football The great moments, coaches & players in Syracuse Football
Boost Social Security Now! Hey Buddy Can You Spare a Dime?
The Birth of American Football. From the first college game in 1869 to the last Super Bowl
Obamacare: A One-Line Repeal Congress must get this done.
A Wilkes-Barre Christmas Story A wonderful town makes Christmas all the better
A Boy, A Bike, A Train, and a Christmas Miracle A Christmas story that will melt your heart
Pay-to-Go   America-First Immigration Fix
Legalizing Illegal Aliens Via Resident Visas Americans-first plan saves $Trillions. Learn how!
60 Million Illegal Aliens in America!!! A simple, America-first solution.
The Bill of Rights By Founder James Madison Refresh *your knowledge of the specific rights for all*
Great Players in Army Football Great Army Football played by great players..
Great Coaches in Army Football Army's coaches are all great.
Great Moments in Army Football Army Football at its best.
Great Moments in Florida Gators Football Gators Football from the start. This is the book.
Great Moments in Clemson Football CU Football at its best. This is the book.
Great Moments in Florida Gators Football Gators Football from the start. This is the book.
The Constitution Companion. A Guide to Reading and Comprehending the Constitution
The Constitution by Hamilton, Jefferson, & Madison – Big type and in English
PATERNO: The Dark Days After Win # 409. Sky began to fall within days of win # 409.
JoePa 409 Victories: Say No More! Winningest Division I-A football coach ever
American College Football: The Beginning From before day one football was played.
Great Coaches in Alabama Football Challenging the coaches of every other program!
Great Coaches in Penn State Football the Best Coaches in PSU's football program
Great Players in Penn State Football The best players in PSU's football program
Great Players in Notre Dame Football The best players in ND's football program
Great Coaches in Notre Dame Football The best coaches in any football program
Great Players in Alabama Football from Quarterbacks to offensive Linemen Greats!
Great Moments in Alabama Football AU Football from the start. This is the book.
Great Moments in Penn State Football PSU Football, start--games, coaches, players,
Great Moments in Notre Dame Football ND Football, start, games, coaches, players
Cross Country with the Parents A great trip from East Coast to West with the kids
Seniors, Social Security & the Minimum Wage. Things seniors need to know.
How to Write Your First Book and Publish It with CreateSpace. You too can be an author.
The US Immigration Fix--It's all in here. Finally, an answer.
I had a Dream IBM Could be #1 Again The title is self-explanatory
WineDiets.Com Presents The Wine Diet Learn how to lose weight while having fun.
Wilkes-Barre, PA; Return to Glory Wilkes-Barre City's return to glory
Geoffrey Parsons' Epoch... The Land of Fair Play Better than the original.
The Bill of Rights 4 Dummmies! This is the best book to learn about your rights.
Sol Bloom's Epoch ...Story of the Constitution The best book to learn the Constitution
America 4 Dummmies! All Americans should read to learn about this great country.
The Electoral College 4 Dummmies! How does it really work?
The All-Everything Machine Story about IBM's finest computer server.
ThankYou IBM! This book explains how IBM was beaten in the computer marketplace by neophytes

Amazon.com/author/brianwkelly
Brian W. Kelly has written 207 books. Thank you for buying this one.
Other Kelly books can be found at amazon.com/author/brianwkelly

www.ingramcontent.com/pod-product-compliance
Lightning Source LLC
Chambersburg PA
CBHW052033090426
42739CB00010B/1889